THE CATHOLIC MOVEMENT

OF

EMPLOYERS AND MANAGERS

STUDIA SOCIALIA

Series published by the Institute of Social Sciences
of the Gregorian University

1. LEONI, ALDO: *Sociologia e Geografia religiosa di una Diocesi.* 1952. (out of print)

2. BELTRÃO, PEDRO, S.J.: *Vers une politique de bien-être familial,* 1957.

3. PELLEGRINI, VINCENTE S.J.: *Algunos Aspectos del Mercado Comun Europeo,* 1960.

4. CARRIER, HERVÉ S.J.: *Psycho-Sociologie de l'appartenance religieuse,* 1960.

5. GREMILLION JOSEPH B.: *The Catholic Movement of Employers and Managers,* 1961.

6. GARRET, THOMAS M. S.J.: *An Introduction to some Ethical Problems of modern American Advertising,* 1961.

GREGORIAN UNIVERSITY PRESS - ROMA

THE CATHOLIC MOVEMENT
OF
EMPLOYERS AND MANAGERS

BY

Rev. Joseph B. GREMILLION, M. A., Sc. S. L.

Priest of the Diocese of Alexandria

GREGORIAN UNIVERSITY PRESS
4, PIAZZA DELLA PILOTTA
ROME
1961

TO THE PARISH OF ST. JOSEPH
SHREVEPORT, LOUISIANA

FOREWORD

Today's industrial economy functions through the combined efforts of two principal groupings of persons: employers and employees, management and labor, bosses and workers.

Their main operative relation is the wage contract, by which the employee agrees to work under the direction of the employer for monetary remuneration, on materials and with instruments which are owned by, or in the charge of, the employer or manager.

In the modern capitalist system these means of production are in very great proportion owned by individuals, families, partners, or incorporated companies (sociétés anonymes). Although through widespread ownership of stocks, bonds or shares title to a particular company is often in the hands of tens of thousands of persons, this system is popularly called private enterprise. This is to be distinguished from ownership or control of productive means by the state or political collectivity through socialization or nationalization of property. In the economies of most Western nations modern capitalism combines in some proportion both these systems of owership in a « mixed economy ».

Currently the Catholic social movement is most active in national societies having such mixed economies as the framework of national production. Within this intermeshing of relations among management and labor, private and state ownership, and other elements, the Catholic social movement aims at the establishment, conservation and perfection of a social order based on social justice and charity, according to principles of natural law set forth by the teaching magisterium of the Church. Since employers and managers fulfil a dominant role in capitalist society, the manner and degree of the influence of Catholic social doctrine on them is of great significance. There exists a relatively young organization of Catholic employers and managers who associate for the purpose of receiving and transmitting this influence. Their national associations and their world federation, UNION INTERNATIONALE DES ASSOCIATIONS PATRONALES CATHOLIQUES (UNIAPAC), is the object of study in this dissertation.

The writer chose this subject because compared to other phases of the over-all Catholic social movement UNIAPAC was barely known to myself and to Catholic social leaders of my country. No parallel association exists as yet in the United States.

And whereas we have there a considerable understanding of workers', farmers ', familial, political, professional and other movements of Christian inspiration, little was known generally about employers' associations. During the period which the writer has devoted to this thesis the situation has begun to change; considerable interchange has occurred of late, interest quickens, the beginnings of an American managerial group of Catholic inspiration seem to appear.

Then, here in Europe, the writer found that while the present Catholic employers' movement has roots going back to the 1870's and today's associations began organizing immediately after World War I, no general, integrated study of the movement has been made. With hearty encouragement from social leaders of the United States, I have made a beginning at covering this gap in the literature of the Catholic social movement, hoping this effort might have some value in itself toward filling in the over-all picture, and might also make some contribution to UNIAPAC's own vision of itself and its mission to the world. Particularly, I thought such a study might help to communicate to leaders of my own country some further understanding of the aims, policy and activity of this managers' movement.

With practicality as a prominent and admitted norm this study is non-theoretical. It deals with actualities and, importantly, it treats principally of very recent and current actualities. While some notice is taken of historical development, the over-riding theme is the composition, orientation and operation of UNIAPAC today. The bibliography reflects this fact; UNIAPAC writings, statements and working papers of recent date predominate. Frequent recourse was also made to interviews, direct contacts with leaders of the movement, visits to their offices and homes, and participation in many meetings, seminars and congresses.

The writer is deeply grateful to the officers of UNIAPAC for the unstinting cooperation they have given me. For eighteen months I have badgered them with questions and poked into their files and at their gracious invitation attended their confidential meetings. Undoubtedly their busy schedules and privacy were often intruded upon during the months which I spent in their headquarters and centers of Holland, Belgium, France, Germany, Switzerland and Italy. The leaders always received me with unfailing courtesy and offered most generously of their assistance and that of their staffs. In many instances too, they arranged personal meeting with leaders of labor, governmental, educational, and economic bodies, which were invaluable in helping me to grasp in some measure the ensemble of the interrelations of which UNIAPAC is a part. I spent more time in Belgium than in the other countries; the reception accorded me there must be singled out for special commendation. And to mention only one person by name, to M. Rik Vermeire, UNIAPAC secretary general, I extend in a particular manner my deepest appreciation.

But before graduate studies and a dissertation were possible, it was necessary that my own Most Reverend Ordinary must grant me leave of absence from my Diocese of Alexandria to pursue them. To him, Bishop Charles P. Greco, D. D.. I express heartfelt and filial gratitude for his permission and for the fatherly encouragement and counsel he has given me in this and in social action undertakings of the past.

Further, I am deeply appreciative to the Jesuit Fathers of the Institute of Social Sciences of the Gregorian University, Rome, and particularly to Father Georges Jarlot, S. J., under whose direction this study was made. I was most fortunate in having a director with such wide grasp of the Catholic social movement in its historical development and concrete manifestations. He offered many background insights invaluable for one freshly arrived on the complex European scene.

For two years I resided in the Graduate Casa of the North American College, the House on Humility Street. It has been good to live again in community with so many fine young priests and under the fraternal charge of Monsignor Joseph Emmenegger and his assistants. To them and to the Most Reverend Rector, Archbishop Martin J. O'Connor, I am profoundly grateful.

During the decade prior to my coming to Europe for social studies, the writer was pastor of St. Joseph's Parish, Shreveport, Louisiana. To the people and sisters and priests of St. Joseph's I dedicate this study. It was my privilege to write about « our parish » in a book inspired by experiences there, published three years ago. Here I can only renew the convictions and sentiments therein expressed; I repeat a hurried « thank you » to the people whom for ten years I called *my* people. It is through their response and cooperation that interest in the social field was nourished and grew within me, and through their generosity, and that of non-Catholic friends, that the financial means of study abroad were afforded me. Most happily, and with renewed gratitude to my Bishop, the pastor who succeeded me was Father Marvin Bordelon, dear friend and close associate. Under his most able leadership the people of St. Joseph's Parish are accomplishing much for Our Lord and His Church, to the profit of their own and many other souls, and of the society of this world as well. To Father Marvin and to his brother, Father Roland Bordelon, also my dear friend and co-worker, I express warmest thanks.

Returning now to the matter at hand, this thesis is not a study of Catholic social doctrine on employers and management, the enterprise and economy. It is rather a study of Catholic employers and managers as interpreters, developers, practitioners and communicators of that teaching. For this reason the sources are not papal or Church or natural law treatments as such, but the positions and practices of UNIAPAC as expressed through their writings, meetings and conversation. The footnotes and bibliography are often topical, and refer overwhelmingly to UNIAPAC sources. Most of these were not in the English tongue; unless otherwise noted, all translations are the responsibility of the writer, who was at times assisted by UNIAPAC officers. The text and translations have been read by M. Rik Vermeire, international secretary general: he has made no objection to the translations; he has offered several highly valued suggestions regarding certain points in the study, some of which have been followed and others have not. At any rate this study is in noway the responsibility of UNIAPAC or its officers. Any inaccuracies of fact, faults of judgement, lapses of discretion, or errors of interpretation are the sole responsibility of the present writer.

TABLE OF CONTENTS

CHAPTER I

INTRODUCTION TO UNIAPAC

The confederation known as UNION INTERNATIONALE DES ASSOCIATIONS PATRONALES CATHOLIQUES (International Union of Catholic Employers Associations) unites sixteen national organizations of Catholic employers. The purpose of this study is to set forth the development of this movement and its affiliates, their basic concept and structure, their aims, doctrine and mode of action, their relation with other organizations, and finally to attempt an evaluation of the federation's position in the ensemble of the Christian social movement in the recent past, and its possible role for the future.

This study treats then of a concrete actuality, of a particular grouping of existing organizations. The overall affiliation, Union Internationale des Associations Patronales Catholiques (hereinafter called UNIAPAC, its own official abbreviation), has its world headquarters at 71 Rue de Cortenberg, Brussels, Belgium. Its affiliated national associations are as follows [1] :

Argentina: Asociación Católica de Dirigentes de Empresa (A.C.D.E.), Avenida Paraguay 1931, Buenos Aires.
Belgium: Fédération des Patrons Catholiques de Belgique (FEPAC), 71 Rue de Cortenberg, Brussels.
Canada: Association Professionnelle des Industriels (A.P.I.), Avenue Papineau 5875, Montreal.

---

[1] « UNIAPAC Summary: International Union of Catholic Employers Associations », pp. 14-15. In English language publications the English title given here is used. Officials of UNIAPAC refer to the movement by this combination of letters which are pronounced as one word and written usually without periods after the individual letters. Some national affiliates also form the initial letters of their titles into a word, e. g., UCID, or FEPAC. The other organizations habitually utilize their initials as call letters, e. g., C.F.P.C., or B.K.U., written normally with periods after each letter, because these do not in most cases form a pronounceable combination. The custom of the respective affiliates will be followed in this work.

1

Chile: Unión Social de Empresarios Católicos (USEC), Agustinas 1350 (Int.) Of. 340, Santiago de Chile.

Cuba: Asociación Nacional de Empresarios Católicos, Calle J., 152, Vedado Habana.

France: Centre Chrétien des Patrons et Dirigeants d'Entreprise Français (C.F.P.C.), 100 rue de l'Université, Paris 7e [2].

Germany: Bund Katholischer Unternehmer (B.K.U.), Bernhard Letterhausstrasse, 26, Cologne.

Holland: Algemene Katholieke Werkgevers Vereniging (A.K.W.V.), Raamweg 32, The Hague.

Great Britain: Catholic Industrialist's Conference (C.I.C.), Shearer House, 9 Lower Mosley Street, Manchester 2.

Italy: Unione Cristiana Imprenditori Dirigenti (UCID), Via del Tritone, 201, Rome.

Mexico: Unión Social de Empresarios Mexicanos (USEM), Palma 30, Mexico 1, D. F.

Peru: Unión Nacional de Dirigentes y Empleadores Católicos (UNDEC), Ant. Miro Quesada, 376-403, Lima.

Portugal: União Catolica de Industriais e Dirigentes de Trabalho (UCIDT), Rua Antonio Jose d'Almeida, 117, Coimbra.

Spain: Acción Social Patronal (A.S.P.), Arapiles, 18, Madrid.

Switzerland: Vereinigung Christlicher Unternehmer der Schweiz (V.C.U.), Alpenstrasse, 5 Luzern.

Uruguay: Asociación de Patronos y Dirigentes Católicos de Empresa, Yaguaron 2042, Montevideo.

UNIAPAC took on the title of « Union » only in May 1949. However, the body has had organized existence as Conférences Internationales des Associations Patronales Catholiques since 1931. The oldest national associations are those of Holland, Belgium and France, dating to 1915, 1921 and 1926 respectively. These, in turn, had been preceded by various local or sporadic groupings, such as those inspired in the closing decades of the last century by the French leader, Léon Harmel [3].

The employers have been latecomers in modern Catholic social organization compared with other groups. Michael P. Fogarty observes: « Even after the new foundations and consolidations of 1915-25, the Christian employers' and middle-class movements were in much less finished form than,

---

[2] On March 23, 1958, the French organization took on its present denomination, dropping the former title of Centre Francais du Patronat Chrétien. It has, however, retained the identifying initials, C.F P.C.

[3] Charles Harmel, « Le Sens du Mouvement Patronal Catholique International », *Rapports du Congrès de Rome, du 7 au 10 mai 1949* pp. 19-21; Joseph Zamanski, *Nous, Catholiques Sociaux*, pp. 152-156; Georges Guitton, S. J., *Léon Harmel, passim;* by the same author, *Léon Harmel et l'Initiative Ouvrière, passim.*

at the same date, the farmers' or workers' movement. It is
not surprising that the next generation saw much more marked extensions and modifications » [4].

Since World War II Catholic employers have formed
organizations in Italy, Germany, Switzerland, Spain and Portugal; the movement has jumped the Atlantic to Canada
and Latin America; unaffiliated embryonic groups exist in
the United States and Vietnam, and a Belgian off-shoot takes
root in the Congo. Only in 1957 did UNIAPAC set up a permanent secretariat and project a vigorous program of expansion and deepening. Writing in 1953, Fogarty continues:

> The workers' movements' age of experiment lies forty or
> fifty years in the past ... But when one comes to the em-
> ployers' movements ... the impression is still very much one
> of a formative stage. No doubt certain tendencies are visible
> already ... But the dominant impression in this field is not
> in any case one of fixed aims and agreed methods. It is one
> of expansion and multiplication — very rapid since the
> Second World War — and of experiment. And for this reason
> the middle-class movements constitute today an exciting field,
> in a way which they certainly did not a generation ago [5].

The subject of this study is not then a *fait accompli*.
UNIAPAC is not a static structure of well-defined lines, hard-
ened by time. It is very much *in fieri*. Its leaders do possess doctrinal convictions and agreed general goals, and in
several instances marked accomplishment and experience.
But theirs is not a complacent mood. They seem convinced
that the entrepreneur of today cannot rest upon his laurels
and his profits, that a new society is in the making, and that
the employer and manager *as Christian* must commit himself to the work of its design and achievement.

In ordering their thought and program towards this end
the operation of the employers' organizations can be divided into four concentric circles of concerns: 1) those of the
enterprise-community (communauté de travail), i. e., the
local factory or mine or service establishment; 2) concerns
of the professional or industrial group, i. e., the textile producers as a whole compose such a group, iron and steel
producers compose another, coal mines a third, others being

---

[4] Michael P. Fogarty, *Christian Democracy in Western Europe 1820-
1953*, p. 256.
[5] *Ibid.*, p. 263.

chemicals, food processing, construction, etc.; 3) those of
the nation as a socio-economic unity, with the grave implications of government's role in the economic sphere today;
4) and finally, those concerns which are of international
scope, as the Common European Market and that projected
for Latin America, the United Nations specialized agencies,
and world trade.

In addition, the UNIAPAC associations address themselves to what might be termed the great issues. These
concerns by their nature overflow the circles outlined above.
Either they cannot be contained in one or the other circle,
or they have roots and implications over and above the
economic sector. Such great issues are, for instance: the
nature of property and access to property for workers; the
survival of non-governmental ownership of the means of
production under pressures toward nationalization; dehu-
manization of work conditions and the mass society; the
family; the inter-relations of the work-community (communauté de travail), syndicates and co-management, and
their relation to social classes; research, automation and
rationalization of processes; cooperation for the advance of
underdeveloped countries; socio-economic ideologies; the
relation of the intellectual and the entrepreneur-manager.

Adequate or even introductory treatment of these subjects is of course here impossible, and they are not in themselves the objects of this study. In regard to these issues,
the present aim is very modest: to uncover and review the
approach of the UNIAPAC associations, or at least to register their awareness, to these issues, with some modicum of
evaluation.

These organizations have two characteristics which
taken together distinguish them from all others: first, they
are *Christian* movements rooted in Catholic social doctrine;
and secondly as distinct from other Christian social groups,
they are *entrepreneurial*, composed of employers and managers. Faced with these four circles of concerns and with
the great issues the entrepreneur *prima facie* is expected
to react in a manner somewhat different from the trade
unionist or university professor or clergyman, and the Christian might well regard these matters in a light different
from the viewpoint of the non-Christian, especially if he
views them according to Catholic social teaching. The Chris-

tian as entrepreneur can develop his own characteristic outlook. Further, this study of the UNIAPAC movements does not in the main consider the Christian employer as an isolated individual, but concentrates rather on his participation in a group endeavour. So, to the two distinguishing notes of Christian and entrepreneur, this study incorporates a further mark: its object is Christian entrepreneurs *as forming a group* movement, and *being formed* by this group movement.

The sixteen national associations listed above by name are such group movements of Christian employers. Together they federate into UNIAPAC, Union Internationale des Associations Patronales Catholiques. The sixteen affiliates preserve their autonomy in their respective nations. They have formed the world federation to serve as communication center and coordinator, to promote the common purposes of the associations in the extra-national sphere and in relation with other international bodies, and to assist the establishing of new associations and the strengthening of existing ones. The constituent organizations differ greatly in numerical strength and activity. The movements in Holland, Belgium and France are the oldest and are solidly established in the economic life of their nations. The program of Italy's UCID approaches these three, and in some aspects surpasses them despite its recent founding date, 1947. Switzerland, Spain, Germany and Canada are developing rapidly. The others, mostly of recent date, show varying degrees of life, from youthful bounce to barely embryonic viability.

Overall the movement pushes ahead at a steady pace, with notable bursts forward since World War II. This recent growth is not mainly an automatic unfolding of interior potencies. The current rise of UNIAPAC seems to come as a response to exterior stimulus: without artificially creating and conveying a sense of desperation, one receives the impression that the entrepreneurial world is fearful of its life and has banded together to assure survival. The *Christian* employers' associations seem to want more than mere survival as employers. While seeking survival certainly, they do manifest concern for the continuance and advance of the free society of Judaeo-Christian tradition; they look beyond the West to the nations now arising and ponder over the role they must fulfill in the emerging world community.

CHAPTER II

CONCEPT AND HISTORY

1. Preliminary Concepts.

On the front page of each issue of its fortnightly publication, *Professions*, the Centre Chrétien des Patrons et Dirigents d'Entreprise Français (C.F.P.C.) sets forth in boxed format this definition of itself:

> C. F. P. C. is a movement which unites employers and managers,
> ★ desiring as Christians to meet their proper responsibilities in their enterprises, in their industries and in the economy as a whole,
> ★ wanting themselves to understand the social doctrine of the Church,
> ★ and to make it known to others,
> ★ to promote its applications in their research and initiatives [1].

This is the concept that the organization offers of itself to the public at large, trying by the very type arrangement to present a clear image. This self-definition is incorporated in the statutes of C.F.P.C. [2]. In a commentary on this definition at the time of its formulation, the movement's secretary general, André Aumonier, explains that the phrase « dotrine sociale de l'Eglise » used here embraces the economic as well as the social sphere, that unless C.F.P.C.'s research and initiatives penetrate minds and are realized in actions this teaching remains a dead letter, and that the

---

[1] *Professions*, no. 420, décembre 1957, p. 1. This boxed formula first appeared in the issue of this date and has been repeated on the front page of the publication to this writing. It is a direct quote from art. 2 of the statutes of C. F. P. C. *Professions* carries also a sub-title, « Le Journal Chrétien du Chef d'Entreprise ».

[2] *Statuts*, C. F. P. C., art. 2. (23 mars. 1958).

Church's doctrine is enriched and completed to the measure of its application by the Christian community [3].

Less formal concepts of itself are conveyed in C.F.P.C. promotional material such as one piece entitled « Le Patron — Cet Homme Seul ... » [4]. This folder keynotes the solitude of the employer, « that man without a boss », faced with a sudden difficulty or an important decision, feeling that his most loyal collaborators, his friends, « your wife herself », regard him with questioning anxiety, while interiorly he experiences « a strange sensation of emptiness ». What the solitary employer needs is solidarity with his peers. The folder highlights the necessity of communication with others, that to resolve individual problems there must needs be comparison with the efforts and problems of others, sharing their confidence and lucidity in « a center which forms a fellowship ... which gives a soul to the manager's milieu ». C.F.P.C. claims distinctiveness in that it proposes to employers a definition of their function by reference to the transcendental order, a conception of human relations based on the dignity of men as sons of God and the demands of the common good, and a conviction of the grandeur and challenge of their providential mission. The center permits employers to unite toward bold initiatives and, quoting Cardinal Feltin of Paris: « to make the French employers of today a conquering management, in order that it can be a management of service » [5].

Another promotional folder, « C.F.P.C., Son But, Ses Moyens, Ses Réalisations », is more direct, resorting less to psychological persuasion [6]. This leaflet stresses the goal of promoting an economic and social order inspired by the Church's social doctrine. However, the important mark added here is that C.F.P.C. is a movement of influence into the heart of the French entrepreneurial milieu (au sein du pa-

---

[3] André Aumonier, « Journée de Décisions et d'Orientations », *Professions, op. cit.*, p. 11.

[4] « Le Patron—Cet Homme Seul ... » is a twelve page folder in three colors

[5] Cardinal Feltin, « Les responsabilités actuelles des chrétiens chefs et dirigeants d'entreprise », *Documents et Commentaires*, no. 106, juin 1956, pp. 11-20. This is an address given to the Assises Nationales of C. F. P. C., March 17, 1956.

[6] « C. F. P. C., Son But, Ses Moyens, Ses Réalisations », is a six page folders in two colors.

tronat francais), bringing to the employers of the nation
rich truths drawn from a living Christianity. It declares
that it is neither a syndicate, nor tied to any political party.
The leaflet quotes testimonials: excerpts from talks to C.F.
P.C. by Henri Daniel-Rops and André Siegfried, statements
by Pope Pius XII, Cardinal Feltin of Paris and Cardinal Richaud of Bordeaux. The Holy Father expresses the pressing fear that today when giantesque organizations exert such
weight in social affairs, the public issues will be settled without the participation of Christian employers. He stresses
that heads of enterprises have a right to be heard and to
exercise vigorous influence in view of their peculiar competence for passing judgement on the grave dangers and issues
of the present age[7]. Cardinal Feltin feels dismay that so
many faithful Christian employers conceive their work in
such a utilitarian and narrow perspective, without grasping
the grandeur and challenge of the entrepreneur's mission[8].
Cardinal Richaud directly urges adherence to the C.F.P.C.:
« I believe that an employer who is Christian by education,
mentality or aspirations, can no longer hold himself outside
the Christian employers' movement, can no longer dispense
with membership in C.F.P.C. »[9].

The Fédération des Patrons Catholiques (FEPAC) of Belgium in its promotional literature adds further precisions
to this general concept of the employers' movement[10]. It
appeals to employers to take on their responsibility of action
as the elite which they are. The folder states that FEPAC
is a national cohesion of twenty-seven regional sections
— « cellules vivantes » — in as many industrial centers. It
interests itself in the law-making process of the contemporary social and economic evolution. It preserves constant
contact with other organizations, communicating its policies
to them: Fédération des Industries Belges (F.I.B.), Confé-

---

[7] Pope Pius XII, « Les Employeurs face au Bien Commun », allocution
to UCID, June 6, 1955. Full text in French is given by Marcel Clément,
Le Chef d'Entreprise, pp. 261-266; full text in Italian is in *Avanzate e Lavorate*, a collection of papal talks published by UCID, pp. 19-27. (*Discorsi e Radiomessaggi di Sua Santità Pio XII*, XVII, 117-123).

[8] Cardinal Feltin, *op. cit.*, pp. 14-15.

[9] Cardinal Richaud, « Mission actuelle du patronat chrétien ». *Documents et Commentaires*, no. 97, janvier 1954, p. 24.

[10] « LA FEPAC », is a sixteen page booklet illustrated by photographs
in color.

dération des Syndicats Chrétiens (C.S.C.), Parti Social Chrétien (P.S.C.), Benelux, UNIAPAC, and is present also « in those organisms and economic, social and cultural institutions in which Catholic managerial opinion should be represented »[11]. FEPAC declares clearly its educational goal and content as « papal teaching on social issues », and at the same time, re-stresses its actionist mission: to organize the collaboration of the classes, to provoke creative concretizations of the Catholic social concept, to struggle against proletarisation especially by accession to property by the workers, to aid and sustain the worker family as the cell of social stability and the guardian of religious and moral life. The booklet avows certain defensive characteristics; it cites especially the dangers of progressive nationalization, Communism and a misunderstanding of the employers' function[12].

The first paragraph of the statutes of Italy's Unione Cristiana Imprenditori Dirigenti (UCID) states simply that it is constituted to promote the knowledge, spread and actualization of Christian social doctrine[13]. The *Rubrica Soci UCID*, a confidential directory listing all its members by name, address, telephone number and business connection, sets forth four « caratteristiche », all similar to those of the French and Belgian associations. One of these cites the desire of UCID to integrate into Italian and international society the social efforts of entrepreneurs and managers, « conscious of their obligations to the common good and to Christian civilization »[14].

By now these references from the literature of various national associations merge to construct an image of the movements as a whole. It is unnecessary indefinitely to repeat such citations, especially where they merely rephrase and re-enforce each other. However, two more references might be permitted, from the German and Swiss organizations. Both treat of their religious motivation and Christian message to the beleaguered and doubt-filled free world.

« Has the West an Idea? » asks a slim German B.K.U. booklet entitled, « Was Will der Bund Katholischer Unter-

---

[11] *Ibid.*, p. 8.
[12] *Ibid.*, pp. 5-6.
[13] *Statuto*, Unione Cristiana Imprenditori Dirigenti, art. 1, p. 1.
[14] *Rubrica Soci UCID*, 1958, p. 12.

nehmer? » [15]. To be sure, it answers, the West does have
an idea, the Christian idea; the man of faith knows and
feels this. Let us see to it then that all become aware of it.
B.K.U. wants to employ this idea in *that* field which Christians have until now forsaken to the atheist and rationalist:
to the arena of the economic order, social justice and the
organized common good. « The Christian West is not at
its finis, but on the threshold of a new beginning. We have
more to promise and more to offer than does the welfare-
apostle of Communism and state control » [16].

A Swiss promotional folder introduces the same idea
by quoting twelve lines from John Foster Dulles, « ein ame-
rikanischer Christ » [17]. The Vereinigung Christlicher Unternehmer embrace and apply to their own program the three
theses of Dulles: first, that the dynamic usually wins out
over the static, the active over the passive; second, that
in all human affairs, the immaterial, spiritual element has
preponderance over the material; and third, that right
and wrong are determined not by created mores, but by
the natural law, the following of which is indispensable for
human welfare. « We have departed from our Christian
principles in our behavior toward each other », the Dulles
quote continues, and while Soviet Communism does not
care much for moral principles, we too remain about as
indifferent. The V.C.U. hopes that this citation will help
to explain why Catholic employers have formed their own
organization: not to compete with existing economic associations, but to bring its particular Christian contribution for
strengthening the free enterprise system [18].

This bare perusal through a few publications shows then
the UNIAPAC affiliates to be organs of education, formation,
inspiration and influence. Definitely this is the characteristic
conception of all the movement taken as a whole [19].

---

[15] « Was will der Bund Katholischer Unternehmer? » is an eight page
booklet in black and white.
   [16] *Ibid.*, p. 2.
   [17] « V. C. U., Vereinigung Christlicher Unternehmer der Schweiz » is
six pages, dated 1955.
   [18] *Ibid.*, p. 2.
   [19] Henry W. Ehrmann, *La Politique du Patronat Français*, devotes a
section to « Les groupes d'opinions ou avantgarde », pp. 164-181. The author, a German-American, includes the C. F. P. C. among the four groups
which he describes as having for their goal the elaboration of a philosophy
within the ranks of the « mouvement patronat officiel », by which

In addition to its organizational responsibilies vis-à-vis its existing affiliates and for the begetting of new ones, UNIA-PAC strives to intensify its work of education, inspiration and influence in the international sphere by rapport with the specialized agencies of the United Nations and other bodies, governmental and non-governmental, Catholic and non-Catholic.

2. HISTORY

A. *Holland*

The first professedly Catholic employers' association was founded in Holland, September 2, 1915. Catholic « Stand », or socio-professional class, organizations of Dutch workers, farmers, small traders and craftsmen were already existing or in formation. The Catholic Trade Union Federation had organized in 1908 and the Catholic Farmers' Union had begun back in 1896. Shopkeepers and craftsmen had set up diocesan federations in 1912 and combined into the present Catholic Middle Class Union in 1915 [20]. Dutch Protestants had parallel « Stand » movements and an employers' organization dating back to 1891 [21]. The present secretary

---

he means the Conseil National du Patronat Français (C. N. P. F.). Ehrmann says of C. F. P. C. and the three other avant-garde associations: « Les groupes insistent, il est vrai, sur l'adoption de nouveaux points de vue dans beaucoup de domaines, sur la transformation de l'état d'esprit des patrons et des organisations patronales, sur les pratiques dynamiques plutôt que restrictives, sur des plans plus constructifs et sur une interférence politique moindre ». The author opines that unless a serious crisis similar to that of 1936 shatters the passive confidence of leaders now controlling French entrepreneurial circles, these « groupes d'opinion » will not have « la force de modifier de l'intérieur ou de l'extérieur l'orientation et la politique du C. N. P. F. »; p. 181. Aumonier, C. F. P. C. secretary general, who called this book to the attention of the writer, thinks Ehrmann's analysis of C. F. P. C. is already outdated.

[20] Fogarty, *op. cit.*, pp. 211-263, gives excellent brief histories of each of these organizations. Also, he explains the practical motives and sociological actuality which have sustained the « Stand » concept in Holland and Belgium, pp. 377-397. « It may be, as the Belgians and the Dutch so often point out, a case of hanging together or hanging separately; knock one key item out of the complex of influences which help Christians of a given country or class to live their lives and make their decisions in the light of their principles, and the complex as a whole will fall to pieces »; p. 395.

[21] « What We Believe and What We Do », promotional folder of the Verbond van Protestants-Christelijke Werkgevers in Nederlands, English

of this association volunteered his analysis of this devolep-
ment: In response to *laissez-faire* liberalism, Europe in the
late 1800's offered two reactions, the socialist and the Christian, each with its own ideas and ideals in the social and
economic fields, ideologies then regarded as irreconcilable.
The Christian movement developed two branches, the Protestant and the Catholic, in keeping with the religious division of Holland, which fifty years ago was almost a neat
geographical division of north and south as well. And these
two religious movements followed the social strata and economic interests of workers, farmers, middle class, professions and employers [22].

This explanation of ideological currents and sociological framework offers valid background for the historical
survey presented in matter-of-fact fashion by Holland's Catholic employers' association [23]. In 1907 a union of Catholic
tobacco and cigar manufacturers was already in existence
and issuing a modest journal, *Ons Dekblad, (The Wrapper)*,
the linear antecedent of today's *De Katholieke Werkgever*,
(The Catholic Employer). In 1910 following a strike at the
Tiglia brickworks, Tegelen, clay and metal industry employers of the Venlo district formed an association upon which
episcopal and royal approval was bestowed. Professor L. van

edition, p. 8.   This first Protestant employers' organization, known as
« Boaz », was a heterogeneous mixture including small traders and even
some farmers.   The folder states on p. 8: « In 1918 the late Minister of
State, Dr. H. Colijn, a big businessman and a true Christian, took the
lead in improving work of the organization, so as to divide it into three
organizations: one for big businessmen and wholesalers, one for small
businessmen and retailers, and one for farmers and gardeners ». Cf. also,
Fogarty, *op. cit.* p. 246.

[22] From an interview with H. H. DeKlerk, secretary of the Verbond,
September 16, 1959, in their headquarters, Alexanderstraat 8, 's-Gravenhage.   Two recent books, recommended by the secretary, give full cover-
age of the Dutch Protestant organization: R. Hagoort, *De Christelijk
Social Beweging, (The Christian Social Movement)*, 1955, and *De Verantwoordelijke Maatschappij (The Responsible Society)*, T. Wever, editor,
1958.

[23] « General Catholic Employers' Association, Catholic Federation of
Employers' Trade Associations », *passim;* this is a seven page leaflet of the
Algemene Katholeike Werkgeversvereniging (A. K. W. V.), in English, giving a short history and an account of the work of the A. K. W. V. and
its close counterpart the Katholiek Verbond van Werkgeversvakerenig-
inger (K. V. W.).   *Waar Voor Wij Staan*, edited by A. H. M. Albreghts,
pp. 49-66, gives the history of A. K. W. V. and K. V. W. up to 1950.   The
larger half of this book is devoted to current issues (Onze Problemen) of
the Dutch association in chapters written by seven members.

Aken, a priest of the Abbey of Berne, Heeswijk, began in February 1913, promoting an Algemene Katholieke Werkgevers Vereniging (A. K. W. V.: General Catholic Employers Association). This fructified formally on September 2, 1915, and with the appointment of L. G. Kortenhorst as general secretary on November 25, 1915, the A. K. W. V. began its work in earnest[24].

The original intention was to build up a single organization for the whole country, which the individual employer would join directly. But the tendency to regionalism frustrated this. On April 29, 1917 an employers' association was set up in the diocese of Breda, followed on July 22, 1918 by one for the diocese of Limburg, which absorbed the pioneer Venlo group of 1910. The dioceses of 's-Hertogenbosch, Utrecht and Haarlem established similar organizations in due course, January 20, 1919, September 22, 1922, and November 6, 1922, respectively. All were united in a federation in 1922; individual employers became members of their particular diocesan association, which in turn adhered to the national group.

Simultaneously the trade associations took shape as economic parallels to this educational and inspirational goal. The cigar manufacturers have already been mentioned. In 1918 clay products' manufacturers formed a trade association covering the whole of Limburg, building from a nucleus of the older Venlo group. At the same period in Eindhoven a meeting was called by the workers' organization in the metal industry inviting Catholic employers in that industry of south Holland in order to discuss the possibility of a collective agreement. In preliminary meetings all workers and employers alike agreed that the common interest would be served by the establishment of an association of employers in the metal industry. A committee appointed for the purpose drafted a constitution, rules and a collective agreement, and in short time the Roman Catholic Union of Employers in the Metal Industry came into being, in virile existence to

---

[24] *Ibid.*, p. 50: J. B. van Dijk was the first president, a « mercator sapiens » of Amsterdam, described as imbued with Catholic thought, ideal principles of life and a warm heart: « het tupe van de ' mercator sapiens ', ... een man van door en door katholiek denken, van ideele levensopvatting, volbloed Amsterdammer en bovenal een man met een warm sociaalvoelend hart ».

this date [25]. Other branches instituted associations in rapid
order. The need for a national federation was immediately
felt; it was constituted January 8, 1919, and survives to this
day as the Katholiek Verbond van Werkgeverswakverenigi-
gen (K. V. W.).

> Just as, on the labour side, there was the « R. C. Trade
> Bureau », which acted as a central body for the national trade
> unions, so now a « R. C. Federation of Employers' Trade As-
> sociations » was founded.   On the 8th of January, 1919, the
> R. C. Federation of Employers' Trade Associations was brought
> into being by the R. C. Employers' Associations in the Cigar,
> Leather, Biscuit Manufacturing, Clay, Printing, Metal and
> Textile industries [26].

From the start, then, the Dutch employers instituted two
parallel organizations.   One was a general movement, the
A. K. W. V., educational, social and inspirational in character and conformed to diocesan boundaries in its structure,
and today a member of UNIAPAC; the other was expressly
syndical in purpose, the K. V. W., structured according to
the various branches of industry, with definite economic
functions, like defense of employer interests and collective
bargaining.   K. V. W. is not a member of UNIAPAC.   From
the beginning, however, the two Dutch associations worked
closely together, and later combined forces to share a joint
secretariate and other organs in common, while remaining
separate organizations [27].   No Catholic employers' association other than K.V.W. retained a distinctly syndical character, although some have at times shown interest in economic functions [28].

---

[25] *Ibid.*, pp. 52-53.

[26] « General Catholic Employers' Association » *op. cit.*, p. 3;   *Waar
Voor Wij Staan*, p. 49, says « Roman » was dropped from the titles in
1938.

[27] A. K. W. V., the general employers association, and K. V. W., the
federation of trade associations, are separate organizations, but since
1921 through today they are closely linked at the national level by a
common executive board (Dagelijks Bestuur) composed of members selected by each group in paritary fashion. Together they publish a monthly,
De Katholieke Werkgever, and operate a joint secretariate, the staff of
which perform duties of an economic nature for the trade associations, as
well as educational work for the A. K. W. V. at the national and diocesan
levels.   The K. V. W. and A. K. W. V. retain, however, separate consti-
tutions and governing bodies.   Most of the forty-five trade associations
in K. V. W. have their own secretariates in addition.

[28] The Association Professionnelle Industrielle (A. P. I.) of Canada,

It must be noted that the employers of Holland organized with the approbation and, one might say, with the blessing of workers' associations. At a meeting to discuss a collective agreement, the metal workers saw the desirability of having an employers' syndicate across the table from them. To a marked degree the employers' associations completed the nation's social blueprint: it seemed normal that besides workers', farmers' and middle class groupings, the employers should organize as well, fitting automatically into the Dutchman's interior vision of how exterior socio-economic relations should be structured [29]. And as already noted, these followed more or less the ideological streams of Dutch national life: socialist, liberal, Protestant and Catholic. The last three formed distinct employers' syndical associations, which continue to this day [30].

While only the non-syndical, educative Catholic movement, A. K. W. V., is a member of UNIAPAC, its parallel trade grouping, K. V. W., will also be adverted to in this study because of their close inter-relationship.

B. *Belgium*

As the first established, the Dutch movement often performed the role of missionary toward other nations. Log-

---

founded in 1943 and a member of UNIAPAC, has at times offered certain services of a juridic and economic nature to its members. But it is not a syndicate or trade association as is K. V. W. of Holland.

[29] In a certain context the Dutch and Belgian Flemish use the concept of « Stand » to signify these groupings. « Stand » might be translated as class, rank, level, state, condition or profession. Some UNIAPAC leaders object to the application of « Stand » to employers' associations. Rik Vermeire, secretary general of the world affiliation, makes such an objection. He points out that « de Stands-organisatie » in the thoroughgoing sense is the complete organization of a single determined class. Such, for example, is the case with Catholic workers in Belgium: they have youth movements as the Jeunesse Ouvrière Chrétienne (JOC), labor unions, mutual insurance programs, consumer cooperatives, credit unions, banks, summer colonies, hospitalization, sport and cultural clubs, etc. Farmers' organizations have a similar all-embracing socio-economic system for their own « Stand ». But, continues Vermeire, such is not the case among employers, and UNIAPAC expressly renounces any desire to foster « Stands-organisatie » and particularly renounces any intent to separate Catholics from the general employers' milieu. From interviews of September and October 1959, and a letter to the writer, January 6, 1960, in response to a request for clarification.

[30] The liberals of Holland have two employers' associations, one for

ically their first conquest was their near neighbor, Belgium.
In 1920 the chaplain of the Limburg group visited Liège
and Louvain to probe the possibilities of launching a Belgian movement. His failure was complete. An encounter
with a Louvain university professor who was also a leading
developer of the Campine coal-fields is retold: « Nothing
doing! The interview lasted two minutes, on the doorstep.
The Professor simply could not see what it was about.
A Catholic organization for leaders in business life? But
that sort of leadership had nothing to do with Catholic
principles! » [31].

In the specifically Flemish sector the first embryoes
appeared. Notably through contacts with the original Dutch
association of cigar firms, a group took shape in Antwerp
in 1923, at first with economic functions on the Dutch model.
Another group flowered forth at Coutrai under the stimulus
of Father A. H. van Overbeke, professor at the College of
St. Amand. It was he who spotted Léon Bekaert at nearby
Zwevegem and won to the movement this manufacturer,
who is now a dominant figure in European industrial circles
as well as in UNIAPAC. Father van Overbeke pushed the
development in Flemish Belgium, with the close support
of Bishop Henri Lamiroy of Bruges [32].

Almost any study of Belgian society must note the division of the country into the Flemish and French Walloon
halves, because most initiatives must have two-fold organizations, one proper to each of the two language and culture groups. So it was among the employers. While they
were moving ahead in Flanders, a simultaneous growth

---

economic affairs, Verbond van Nederlandsche- Werkgevers, and a second
for social issues, Centraal Sociaal Werkgevers-Verbond. The relative
strength of the Protestant, Catholic and liberal associations is discussed
below, chapter III. section 2.

[31] *Waar Voor Wij Staan,* p. 79.

[32] From an interview with Léon Bekaert, Zwevegem, September 13,
1959. Bekaert gives great credit to these efforts of Father van Overbeke
in the mid-twenties, and emphasizes the support given by the Bishop of
Bruges. According to Bekaert the priest was appointed to sinecures in
order to leave him much free time to promote the movement, first as
vicar of Heule, then in 1933 as chaplain of the Madeleine Cemetery, Coutrai. After being bombed out of his home in 1944, Father van Overbeke
lived for several months at the Bekaert residence. This detail introduces
the fact of the unusually close relations that have obtained between
chaplains and lay leaders of the movement. For Bekaert's own role, cf.
chapter IV.

went on among the French-speaking. Charles Harmel [33], pioneer of the movement and honorary president of UNIAPAC, recounts the feverish mood of post-World War I reconstruction and the uneasy social temper in which this occurred:

> But simultaneous to the upswing of material activity (of rebuilding after the first War), the class struggle became ever more acute than ever. Labor's demands became ever more pressing despite governmental intervention and efforts at pacification. The chasm between employers and the working class constantly deepened. Wage raises were followed by price increases, which in turn brought on new waves of wage raises, and the spiral thus put in motion would have continued indefinitely to bring on a fatal economic crisis [34].

Employers began meeting informally. They asked Father Demain to be their moral guide « in the study of the papal directives contained in the encyclical *Rerum Novarum* ». On November 16, 1921 the Association des Patrons et Ingénieurs Catholiques (APIC) was founded at Brussels, with Georges Dallemagne as first president. He was then president of the Fédération des Industries Chimiques et Céramiques of Belgium. Other charter members were: Victor Defays, engineer, professor at Louvain University; Victor Thiran, manager of coal mines; M. Defourny, Louvain professor; A. Broussier, president of the Groupement Marbrier Belge; J. Choppinet, manager of the Antwerp Bell Telephone Co.; A. Demeure, industrial manager; Baron de Moffarts, manager of the Ferronnerie Bouillonaise; H. Ferauge, executive of coal mines; M. Gilbert, industrialist and president of the Chamber of Commerce of Mons; A. Hanet, director of textile mills, Ghent; I. Isaac, manager of construction works of Enghiem, St. Eloi; H. Lagache, executive at Renaix; A. Legrand, director of Legrand Mills, Brussels; Th. Lhoest, director of a lime quarries and furnace company, on the Meuse; J. Velings, manager of coal mines; Count Vilan XIIII, senator; and J. Waelkens, industrialist [35].

---

[33] Charles Harmel, now 85 years of age, is still active in business and employers' circles. He has served since 1955 as president of the Union Internationale des Transports Publics. On October 9-10, 1959, he attended in Rome the meeting of UNIAPAC's governing body, « comité central des délégués ».

[34] Charles Harmel, « Une Grande Association Patronale », *Revue Générale Belge*, no. 14, décembre 1946, p. 107.

[35] *Ibid.*, p. 208.

In 1935 the Flemish groups federated into a national (language) association, Landelijk Algemeen Christelijk Verbond van Werkgevers (L. A. C. V. W.). For a while they had experimented along the Dutch model with trade functions, but in time the Walloon APIC educational concept prevailed. Soon the Flemish dropped economic work, retaining today only general services for members, as handling of family allowances, mutual insurance, and advice on taxation and labor problems. While remaining autonomous organizations APIC and L. A. C. V. W. combined into the Fédération des Patrons Catholiques (FEPAC) in 1937, which was given its present form in 1945.

Together with Bekaert and Harmel, Father Jean-Marie Laureys, S.J., is a dominant FEPAC figure in Belgium through-out the twenty-five years until his death in 1956. In 1930 he became chaplain of APIC. Finding a vague assemblage of good will and self-interest, he joined the lay leaders in forging these impulses into an institution. He created a library and study center, and launched the *Bulletin Social des Industriels*, now a respected monthly review. He authored brochures, led numerous study commissions, and played the leading role in preparing national congresses which developed major doctrinal themes closely linked to current socio-economic issues.

It is instructive to glance over some of the subjects to grasp the interests of the Belgian employers over these years. Some brochure titles are: « Entre l'Usine et le Foyer, l'APIC et le Chômage, L'Organisation des Professions dans les Encycliques Pontificales, La Moralité au Travail, Conflits de Travail, La Noblesse et la Sainteté du Travail ». Among others there were study commissions on: Women Workers in Factories, Housing, City Planning, Social Security, The Guaranteed Weekly Wage, Nationalization, Labor — Management Committees. And a few of the congress themes were: Tradeunionism, Management and De-proletarization, Industrial Organization, Solving Labor Conflicts [33].

Undoubtedly, however, the all-important and lasting

---

[36] Data on Father Laureys are from FEPAC and UNIAPAC archives, from personal interviews with some of his friends, and from a twenty-eight page booklet, *Hommage au R. P. Laureys, S.J., Aumônier de l'APIC*, issued on the occasion of his twenty-fifth jubilee as chaplain, January 18, 1956.

contribution of Father Laureys was the formation he gave
to the men with whom he worked. His very photograph
gives a virile impression of strength and vigor. During the
first World War he received grave wounds and was a prisoner during the last War [37]. He formulated doctrine allied
to reality; he prepared the men who were to lead the association and deepen the concepts in succeeding years. If he,
a priest, seems somewhat to dominate for a quarter of a
century a layman's movement in the temporal order, it was,
by today's testimony of his associates of yesterday, because
he appeared to fulfill an indispensable vocation: not mainly
forming up an organization, but rather the forming of leaders
for the employers' apostolate.

This principal work did not enter into seminar minutes
and congress reports. Consequently it is elusive and hard
to pin down. Conversations with the men who surrounded
him bring out this unrecorded and quasi-unofficial role
above all.

René-Hubert Frings was one of Laureys' « disciples » [38].
He reports that experience today with unabashed emotion
and gratitude. His first contact with Father Laureys came
in 1934. Until then, Frings admits readily that his inherited
faith meant little to him. In time he found himself in the
chaplain's « entourage » of some thirty men, fifteen of whom
were particularly close to the priest. In addition to organizational and study sessions with others, Frings went to
Laureys privately some two or three times a month for an
hour's conversation, or more properly « spiritual direction »,
to use Frings' own words. He continues: « He changed my
whole view of life. His formula in these encounters was
directly religious. Father Laureys demanded total response
to duty in one's state in life, without compromise ». The

---

[37] Jean van Houtte, former prime minister and currently minister
of finance of Belgium, recounted to the jubilee audience war-time experiences with Father Laureys in a prison camp. These war memories
provided later bonds among the national leaders, and as frequently
served to divide the Catholic employers of Europe. Van Houtte's talk
highlights the astonishing rapprochement effected since 1945, toward
which UNIAPAC members are making a most creditable contribution.
Ibid., pp. 15-17.

[38] This account is from interviews of September 5-6, 1959, at Hervelé-
Louvain. Among other intimates of Father Laureys to whom the writer
is especially indebted for interviews and insights are Léon Bekaert, president of FEPAC, Emmanuel Vaes, Jean Perrot and Jan De Spot, all
leaders of the Belgian association, as is Frings, cited here.

priest would offer the men books on issues then current, and
on the return visit the subject was informally discussed.
« He knew we business men had little time for reading », reports Léon Bekaert, another of Laureys' intimates, « so he
would point out a particular chapter or mark a relevant article in a magazine which he divined would fill a pressing
need or gap in our knowledge. I, too, saw him almost
weekly ».

Frings adds that, he being a technologist, the relation
of science and religion often entered into the conversations,
and, « Father Laureys often cited Teilhard de Chardin ».
From his wallet Frings pulled out a frayed copy of a prayer
composed by his chaplain some twenty-five years back expressly for the blessing of his new business offices. The personal concern reached also the family; a daughter of Frings
was led by Laureys into the Jeunesse Ouvrière Chrétienne
Feminine to enable her to contact workers and to grasp something of their problems and mentality. During the second
War, the FEPAC library and archives found refuge in the
Frings' home.

Testimonials to Father Laureys' accomplishment come
from men of state as well as his closest personal friends.
The banquet celebrating his twenty-fifth jubilee of cha-
plaincy heard encomiums from three former prime ministers: Jean van Houtte, Georges Theunis and Paul van Zeeland, the last two being also *ministres d'état* [39].

But the best testimonials to Father Laureys are the organization and leaders he left behind. He died August 1956,
at the Bekaert residence, Zwevegem, where he had gone to
seek rest in view of a worsening heart condition. The writer
accompanied a dozen of the men now leading FEPAC on an
informal pilgrimage to the Laureys grave in the cemetery
of the Jesuit house of studies, Hervelé. Their avowals of

---

[39] George Theunis has been president of FEPAC and of UNIAPAC,
1933-39. The presence of the three former prime ministers as speakers
at the Laureys' anniversary introduces the fact of the close relation of
FEPAC with leaders of the Christian Social Party, a relation through
persons and program which conceives of the employers' and « Stand »
organizations as complementary currents in the overall Christian Democratic movement, the political expression of which is the party. A
similar close tie is found in Holland, and to a lesser degree in other
countries.

devotion, admiration and gratitude flowed freely.   They still feel his stimulus, which they pass on to other men and other national movements over the world.

C. *France*

Next to Holland and Belgium, the oldest Catholic employers' association is that of France.   While it received juridical form only January 9, 1926, the C.F.P.C. has roots reaching further back than those of her two northern neighbors.   In the 1870's Catholic employers of the North of France, especially in the textile industry, felt the need of conjoint action to carry out their responsibilities as Christian entrepreneurs.   The most dynamic witness of this « prise de conscience » was Léon Harmel of Val des Bois [40]. He introduced an impressive system of welfare services and worker-management consultation.   Others came to observe. In 1884 they founded the Association Catholique des Patrons du Nord de la France.   This grew to wide influence until dissolution in 1892 because its religious objects put it outside the law permitting professional unions.   It resurrected in another form, as Conference des Etudes Sociales.   They promoted mixed syndicates and pioneered in the fields of mutual insurance, consumers' cooperatives, housing and dispute settlement by conciliation and arbitration.

In 1889-91 Harmel collaborated with Father Alet of Paris to found an Union Fraternelle du Commerce et de l'Industrie [41].   They published a trade directory, provided information on advertising, insurance, transport, taxation, and strove for the personal and religious formation of the members.   The Union's peak membership was some 7000, with 1200 in Paris alone.   But despite the fact that its founder, Harmel, was a manufacturer, it drew mostly shopkeepers or small employers, and only a few large industrialists.   The builders' section pulled out of the Union in 1896

---

[40] Georges Guitton, S.J., *Léon Harmel*, 2 vols., *passim;* Joseph Zamanski, *Nous, Catholiques Sociaux*, pp. 52-65, 143-160.   The writer is indebted to the C.F.P.C. secretariate and archives; especially helpful for this early period are four pages of typed notes entitled, « Origines Lointaines du C.F.P.C. » As usual, Fogarty, *op. cit.*, pp. 251-252 covers this period with a pithy summary.

[41] Guitton, *op. cit.*, vol. II, pp. 30-34.

to form their own group[42].   Other branches followed suit.
Twenty-six of these trade groups affiliated in 1901, mainly
through the efforts of Father Puppey-Girard[43], to institute
the Unions Fédérales Professionnelles des Catholiques.
They published a monthly organ, *Moniteur*, and pursued
an active course for several years, particularly on issues
as legal provision for arbitration, workers' pensions and
Sunday observance.   The builders' section organized in 1902
a joint conference with the clerical and manual workers'
unions, perhaps the first such case of combined action in the
French Christian social movement.

Joseph Zamanski now enters the story, to remain near
its center until the present day.   In 1925 he became head
of the Union Fédérale.   Already in 1905 at the age of thirty
years Zamanski had founded at Paris the first social secretariate of France.   During the prewar years he contributed
notably in the creation of workers' unions which laid ground-

---

[42] Fogarty, *op. cit.*, p. 251, writes that the builders « broke off. »
« Origines Lointaines du C.F.P.C. », p. 1, seems sensitive toward the implication that a break actually occurred.   They offer the picture rather
of a logical and acceptable growth: « Dès sa fondation, l'Union fraternelle se préoccupe de constituer sous son égide des *syndicats professionels patronaux*.   Quelques années, les syndicats du batiment se con-
sidérent comme suffisamment organisés pour *voler de leurs propres ailes*.
Il ne s'agit pas d'une scission mais plutôt du désir manifeste de pour-
suivre plus activement l'action syndicale, sans entrainer l'Union fraternelle dans les difficultés qu'elle peut faire surgir.   Successivement 26
syndicats professionels sont ainsi créés » (Emphasis is from the original).
Zamanski, *op. cit*., pp. 149-150, conveys the same atmosphere: « ... les
syndicats du bâtiment qui sont sortis de l'Union fraternelle, il va les
prendre comme point de départ d'un plus vaste syndicalisme patronal.
Comme l'Union fraternelle s'était créee dans le recueillement de Manrèse,
les syndicats naîtront d'une méditation à Epinay.   Quelques heures de
retraite, quelques moments de silence et voici de l'action ».   The latter
remark serves to introduce a characteristic of the French movement:
the great stress upon spiritual deepening and supernatural motivation,
a quality shared by the Belgian APIC.   Also, to be noted here is the
early dichotomy between educational and syndical functions, as already
seen in Holland and Belgium.
[43] Father Puppey-Girard was also responsible for founding in 1892
what became presently, and is to this day, the Union Sociale des Ingénieurs Catholiques (USIC), 18 rue de Varenne, Paris 7e.   Its members
are engineers, technologists and middle-level staffmen, united into regional
sections all over France.   They publish a monthly, *Responsables*, and
have amicable relations with C.F.P.C.   Some members of USIC are on
the same level of management as are some of the « Ingénieurs et Cadres »
of APIC of Belgium, but USIC is not an UNIAPAC affiliate.   From an
interview with Father Joseph Thomas, S. J., ecclesiastical assistant of
USIC, December 23, 1958, Paris.   Cf. also, Zamanski, *op. cit.*, pp. 143-145.

work for the appearance in 1919 of the Confédération Française des Travailleurs Chrétiens [44]. Upon assuming office Zamanski turned his attention to the urgent need for uniting the two entrepreneurial groups into one single organism. The chance came with the election of a friend of Zamanski's youth to the leadership of the Union Fraternelle, Eugène Delcourt-Haillot. They had been militants together in the Association Catholique de la Jeunesse Française. The Union Fédérale and Union Fraternelle combined on January 9, 1926; Zamanski occupied the post of president-general, and Delcourt-Haillot that of president. The fusion called itself La Confédération Française des Professions (C.F.P.), and the further modifiers « commerciales, industrielles et libérales » were added on to the full title. The foundation statement says:

> It is necessary to re-integrate morality and conscience into the modern world and, especially for us of the business world, into labor and the material occupations which represents a third of man's life ... Production does not find all of its purpose in itself; it has a social function. *It is the Christian spirit which we are striving to re-integrate into the world of business* [45].

The C.F.P. experienced noteworthy growth in the next decade, from 3500 members in 1926 to 12,000 in 1935 [46]. Concerned with the preparation of young entrepreneurs, the C.F.P. initiated on December 7, 1929 the Jeunesse Patronale Catholique as an orbital group [47]. In the meantime, Za-

---

[44] *Ibid.*, pp. 95-101, 129-142 « ; Origines Lointaines », p. 2.

[45] *Ibid.*, p. 3. Emphasis is in the original.

[46] *Ibid.;* and from an interview with André Aumonier, C.F.P.C. secretary general, Paris, July 8, 1959. Also, for the whole period since 1926, an excellent history is afforded in « Vingt-cinq Ans d'Action Patronale », *Professions*, no. 262, 27 janvier 1951, pp. 2-3.

[47] National youth branches are especially strong in Germany and Belgium. Organized loosely as the Jeunes du Patronat Chretien, they held their own international congress at Strasbourg, May 1-3, 1959. This specifically Catholic group is distinct from the Centre des Jeunes Patrons (C.J.P.). This latter influential French avant-garde movement carries no confessional title. It insists on its secular character. However, the great majority of the members and leaders, as well as their ideological orientation, are Christian. In fact, C.J.P. appeared in 1936 as something of an off-shoot of the C.F.P.C. Ehrmann, *op. cit.*, p. 167, says: « En 1948, le fondateur des J. P. (Jeunes Patrons), Jean Mersch, affirmait, sans crainte d'être contredit, que les vrais ancêtres du mouvement étaient la Tour du Pin et Albert de Mun. Bien que le mouvement désavoue toute

manski, Delcourt-Haillot and other French leaders took up contact with the employers' movements of other counties toward creating the international conference of 1931 which UNIAPAC continues today. The C.F.P. changed its title to Centre Français du Patronat Chrétien (C.F.P.C.) on June 16, 1949, and again on March 23, 1958 to Centre Chrétien des Patrons et Dirigeants d'Entreprise Français, but retains the identifying initials C.F.P.C.[48].

D. *Harmel and « Patrons du Nord ».*

This rapid survey skips over so much of the ferment and drama of the fifty years preceding the first World War that a second look is necessary to flesh out somewhat this bare historical skeleton. This was the half-century of the great social initiators. The image of Léon Harmel in particular must needs be evoked to recapture to some degree the matrix events of those decades and their turbulent setting[49]. He stands out among Christian entrepreneurs as-

appartenance catholique, il ne fait guère appel à des non-catholiques, pourtant assez nombreux parmi les patrons francais ». C.J.P. is not an UNIAPAC affiliate.

[48] *Statuts, C.F.P.C.*, art. 3 (modifiés par l'Assemblée Générale du 23 mars 1958). The inclusion of the term « dirigeant » in the title denotes acknowledgment of the ascendancy of the manager type enterprise over the family firm. The other innovation, of having « Chrétien » modify « Centre » instead of the persons who are members, was commented on by André Aumonier, secretary general, to the UNIAPAC congress, Luzern, June 4-7, 1959. He volunteered that it is an « ouverture » by C.F.P.C. toward non-Christians. The French now welcome non-Christians to full membership in their movement, Aumonier explained, which movement is expressly, in its origins and orientation, based on the Catholic social doctrine. (From the writer's private notes of the discussion, June 4, 1959). Tensions over the tendencies of confessionalism versus « openness » appear today in the employers' associations, as they show up in the workers' and political manifestations of Christian Democracy. The C.F.P.C. has opted « openness ». A third important implication of the French change of title, and also cited by Aumonier, is the dropping of the abstract concept « patronat », because, he said, « patronat » seems opposed to « salariat ».

[49] Material for this section on Harmel is mainly from the following sources: Georges Guitton, S. J., *Léon Harmel*, 2 vols., *passim*, (vol. I bears a sub-title, *Jusqu'à l'Encyclique Rerum Novarum*, vol. II, *Après l'Encyclique Rerum Novarum); and also by Guitton, Léon Harmel et l'Initiative Ouvrière, passim;* Zamanski, *op. cit.*, pp. 53 ff.; « *Léon Harmel* », *Anthologie du Catholicisme Social en France*, Jean Megret and Pierre Badin, editors, pp. 131-140; and the already cited « Origines Lointaines du C.F.P.C. ».

having perceived the necessity of an apostolate in the employers' milieu, a concept warmly seconded by Pope Leo XIII, who became Harmel's strong supporter and personal friend.

Harmel was born in 1829 into a family of wool textile manufacturers. He became in time head of the family firm at Val des Bois in Northern France. During 1870 to 1900 Harmel introduced into his factory a long series of reforms affecting worker-management relations. His basic principle was that the worker must have a voice, that no serious change in plant administration affecting the workers should be initiated without their having understood the reasons and their having a chance to be heard. To provide social security Harmel introduced the old age and retirement pensions, family subsidies, credit union and family mutual insurance (with 1038 members in 1909). To promote cultural advance there were offered night courses and a complexus of sports, artistic, music and dramatic clubs. And to facilitate a constant communication between labor and management, Harmel established bodies to treat of diverse areas of interest, « conseil de perfectionnement, conseil syndical, conseil d'usine », each composed of workers as well as management [50]. The last named, factory council, was the ultimate attainment of a gradual evolution, comparable in a way to the present day « comité d'entreprise ». In 1909, article 7 of the official regulations of the Val des Bois factory described the factory council as follows:

> The factory council establishes real cooperation by the workers in the industrial and disciplinary management of the factory.
> Its purpose is to maintain a close relationship between employers and workers, based upon reciprocal confidence.
> It is composed of ordinary workers who are elected and who meet with the management every fortnight.
> They are requested to give their counsel on all wage changes, on disciplinary measures to be taken, on questions of safety, hygiene, apprenticeship and work.
> They are the spokesmen of their comrades in demands to be made of the employer.
> Finally, they study reforms which could facilitate their work and render it more profitable.

[50] Georges Guitton, S.J., *Léon Harmel*, vol. II, « Tableau des Institutions Ouvrières du Val des Bois », facing p. 274.

Women workers have their own special council which has the same attributes [51].

Of lasting interest in the history of the development of Catholic social doctrine is Harmel's relation with Pope Leo XIII. The pontiff already in 1879 had invited « all employers and all workers in large factories to strive to follow the example of Val des Bois » [52]. Harmel began receiving invitations to speak to employers' groups on his experiences. On February 2, 1879 he wrote to René de La Tour du Pin: « I will begin attending various industrial meetings starting with a trip to Saint-Chamond on March 23rd ». A few days later he sent La Tour du Pin a lecture prepared for this occasion entitled, « L'Oeuvre des Cercles catholiques et l'Economie libérale », asking La Tour du Pin's comment and approbation. On March 13, after having received his friend's approval, Harmel returned a second draft of his address for La Tour du Pin's rieview, explaining that other friends had suggested changes [53]. These interchanges show how a group spirit began to develop very early, leading in 1884 to the Association Catholique des Patrons du Nord de la France.

Urged by socio-economic considerations as well as by Church-State issues, Harmel understook in 1885 the leadership of a pilgrimage to Rome as an act of homage and condolence to the « prisoner of the Vatican ». This sparked the workers' pilgrimages which followed under the banner of « France du Travail » [54]. The first Roman voyage of 1885 was in no way a workers' affair; *Civiltà Cattolica* (February 26, 1885) reported as composing it only a hundred employers, a few factory chaplains and a few white-collar employees. Harmel saw the need of having workers also call upon the Holy Father, so that they and the employers together in solidarity could receive instructions and counsel from him. The second pilgrimage, 1887, had 1400 workers, 300 chaplains in charge of workers' interests, and a hundred employers. Succeeding pilgrimage grew to reach the top figure of 12,000 workers. It was during the 1887 visit that Leo XIII said, « It is necessary that Harmels be multiplied. Harmels must

---

[51] *Ibid.*, pp. 261-262.
[52] *Ibid.*, vol. I, p. 228.
[53] *Ibid.*, footnote.
[54] *Ibid.*, Chapter XII, « Les premiers pèlerinages de la ' France du Travail ' 1885-1889 », pp. 202-226.

be multiplied » [55].   In a true sense this was the purpose of the « Patrons du Nord », as well as of the Conference des Etudes Sociales which succeeded it in 1892 and the Union Fraternelle du Commerce et de l'Industrie founded with Father Alet in 1891 for the whole of France.

Already in 1877 Harmel had written a *Manuel d'une Corporation Chrétienne*; in 1889 he published his *Catéchisme du Patron*.   These spread his ideas and experiences further; they also show that Harmel's thought was known and studied by Catholic theologians.   His biographer, Father Georges Guitton, S. J., records that Father A. Lehmkuhl said of the *Catéchisme,* « It is a perfect book »; and Guitton quotes Father J. Costa-Rossetti as praising it, « It is a masterpiece ». Lehmkuhl made a few reservations, particularly concerning the scale advanced for proportioning wages.   Costa-Rossetti regretted mainly that the book based the family wage simply « in the name of social interest and of Christian charity ». (Harmel's words, page 79 of the *Catéchisme*).   « It is the word *justice* », said Costa-Rossetti, « which should suitably replace the word charity » [56].

Harmel joined with Charles Maignen and Albert de Mun in promoting the Christian workers' movement, L'Oeuvre de Cercles Catholiques d'Ouvriers.   On November 5, 1893 de Mun came to Val des Bois to speak at an enrollment campaign to a thousand workers.   Two weeks later, November 19th, de Mun strove to counter labor-inspired criticism of « le Bon Père », Harmel; at Saint-Brieuc he recalled that « the first initiator of the movement embracing the working masses was Léon Harmel ... Maignen at our cradle, Harmel in our mature years, these have been our two guides ...   Today, he draws us toward a new development, ... a great hope for the future, I refer to the workers' congresses » [57].   De Mun goes on in the same address to acclaim these germinating Cercles Catholiques d'Ouvriers as the beginnings of industrial-professional organization, and he betrays in one phrase the over-whelming concern of that generation, and probably the prime motivation of many em-

---

[55] *Ibid.,* p. 228.   Guitton cites Henri Bayart as one of the witnesses to Leo XIII's statement; Bayart recalled this in a public talk at Lille, December 3, 1887.

[56] *Ibid.,* p. 234.

[57] *Ibid.,* vol. II, p. 21

ployers: « Now at last we will have worthwhile power, a truly popular force to oppose to the socialist army » [58].

Despite criticism of Harmel by both labor and fellow patrons, his biographer, Guitton, believes that his promotion of these workers' circles was in keeping with the desires of Leo XIII: « That which the Pope had so often said to the ' Bon Père ' in private audience, he now willed to repeat in a public letter of Cardinal Rampolla: (March 31, 1894).

> His Holiness has learned with joy that the good workers of France, among whom many have given him the pleasure of having received them during their pilgrimages of happy memory, plan to meet today to strengthen themselves further in the knowledge and appreciation of practical truths, without which we will but vainly hope to attain the welfare of the social classes ... Also, the Holy Father desires that you, who have been so justly acclaimed honorary president of the Christian workers' congress at Rheims, should convey to the organizers and members of the future assembly assurance of his very special good wishes and of the interest which he takes in their work [59].

Such is the image of Harmel, presented in his lifetime as the model Catholic employer: the *Bon* Père who brings his children to see the *Saint*-Père; who looks after every need and many mere wants of his extended family (after the manner of the biblical patriarch and the patron of imperial Rome); who, as they reach adolescence as social beings, permits his worker-wards to talk back a little at the family table; and who even presides over their moderated discussions with the better-bred brats of other factory-families in the *soi-disant* « workers » congress.

Such is the negative side of this image, a criticism of hindsight today. Still, despite all its faults revealed in retrospect, Harmel's paternalism was a great step forward when he began it. That workers should be treated as human *children*, rather than a cut-to-the-bone production cost, was at the least, a Christian advance over neutral *laissez-faire* liberalism. It was, in fact, such an advance that it seemed sufficient years after it became obsolete.

Henri Rollet, a C.F.P.C. leader of today, sums up the deficiencies of Harmel and his associates: In 1895 an out-

---

[58] *Ibid.*, p. 22.
[59] *Ibid.*, p. 23.

standing « patron du Nord », Camille Feron-Vrau, said, « We must educate the workers further, and accustom them to respect the sphere reserved for the employer ». This sphere reserved to the employer was exprssed by a pervading mentality which exteriorized itself by the employer's wife who comes to the plant and without more ado dismisses non-Catholic women; by the chaplain at Formies who pointedly preaches the peace of the Gospel in the factory council; by the Roubaix employers who control spending at the public house instead of increasing wages; by the nuns at Vrau who take the mothers' place in training the children and are sent to workers' households to arbitrate domestic disputes; « ... always the idea of the worker as a minor, a child to be looked after » [60].

The ensemble of this behavior earned the depreciatory label of paternalism. And again these employers cannot be condemned a priori. In the context of their times they were daring pioneers — for employers. Feron-Vrau, the very man who wanted to educate the workers « to respect the sphere reserved for the employer », was thought a revolutionary by his colleagues in the Conference des Etudes Sociales for permitting his factory workers to elect their own delegates to the factory council instead of hand-picking them himself. When he defended his practice before the Conference, the minutes recorded « general cries of dissent ». And while paternalism inspired valuable social services, relieved much misery and initiated various volunteer committees which grew later into contemporary institutions, it fast went out of date, so fast that many sincere men never noticed the anachronism. Rollet states that Harmel-type paternalism was acceptable in 1885, but combatted ten years later by the workers; such was the rapid flow of events. « At that point », he concludes, « its rigidity and tenacity helped to prevent the fusion of new ideas with the old ... It rendered great services, which it would be unjust to forget. But its condemnation lies in the fact that it made it impossible to unite the organized Catholic forces in industry [61].

The work of Harmel can be evaluated also for its more

---

[60] Henry Rollet, *L'Action Sociale des Catholiques en France, 1871-1901*, translated by Fogarty, *op. cit.*, p. 234. Guitton, *op. cit.*, vol. I, pp. 276-299, treats of paternalism and the corporative concept.

[61] Rollet, *op. cit.*, p. 322.

direct influence on Catholic social doctrine and on the corporative concept of industrial organization in particular.
Studies of the first draft of *Rerum Novarum*, ascribed to
Father Liberatore, show the original text to be without sym-
pathy for purely workers' associations, or what are called
today trade unions [62]. The corporative organization prevailed, with mixed membership of both workers and entrepreneur, a throwback to the medieval corporation-guild and
the future means of dissolving the class struggle. Paternalistic good works are to flow from this mixed confraternity. Father Georges Jarlot, S. J., sees in these proposals
of 1889-90 the influence of Harmel and his associates:

> How these ideas are familiar! For fifteen years La Tour
> du Pin and the Comité d'Etudes de l'Oeuvre des Circles had
> repeated them each month in *Association Catholique*. Léon
> Harmel, with a more paternalist accent, incorporated them
> in his *Catéchisme du Patron* (1889) and in his *Manuel d'une Cor-
> poration Chrétienne* (1879). He put them into operation at Val
> des Bois. To dismiss all doubt, Father Liberatore cites him
> abundantly in the article of *Civiltà Cattolica* (November 25,
> 1889) in which he defines what he understands by « corporation
> chrétienne ». Here are its characteristics: it results from a
> voluntary consensus of adherence; it is founded on religion;
> it exercises vigilance over family relations; it manages the
> economic institutions and controls a corporative treasury; it
> asks of the government nothing but that legal recognition
> which grants it juridic personality [63].

Jarlot is discussing the « anciennes corporations » in
the « avant-projets de *Rerum Novarum* »; he thinks that
Liberatore was transposing into this original draft of the
encyclical the true thought of Leo XIII as developed to that
date and manifested earlier on several occasions. Jarlot
notes that on April 20, 1884, in the encyclical *Humanum
Genus*, Leo alludes to the medieval workers' corporations
as institutions to be re-established and adapted to modern
circumstances. Then in *Humanum Genus* the Pope goes
on: « It is for us no slight consolation to learn that already
in several localities such associations have been re-constitut-
ed, as well as associations of employers, the common goal

---

[62] Georges Jarlot, S. J., « Les avant-projets de 'Rerum Novarum' et
les 'Anciennes Corporations' », *Nouvelle Revue Theologique*, t. 81, no. 1,
janvier 1959, pp. 60-77.
[63] *Ibid.*, pp. 63-64.

of which is to relieve the interested working class ... » [64].
Of course, they exist, Jarlot repeats, « that which already
exists is the ' corporation chrétienne ' of Léon Harmel, the
Association des Patrons du Nord ... », and in Italy the comparable work of Giuseppe Toniolo [65]. But mixed syndicates
are a far cry from the combative, purely workers' unions
which ultimately received Leo's approval in *Rerum Novarum*. The ideal of the Harmel corporation was that economic organization must come forth from an existing religious
solidarity; he did not understand the right-to-organize as
a right in justice independent of Christian brotherhood. In
the mixed syndicate, Jarlot explains, « the moral and religious association precedes the economic association : the corporation is a sort of confraternity ... The employer presides,
the employee has a consultative voice » [66].

A second draft of *Rerum Novarum* by Cardinal Zigliara
leaned away from the Harmel corporative concept and more
towards the ideas of his friend, La Tour du Pin, on professional organization, which, while defining the rights of the
worker precisely and rooting them more solidly, retain a

---

[64] *Ibid.*, p. 64. It is well to reproduce the entire section from the
original Latin: « Una quaedam res est, a maioribus sapienter instituta,
eademque temporum cursu intermissa, quae tamquam exemplar et forma
ad simile aliquid valere in praesentia potest. Scholas seu collegia opifi-
cum intelligimus, rebus simul et moribus, religione duce, tutandis. Quo-
rum collegiorum utilitatem si maiores nostri diuturni temporis usu et
periclitatione senserunt, sentiet fortasse magis aetas nostra, propterea
quod singularem habent ad elidendas sectarum vires opportunitatem.
Qui mercede manuum inopiam tolerant, praeterquam quod ipsa eorum
conditione uni ex omnibus sunt caritate solatioque dignissimi maxime
praeterea patent illecebris grassantium per fraudes et dolos. Quare
iuvandi sunt maiore quam potest benignitate, et invitandi ad societates
honestas, ne pertrahantur ad turpes. Huius rei causa collegia illa magno-
pere vellemus auspiciis patrociniisque Episcoporum convenienter tem-
poralibus ad salutem plebis passim restituta. Nec mediocriter Nos de-
lectat, quod pluribus iam locis sodalitates eiusmodi, itemque coetus pa-
tronorum constituti sint: quibus propositum utriusque est honestam
proletariorum classem iuvare, eorum liberos, familias praesidio et custo-
dia tegere, in eisque pietatis studia, religionis doctrinam, cum integritate
morum tueri ». Encyclical *Humanum Genus, Acta Sanctae Sedis*, XVI,
341, (April 20, 1884).
The pastoral and moral role assigned here by Leo XIII to these
resurrected guilds seems to be so dominant that he appears to con-
cede them little economic purpose. In a way this passage amounts,
too, to commendation for the paternalistic conduct of the « patrons »
retold above by Rollet.
[65] Jarlot, *op. cit.*, p. 64.
[66] *Ibid.*, p. 72.

mixed character, employers and workers together. Only the very last text of *Rerum Novarum* through the personal intervention of Leo himself, an intervention ascribed by Jarlot in great part to the influence of Cardinal Gibbons, contains the definitive teaching that workers can form their own separate unions [67]. Even this is preceded by an encomium to the « beneficent achievements of the guilds of artisans among our ancestors ». In the next sentence the Pope allows that these must be brought up-to-date:

> In our present age of greater culture, with its new customs and ways of living, and with the increased number of things required by daily life, it is most clearly necessary that workers' associations be adapted to meet the present need. It is gratifying that societies of this kind, *composed either of workers alone or of workers and employers together,* are being formed everywhere, and it is truly to be desired that they grow in number and active vigor. (Emphasis supplied) [68].

That « workers alone » might organize was, according to Jarlot, introduced into the text between the penultimate version of April 21, 1891, in which the phrase underlined in the quote was absent, and the final text of May 15th [69].

The principal purpose of the present writer is to reiterate the influence in high places and the staying-power of the corporative and mixed association idea, exemplified par excellence by Léon Harmel and the Patrons du Nord, since they were the direct ancestors of the UNIAPAC movement.

Despite today's hindsight criticism, Harmel and his closer collaborators — by no means can all the Patrons du Nord be included here — did accomplish much good. One signal achievement was the stimulation they caused for the awakening of social leaders, laymen and priests alike. Such a priest was Monsignor Paul Six, cited as the « Premier Missionnaire du Traval », chaplain of the Notre-Dame-de-l'Usine

---

[67] *Ibid.*, pp. 67, 73-77. Guitton, *op. cit.*, vol. I, p. 279, recounts that Cardinal Gibbons visited Harmel and Val des Bois on May 5, 1887. Gibbons was returning to the United States from Rome where he had successfully defended the right of Catholics to participate in the Knights of Labor before Leo XIII. The Knights of Labor were, of course, a non-mixed association of workers only.

[68] Pope Leo XIII, *Rerum Novarum*, (National Catholic Welfare Conference translation), *Principles for Peace*, Harry C. Koenig, editor, pp. 74-75; A.A.S., XXIII, 641-670-(1891).

[69] Jarlot, *op. cit.*, p. 67.

at Tourcoing, and for years diocesan director of social works for the diocese of Lille » [70]. His biographer, Monsignor J. Lamoot, records that a turning-point in the vocation of young Père Six was the Harmel « France du Travail » pilgrimage he made in October 1889. Thirty years after the great post-*Rerum Novarum* turmoil over mixed syndicates and the corporative concept in which he was also intimately embroiled, Monsignor Six writes:

> I consider Léon Harmel, not as the greatest leader in social works (oeuvres) of the nineteenth century — this word social works having so often acquired a narrow and parsimonious meaning — but as the most extraordinary creator of essential or timely social organizations, and, too, as the greatest inspirer of social vocations [71].

The years immediately following *Rerum Novarum's* appearance are called by Guitton, « L'heure douloureuse des polemiques » [72]. The Patrons du Nord feared exceedingly any encouragement toward worker organization of any sort. Harmel was subjected to constant bitter attack by his employer colleagues:

> « Do you realize what you are doing by this arousing of the worker class? You are organizing them against yourself ». To which the « Bon Père » would answer energetically: « They will organize anyway without you. What have you got to gain? And above all — for that's what really counts — what will Jesus Christ gain from it all? » [73].

Guitton adds wistfully, « Upon seeing what is happening today forty years later among those misled men who turn to Moscow, how we would like to be able to say that our apostle (Harmel) had erred ». Guitton sees a development in Harmel's position on separate workers' syndicates [74]. After *Rerum Novarum* he did not remain obdurate in support of the mixed union which underlay the corporative concept. By 1897 Harmel's emphasis was that the worker

---

[70] J. Lamoot, *Monseigneur Six, Premier Missionaire du Travail*, pp. 73-78. It so happens that Msgr. Lamoot, Six's biographer, is currently national chaplain of France's C.F.P.C.

[71] Guitton. *op. cit.*, vol. II, p. 406. The quote is from a private letter to Guitton from Monsignor Six.

[72] *Ibid.*, title of Chapter XIX, pp. 49-75.

[73] *Ibid.*, p. 48.

[74] *Ibid.*, p. 95.

could not remain autonomous, and « capable of directing
his own affairs », unless he was truly Christian. As cited
above, he told his bitterly reproachful colleagues that labor
would organize independently anyway and that what really
mattered was the Faith. Guitton interprets Harmel's orientation in 1897 as follows:

> He favored the industrial organization of Catholic workers.
> Had it not been for the obstacles erected by rather myopic
> conservatives, unconscious disciples of the old liberalism, and
> had it not been for the side- tracking of 1896, responsibility for
> which falls upon a few immature democrats ... it is not rash
> to conceive that the association which would one day mate-
> rialize under the name of Confédération Française des Trav-
> ailleurs Chrétiens would not have had to wait twenty-three
> years longer to establish itself [75].

A second definite development in Harmel's conception
is observable in his view of the role of the state in social
and economic affairs. The two opposite current opinions
were polarized in meetings and groups which became identified with the cities of Angers and Liège. The « conservative » Angers pole « only asked the state to repress moral
evil and to favor the necessary liberty of good citizens ».
The « radical » Liège pole recognized for the State « the
right and the duty, not only of protecting, but further, of
promoting the common good of society » [76]. Guitton sees
a change in Harmel's position especially after 1890, attribut-
able in part to La Tour du Pin:

> Angers — and Harmel at the first stage of his evolution,
> before the influence of La Tour du Pin — was naturally in
> defiance against a government without counterpoise or control.
> On the other hand, having their antennas toward the future ...
> Liège — and Harmel especially since 1890 — already lived a
> bit in the future and demanded of the state services which
> were really beyond its actual ability of fulfilling with perfec-
> tion [77].

Another marked contribution of Harmel to social thought
and practice was his promotion of the family wage and family allocations. In his study, *Vers une Politique de Bien-*

---

[75] *Ibid.*, p. 98.
[76] *Ibid.*, p. 50.
[77] *Ibid.*, p. 51.

Etre Familial, Father Pedro Calderan Beltrão, S. J., in the chapter on « L'Origine et le Développement de la politique familiale » cites Harmel's initiative in this field as outstanding [78]. After surveying the demographic policies of imperial Rome, modern Britain, and France through Colbert, Louis XIV and Napoleon, Beltrão states:

> But the most significant case — proving besides the influence of social Catholicism in the development of ideas on the subject — is furnished us by the initiative of Léon Harmel in his factory at Val des Bois. According to his biographer (Guitton), the « supplément familial au salaire » instituted by Harmel in 1891 for reasons of social justice was a direct consequence of principles advanced by *Rerum Novarum*. And that was from its inception an institution of such progressive character that it still astonishes us today a half-century afterward [79].

Another Louvain author, Ch. Dieude, corroborates Beltrao: « We do not hesitate to attribuite to Léon Harmel the first practical application of the principle of employer subsidies to larger families » [80]. In fact, after *Rerum Novarum*, Harmel advanced in his position on the family wage far beyond the charity motive for which he was mildly reproached by the theologian Costa-Rossetti, cited above for his comment on the *Catéchisme du Patron*. The family subsidies program praised by Beltrao and others was directed at the unusually large family; Harmel thought that the normal wage must be gauged to the ordinary necessities of life sufficient for the worker and the ordinary family. The basic salary should be a family wage; then came the additional « supplément familial au salaire » for the exceptional large family. The following quote from Harmel is noteworthy not merely in its pertinency, but moreover for its inkling of the influence of the Le Play school of sociology, as well as Leo XIII, on wage theory through the concrete persons and actual experiences of Harmel and his collaborators:

> Already for a long time, explains the « Bon Père », Le Play in the first volume of *Reforms Sociales* gave the defini-

---

[78] Pedro Calderan Beltrão, S.J., *Vers une Politique de Bien-Etre Familial*, p. 126.
[79] *Ibid*.
[80] Ch. Dieude, *Les Allocations Familiales*, p. 15.

tion of wage: « The wage is that remuneration accorded the
worker in exchange for his work. Among model societies, it
is composed of two parts: one, the wage properly speaking,
proportional to the effort of the worker; the other, 'les sub-
ventions', proportional to the needs of the family ».

The Sovereign Pontiff Leo XIII, in his encyclical on *Condition of the Workers*, insists on the importance of the question of justice in wages. He wants the employer to concern
himself not only with the wage current to the locality, but
also with those relations which can exist between salary level
and the necessities of life.

Therefore, we believe that a normal piece of work, performed by a man living in ordinary circumstances, should obtain remuneration sufficient for the worker and a family of
ordinary size. With Le Play we believe that employers should
provide from their general expenses a reserve intended to meet
the needs of the larger family [81].

In view of this progression of their thought — toward
true trade unions, state action for the common good, family wage theory, social security, and the rest — it is difficult
to call Harmel and his closer collaborators paternalists without further qualification. The appellation must be synchron-
ized to the interplay of swiftly moving events and rapidly
evolving concepts. Certainly many of Harmel's colleagues
among the Patrons du Nord were obdurate and static. They
and entrepreneurs in general became justly identified with
a holding operation, defending the status quo. Only conceived within this context can the work and mission of the
Harmel group be evaluated. They were the pushers, the
dynamic initiators in the midst of their fellow entrepreneurs,
striving to think through and apply Christian principles to
the new industrial society. The UNIAPAC affiliates continue
in this tradition. The first president of C.F.P.C. and a UNI-
APAC founder, Eugène Delcourt-Haillot says, « The French
employers' organization is the natural consequence of the
Christian organization of the Val des Bois factory » [82].

However, in general, neither did the latter-day advance
in thinking of the Harmel group, nor did Leo XIII, exorcise

---

[81] Guitton, *op. cit.*, vol. I, p. 290.

[82] « Origines Lointaines du C.F.P.C. », p. 1. Other testimony to the
descendance of C.F.P.C. from Harmel's work is readily available. For
instance, *Professions*, C.F.P.C.'s publication, on the occasion of the association's 25th anniversary in 1951 writes: « Noces d'argent, nous de-
vrions dire de diamant. Car il y a bien soixante ans qu'un homme
dont le nom ne rencontre qu'admiration, même hors de notre milieu,

paternalism from those possessed of property and employer authority. Especially, in family enterprises it remained embedded in the owner mentality for decades. Its vestiges are seen today in the very name « patron » and in occasional invocation of Patrons du Nord earlier initiatives as nostalgic models even today. These latter are, however, mostly ceremonial rubrics without reference to the deliberate utterances of present UNIAPAC affiliates. Rollet of C.F.P.C., quoted earlier, speaks with the authentic voice. In like vein, Paul van Zeeland of FEPAC concludes:

> Paternalism, which was once necessary and tomorrow might again become useful, is actually surpassed by a superior formula which superimposes upon each other the rights and duties of employers and employees. From this there results more security and more dignity for both the one and the other, and for all more nobility and value [83].

E. *The International Conferences.*

The history of the employers' associations of the Netherlands, Belgium and France has been hurriedly traced. These three, almost alone, make up the movement before the second World War. They in consequence dominate UNIAPAC history; all the others by comparison are current events, having come into being only yesterday, and usually as a

---

même hors de notre pays, réunit pour la première fois des patrons chrétiens. En fondant, en 1890 l'Union Fraternelle du Commerce et d'Industrie, notre grand Léon Harmel ajoutait l'exemple d'une action sociale, concertée et conquérante, à la leçon que donnait son admirable Val des Bois d'une union cordiale du patron et de l'ouvrier ». « Vingtcinq Ans d'Action Patronale », *Professions*, no. 262, 27 janvier 1951, p. 2.

A third witness, Monsignor J. Lamoot, conseiller ecclésiastique national du C.F.P.C., writes: « Le Mouvement (C.F.P.C.) ne date pas d'hier. Dès 1889, deux ans avant la publication de *Rerum Novarum*, l'inoubliable Léon Harmel fondait à la demande de Léon XIII l'Union française du commerce et l'industrie, qui groupa jusqu'à 6,000 patrons. Une autre organisation apparut bientôt, sous une forme plus résolument syndicale: les Unions fédérales professionnelles catholiques. En 1926, les deux associations fusionneront sous le titre de Confédération française de professions commerciales, industrielles et libérales (C.F.P.) ». « Le Centre Chrétien des Chefs d'Entreprise de France (C.F.P.C.) », *Facultés Catholiques de Lille*, p. 277.

[83] Paul van Zeeland, « Discours de M. Paul van Zeeland, Ancien Premier Ministre, Ministre d'Etat, Membre du Sénat », *Hommage au R. P. Laureys, S. J.*, *op. cit.*, p. 19.

result of the missionary efforts of the original three. It was they who developed personal contacts into an international conference. Piet J. Spoorenberg, Rotterdam industrialist and past president of UNIAPAC, participated in these early moves across national boundaries [84]. He recounts that in 1926 Holland sent out letters inviting Belgian and French confreres to the tenth anniversary of A.K.W.V. During business trips, contacts ripened [85]; several crossed their borders to attend a September 1930 meeting in Antwerp and the fifteenth anniversary celebration of the Dutch group in November 1930 [86]. An international « comité d'initiative provisoire » was set up, chaired by Max Paul Leon Steenberghe, later minister of economic affairs of Holland.

Benefitting from plans then afoot to have employers represented at Rome for the fortieth anniversary of the encyclical *Rerum Novarum* — Pope Pius XI had invited workers and management from all nations — Steenberghe arranged a meeting in Rome. Zamanski and Delcourt-Haillot were on this occasion again prime movers. About twenty

---

[84] Most details of this section are from an interview with Spoorenberg, September 25, 1959, Brussels, and from *Waar Voor Wij Staan*, pp. 81-89. Spoorenberg has also served as president of the Dutch A.K.W.V.

Material is also provided from the UNIAPAC archives, other interviews already cited, and from an interview with Dr. A. H. M. Albreghts, former secretary general of A.K.W.V. and of UNIAPAC, and editor of *Waar Voor Wij Staan*, September 15, 1959, The Hague. Further data is found in P. J. Spoorenberg, « Le 25ème Anniversaire de *Quadragesimo Anno* et de l'UNIAPAC », *Bulletin d'Information de UNIAPAC*, no. 5 et 6, juin, juillet, août 1956, pp. 51-52; Zamanski, *op. cit.*, pp. 157-158; Charles Harmel, « Le Sens du Mouvement Patronal Catholique International », *Rapports du Congrès de Rome*, pp. 20-21.

[85] According to *Waar Voor Wij Staan*, p. 81-83, close relations had developed between the Dutch and the Belgian Flemish organizations; in 1927 a joint congress was held in Antwerp. Further contacts and motivation resulted from participation of Catholics in meetings of the International Labor Office, Geneva; pp. 82-83. Father André Arnou, S.J., was then associated with ILO; he became very active in C.F.P.C. and UNIAPAC through the next two decades. *Bulletin d'Information de l'UNIAPAC*, no. 9, novembre 1955, p. 3.

[86] *Waar Voor Wij Staan*, p. 83. The Antwerp meet, September 5-6, 1930, called itself « Internationaal Congres van Christelijk Werkgevers en Jonge Werkgevers ». The special session of November 25, 1930 at the Hague was termed « Assemblée Internationale des Délégués des Associations Patronales Catholiques ». Dr. Fonk of Germany, R. Lambert of Belgium and E. Fourmond of France represented their respective groups. The last named was charged with approaching authorities at the Vatican to explore the attitude of the Holy See toward an international organization; pp. 84-85.

men gathered in a hotel room, May 12, 1931 [87]. Besides members of the three national associations, present also were entrepreneurs from Germany, Spain and Czechoslovakia. They established the Conferences Internationales des Associations Patronales Catholiques [88]. Joseph Zamanski was elected first president. This coalition was to become UNIA-PAC eighteen years later.

The employers gathered with thousands of others in the Court of St. Damasus on May 15, 1931, for the Holy Father's message commemorating *Rerum Novarum*'s forty years. That message was the encyclical *Quadragesimo Anno*. « Until three days before we had no suspicion a new encyclical was to be given us », Spoorenberg reports. « We were, of course, pleased at the reference made to our initiatives. The Pope said he was very happy associations of employers were at last moving ahead » [89]. The Holy Father

---

[87] Spoorenberg adds these data: Dr. Steenberghe's mother was for many years president of the Union Mondiale des Organisations Féminines Catholiques (U.M.O.F.C.). The meeting at Rome took place in Hotel Continental. The German contingent were members of an employers' section attached to the Center Party, Handels-und Industrie-Beirate de deutschen Zentrums-partei. Because of this political affiliation it was, of course, suppressed shortly thereafter by the Nazis. Spoorenberg recalled from memory the Czechoslovakian present, Jan Ruckli, who intended to launch the movement in his land. He has not been heard from since the War.

[88] *Waar Voor Wij Staan*, p. 87. The Holy See did not look with favor upon the founding of a true organization. On January 21, 1931 Fourmond, charged by the « comité d'initiative provisoire » with this side the matter, wrote, « Mgr. Pizzardo a fait ressortir son opinion, que Rome n'approuvera pas une internationale catholique. Pendant l'entretien, il ressortait que peut-être à l'avenir, quand on aura observé l'effet et l'action de l'union, on aura une opinion plus indulgente ». The lay leaders clearly wanted a real organization, but in face of Msgr. Pizzardo's opinion they arrived at Rome with two alternative formulas, that of an « Union Internationale », or that of « Conférences Internationales »: « Le texte est conçu en tels termes, qu'immédiatement quand les difficultés sont levées nous puissions revenir au premier projet »; p. 87.

[89] Under the paragraph heading « Associations of Employers », the encyclical, after lauding the formation of associations of workers, farmers and the middle class, states: « But if this cannot be said of organizations which Our same Predecessor intensely desired establishing among employers and managers of industry — and We certainly regret that they are so few — the condition is not wholly due to the will of men, but to far graver difficulties that hinder associations of this kind which We know well and estimate at their full value. There is, however, strong hope that these obstacles also will be removed soon, and even now We greet with the deepest joy of Our soul, certain by no means insignificant attempts in this direction, the rich fruits of which promise a still richer harvest in the future ». *Quadragesimo Anno*, National Catholic Welfare

knew of their presence in Rome, Spoorenberg continues,
but the entrepreneurs did not meet him as a group [90]. For
his part this UNIAPAC founder considers the teaching on
the *ordines* as the most significant part of the encyclical.
« The big point of Q. A. is that economic life must form
a community of ' droit public ', while still not becoming
part of the State. That's the slow development we are
pushing in Holland with our P.B.O. (Publiekrechtelijke Bedrijfsorganisatie, Public Law Industrial Organization). When
we first heard the encyclical we did not, of course, realize
this deep implication. In fact, it pierced very slowly. We
saw it fully only after World War II. Pius XII strongly
re-insisted on professional organization in his talk to us
in 1949. And Father Laureys kept hammering away, too.
In time then the structure of economic society became our
principal preoccupation in Holland, and to a great degree,
in UNIAPAC as well » [91].

Attention must be called to the fact that the 1931 Rome
meet did not constitute a true organization but « Conferences », a loose coalition only. Until 1939, under successive
presidencies of Zamanski, Georges Theunis and Spoorenberg, these international conferences were as follows [92]:

The Hague 1932, Coopération du Capital et du Travail.
Paris   1933, Juste Salaire et Monnaie.
Brussels   1935, Activité des Associations Affiliées.
Paris   1936, Examen d'un Programme Général d'Action.
The Hague 1937, Service Social dans l'Entreprise.
Antwerp   1938, Assurances Sociales dans la Profession Orga-
            nisée.

Conference translation, authorized by the Holy See, par. 38, p. 16 (A.A.S.
XXIII ' 1931 ', 189).

[90] Spoorenberg, *op. cit.*, p. 51, gives further details as a participant
in the encyclical's promulgation: « Ce même jour (May 12, 1931) on apprit
que le Saint Père allait promulguer le 15 mai une nouvelle encyclique.
Tout intérêt était porté vers et toute discussion était concentrée sur ce
nouveau developpement de la doctrine sociale de l'Eglise.
« Dans l'après-midi du 15 mai des brochures en vingt langues conte-
nant un résumé de l'Encyclique *Quadragesimo Anno* furent distribuées.
A quatre heures une foule de 12.000 personnes se trouva dans la Cour
St. Damase où le Saint Père lui adressa la parole d'abord en italien,
ensuite en français et après en allemand ».

[91] All direct quotes are from the Spoorenberg interview.

[92] UNIAPAC archives, « Quelques Informations sur l'Histoire de
l'UNIAPAC », par. 2; also « Brief History », p. 2.

Besides the sponsorship of conferences, the international group strove to promote the founding of new associations in other nations. The only pre-War addition to the original three was Britain's Catholic Industrialists' Conference (C.I.C.), founded in 1938. Paul Kelley, George McClelland and Arthur J. C. Gormley are the men closest to the British movement. The first named has also been chairman of the Sword of the Spirit, both Kelley and McClelland have held office in the Catholic Social Guild and Catholic Workers' College as well as in the C.I.C., showing again the absence of class struggle animus in the outlook and intent of both sides [93].

A war-time contingency brought the movement to Canada. Georges Theunis, who has already figured in this history, was sent in 1940 as Belgian ambassador to the United States. From Washington he took up contacts with French-speaking Catholics of the province of Quebec, and under his stimulus the Association Professionnelle des Industriels (A.P.I.) was constituted on July 7, 1943. Local founders were Eugène Gibeau and Father Emile Bouvier. The rise of the Canadian A.P.I. was very rapid [94]. Despite war-time handicaps they had by 1945 set up permanent offices, established a « Service des Relations Industrielles » for their members, begun publication of a bulletin, stimulated the founding of an Industrial Relations Section at the University of Montreal, financed scholarships for same, published correspondence courses, launched regional groups at Montreal, Quebec and Saguenay, sponsored two study days and a national congress of three hundred participants. This 1945 congress under the theme, « To Safeguard Private Enterprise », featured such name-speakers as J. Schumpeter on « The Future of Private Enterprise in View of Modern Socialist Tendencies », and Goetz Briefs on « Government and Industry ».

---

[93] *Ibid.*, par. 4; also, « Fiches et Personnalités »; and *Rapports du Congrès de Rome*, p. 20.

[94] J. G. Lamontagne, « Regards sur l'A.P.I. depuis sa Fondation en 1943 », leaflet extract of the *Bottin de l'A.P.I.*, July, 1956. The author serves as secretary general; he says of the founders: « Eugène Gibeau, un patron modèle, qu'on a surnommé à juste titre le Léon Harmel du Canada. Le Père Bouvier, un grand apôtre social, un sociologue et un économiste réputé, dont le dynamisme a donné a l'A.P.I. une impulsion irrésistible »; p. 1.

At first A.P.I. undertook limited economic services for its members, but these have of late lessened in importance, ceding to the educative and inspirational character of the movement. In 1957 A.P.I. hosted the UNIAPAC world congress, the first held outside Europe and signalizing the arrival of UNIAPAC to truly international stature [95].

F. *Post-War Europe.*

Before the end of the war, in 1944, a few Catholic industrialists of Milan began meeting informally to consider the physical and social debris Italy had inherited from Fascism and its aftermath [96]. A gathering of ten employers formed on May 11, 1945 the Gruppo Lombardo Dirigenti di Impresa Cattolici. Under stimulation of the Milanese a Gruppo Piemontese, Turin, was established December 22, 1946. These two groups, and informal adherents of other regions, constituted formally on January 31, 1947 the Unione Cristiana Imprenditori Dirigenti (UCID). During the following month, February 22nd and 23rd, the Gruppi Ligure, Genoa, and Emiliano Romagnolo, Bologna, came into existence, joined in turn by Gruppo Toscano, Florence, May 4, 1947. Venice and Rome followed suit in 1948, the year too of the first national congress.

Vittorio Vaccari, himself a prime mover from UCID's earliest years, credits these men with the original and telling initiatives; Pio Bondioli, Enrico Falk, Gaetano Barbieri, Oreste Giletti, Isidoro Bonini, Silvio Cavatorta, Aldo Vanente and Don Alessio d'Este. UCID grew up in and partook of the

---

[95] The economic functions of A.P.I. are not very highly developed. Marcel Allard, vice-president of UNIAPAC and A.P.I. delegate to the same, believes this economic interest is fast weakening and will in time become almost nil, with consequent strengthening of the educational and inspirational program. From an interview, October 9, 1959, Rome. Vermeire insists on this same tendency after his visit to Canada, November 1959: « Rapport du Secrétaire Général sur son Voyage en Amérique du Nord », UNIAPAC Conseil des Délégués, La Haye, 5-6 février, 1960, 11B, pp. 1-2.

[96] Vittorio Vaccari, « 7 Anni di Azione Sociale UCID », p. 5; « UCID Dieci Anni », p. 3-4; « Una Dirigenza Cristiana per un Progresso Sicuro », p. 5; also, *Rubrica Soci 1958*. p. 14; and Pio Biondioli, « Dieci Anni di Azione Sociale UCID », *I Fattori Umani Nello Sviluppo Economico*, pp. 260-264.

post-war struggle to establish Christian Democracy in Italy.
Vaccari captures the stress and uncertainty of those years:

> The post-war years were truly hard for everyone. But this
> is especially true of economic management which was called
> upon to re-establish plants and work opportunities destroyed
> by the world conflict and the civil war. It was a time of
> agitation and ferment, a period during which the nation seem-
> ed certain to perish, convulsed by internal disorder, and its
> traditional civic and cultural values having been eroded by
> the massive offensive of subversive forces.
> The genuis and selfless toil of Alcide De Gasperi, the spir-
> itual dike raised by the Church, the efforts of a band of sincerc
> democrats held back the catastrophe. Day by day the cement
> of solidarity from these earnest men filled in the ruptures and
> restored dignity to public and private sectors, so that at last
> the authority of the state could assure national life with the
> hope of civil and social order [97].

The personal stories of the makers of UCID — and of
Italy's Christian Democracy — during these fateful years
would make absorbing reading, but this is beyond the scope
of this study. The writer interviewed several such men. One
a Turin industrialist who prefers anonymity, in response to
the query as to what motivated his time-consuming devotion to UCID'S birth in the feverish days of 1945-47, shared
these confidences: Since youth he had been a Catholic
« more or less ». He knew nothing of the Church's social
teaching. The last years of the war found him managing
a factory in the Alpine foothills north of Turin. Local Italian
authority broke down completely. A see-saw battle between
the partisans and Nazis ensued. For months his area was
engulfed in semi-guerrilla strife. His factory changed hands
several times, a few weeks in control of the partisans, a
few days under the Nazis, back and forth. Each side would,

---

[97] Vaccari, « Una dirigenza cristiana per un progresso sicuro », pp. 5-
6. Besides documentary sources information on UCID is from numerous
interviews and conversations, in particular with the following: Vittorio
Vaccari, secretary general, March 11, 1959, Rome; Giuseppe Mosca, UCID
past-president and UNIAPAC president, Father Luigi Belloli, chaplain
of Gruppo Lombardo, Giulio Barana and Teresa Lisa, both regional
secretaries of the same group, March 18-20, 1959, Milan; Giuseppe Prever,
Giuseppe Stroppiana and Father Mario Occhiena, vice-president, secretary
and chaplain respectively of the Gruppo Piemontese, G. Arata, regional
secretary, and Rina Oddone, editor of Operare, March 21, 1959, Turin;
Duca Giannandrea d'Ardia Caracciolo, secretary of Gruppo Romano,
April 17, 1959, Rome; Prof. Anacleto Benedetti, director of studies for
UCID, May 8, 1959, Venice.

of course, accuse him and his workers of collaborating with
the enemy. Hostages were executed. Fear weighed upon
all. Families suffered terribly. Hate generated hate. « I
vowed to God », the industrialist concludes, « that if I lived
through that hell, I would do all I could to remedy the
injustice and soothe the hate that caused the dictatorship
and all that human misery. Now God gives me this chance
to do my bit ».

UCID steered a middle course between two tendencies:
« One minority wanted UCID to accentuate the spiritual side
in the formation of its members »; others wanted « a true
and proper confederation of employers, of Catholic inspiration, (they drew a parallel with the workers' efforts, they
being at the time estranged from the extremist labor
unions) »[98].

From its late start, UCID's growth has perhaps been
the most rapid of all the national associations. It became,
hand in hand with the Christian workers' and farmers'
groups, one of the mainstays of Christian Democracy, and
a principal ingredient in the overall Christian Democratic
movement in Europe as a whole[99]. It assumed leadership
in favor of developing Italy's Mezzogiorno, the European
Common Market and other important phases of recent economic life. It hosted UNIAPAC's constitutional convention
in 1949 and provided one of its members, Giuseppe Mosca,

---

[98] Vaccari, « UCID Dieci anni », p. 6.

[99] A decisive distinction must be made between Christian Democracy
and the national Christian Democratic political parties which are one
expression of one phase, the political, of the overall movement — albeit
a most important and more newsworthy facet. Fogarty, in his *Christian
Democracy in Western Europe 1820-1953*, says: « Its (the book's) subject
is Christian Democracy, the area in which lay men and women, inspired
by their Christian faith, take independent responsibility for the running of political parties, trade unions, farmers' unions, and the like »;
p. xiii. « Then what is Christian Democracy? It might be crudely defined
as the movement of those laymen, engaged on their own responsibility
in the solution of political, economic, and social problems in the light
of Christian principles, who conclude from these principles and from
practical experience that in the modern world democracy is normally
best: that government in the State, the firm, the local community, or the
family, should be not merely of and for the people but also by them »;
p. 5.
And the sentence concluding Fogarty's book: « In short: Christian
Democracy can be redefined as that aspect of the ecumenical or catholic
movement in modern Christianity which is concerned with the application of Christian principles in the areas of political, economic, and social
life for which the Christian laity has independent responsibility »; p. 435.

as immediate past president of the international union, 1956-59. Under his affable leadership UNIAPAC became a truly international movement.

Two other latecomers who have attained in short order top position in UNIAPAC ranks are the German and Swiss associations. The date of founding of the Bund Katholischer Unternehmer (B.K.U.) is March 27, 1949 [100]; the place, Königswinter, in the headquarters of the workers' social commission of Germany's Christian Democratic Party. This latter circumstance stimulates two observations from Wilfrid Schreiber, B.K.U. secretary general: First, the B.K.U. is not directly affiliated with any political party, as was the pre-Nazi Handels und Industrie Beirate de deutschen Zentrums-partei. Second, in its very beginnings the B.K.U. had closest associations with the workers' movement; they and the Katholischer Arbeiter-Bewegung (KAB) are friends and, even more than friends, collaborators. Neither want any part of the class struggle. Both seek in every way fullest confidence between workers and employers [101]. And Schreiber cites the physical expression of this collaboration in the fact that B.K.U. rents its offices from the KAB's Kettelerhaus in Cologne.

Besides Schreiber, principal founders of the German group were Peter Werhahn, Franz Greiss and Fritz Burgbacher. Small meetings begun in 1947 among a dozen men moved along with the support of Cardinal Frings and the assistance of Father Oswald von Nell-Brunning, S. J. Mon-

---

[100] Franz Greiss, « Zehn Jahre B.K.U., Rückblick und Ausblick », Jahrestagung, Bad Neuenahr, October 2, 1959; *Bund Katholischer Unternehmer Mitgliederverzeichnis* 1958, p. 4. *Waar Voor Wij Staan*, p. 80, reports opposition to a Catholic employers' association to have been as strong in Germany during the 1920's as it had been originally in Belgium. One vocal opponent was Father Heinrich Pesch, S. J. After recounting the vehement negative of the Louvain professor-industrialist, cited above, *Waar Voor Wij Staan* continues: « De bekende nationaal-econoom Heinrich Pesch, S. J. werd bezocht. Een ' Katholische Arbeitgeberverband? Neen, begin er in Duitsland niet mee. We hebben tot 1912 hier de onzalige strijd gehad tussen de Berliner en de Kolner-richtung. Begint men weer met een katholieke werkgeversvereniging, dan zal die oude strijd weer oplaaien '. Pesch vergat, dat het niet ging als in 1912 om een vakvereniging maar om een standsorganisatie, en dat Duitsland die ook had voor de arbeiders ».

[101] From interviews with Schreiber, September 21-22, 1959; with Bernard Kulp, assistant B.K.U. secretary, March 23, 1959; and with Prelät H. J. Schmitt, national chaplain of Katholischer Arbeiter-Bewegung, March 24, 1959, all in Cologne.

signor Joseph Höffner of the University of Münster added
his interest and influence. At a meeting near Münster some
ten Dutch employers, among them Spoorenberg, explained
their movement to a like number of Germans. « The Dutch
were like missionaries to us », comments Schreiber, still
warmly grateful for the friendship shown himself and associates in the bitter chaos of the after-war. The new UNIA-
PAC president, elected February 1960, is Peter Werhahn, a
B.K.U. founder.

The Vereinigung Christlicher Unternehmer der Schweiz
(V.C.U.) was constituted April 30, 1949 at Einsiedeln, the
outcome of study circles which had been meeting for two
years [102]. Impulse toward organization was supplied especially by inspiration and contacts from the Vorstand der
Akademischen Arbeitsgemeinschaft. The names or Arthur
Fürer, Professor Willi Büchi and Father Jakob David, S. J.,
figure highly in these first moves. The V.C.U. has by now
set up seven regional groups, all in the German-speaking
cantons. They hosted the 1959 UNIAPAC congress at Luzern, and one of their founders, Fürer, was elected treasurer
of the international body, February 1960.

The Acción Social Patronal (A.S.P.) of Spain and the
União Catolica de Industriais e Dirigentes de Trabalho
(UCIDT) of Portugal were established in 1951 and 1952 respectively. Together they introduce a characteristic not yet
encountered among employers' associations. For political
reasons socio-economic groups independent of the state are
not permitted in either country. Consequently both A.S.P.
and UCIDT have juridic status peculiar to themselves. The
Spanish organization states: « Juridic form: Asociación de
Apostolado Seglar, which makes up a part of the Asociación de los Hombres de Acción Católica, with an autonomous organization for its own specific goal ». Portugal's
UCIDT says: « Statutes approved under the concordat with
the Holy See » [103].

---

[102] « Zehn Jahre V.C.U. », *V.C.U. Bulletin*, no. 86, September 1959,
pp. 574-577; *Statuten*, Vereinigung Christlicher Unternehmer der Schweiz,
passim.

[103] UNIAPAC archives, « Cuestionario », q. 6, p. 1. The status of
these two associations is obviously not in keeping with the concept of
Christian Democracy, which characterizes all the other employers' movements, as set forth by Fogarty in footnote no. 99, above. Background

Spain's A.S.P. is exceptionally well-developed for its years. It ranges over the country through ten diocesan commissions, each with secretariates. It publishes two monthlies, one especially on agrarian questions, and a quarterly, and offers numerous courses, institutes and seminars. Juan Vidal Gironella, president of the vigorous Barcelona association and national vice-president, was elected a vice-president of UNIAPAC, February 1960. Portugal and Spain have collaborated in promoting four Iberian congresses since 1953.

G. *Latin America.*

The Unión Social de Empresarios Católicos (USEC) of Chile is the first association to appear in Latin America, 1948. Founders were Manuel Ossa Undurraga, Jorge Matelich Fernandez, José Luis Claro Montes and Padre Ramon Coo Baeza:

> These industrialists met May 24, 1948, to found the Unión Social de Industriels Catolicos (USIC), in order to realize more conscientiously their Christian convictions in the circles where they exercise their functions. Somewhat later, they decided to extend their action among enterprises of all kinds: commerce, agriculture, fiscal institutions, liberal professions, etc. Our association then became Unión Social de Empresarios Catholicos [104].

Sergio Ossa Pretot of Chile has served as an UNIAPAC vice-president since 1958, the first Latin American to hold an international office.

The Asociación Católica de Dirigentes de Empresa (A.C.D.E.) of Argentina dates officially from 1953. But again stirrings are heard a few years before, and again worker leaders played a role:

---

was obtained also by interviews with Xavier Osset Merle, secretary general of A.S.P., May 9, 1959, Venice; with Juan Vidal Gironella, president of the Barcelona section and national vice-president, October 9, 1959, Rome; and with Father João Evangelista Ribeiro Jorge national chaplain of UCIDT, May 4, 1959, Rome.

[104] UNIAPAC archives, « Fiches et Personnalités »; and Sergio Ossa Pretot, « Version Grabada del Historial del Movimiento Patronal en Chile », typewritten report. Also, interview with Ossa Pretot, June 7, 1959, Luzern.

In 1950 on the occasion of a visit by Canon Cardijn, a dinner was organized to which many Catholic employers were invited. At this gathering Canon Cardijn stated that a Catholic employers' movement was very necessary, and that he considered such a movement as much needed for obtaining a Catholic social order as was his own J. O. C. ... Those present were invited to a new series of meetings for the purpose of constituting such an association, and step by step it progressed ... so that in December 1952 the Archbishop of Buenos Aires gave it his approval and blessing ... The official foundation took place December 3, 1953 ... [105].

In the meantime across the River Plata in Uruguay, the Asociación de Patronos y Dirigentes Católicos de Empresa had been launched in October 1952 [106]. Plans to hold a Latin American continent-wide congress at Montevideo in the autumn of 1960 witness to the progress and solidity of the Uruguayan endeavor.

The associations of Peru and Cuba count only a score or so members each. They have barely launched forth. The fate of the Cuban group, who were mostly agriculturists, is, in fact, still in the balance in the wake of the 1958 revolution.

The organization in Mexico has existed since October 4, 1957. A meeting on that date, attended by Vittorio Vaccari and Lorenzo Bona, secretary general and president of Italy's UCID, founded the Unión Social de Empresarios Mexicanos (USEM). Study meetings and round tables followed. It was visited by Rik Vermeire, UNIAPAC secretary general, in December 1959, and affiliated with the international federation in February 1960. USEM now has a full time secretary, a well organized section in the national capital, budding groups in Monterey and Guadalajara, and shows excellent promise of rapid development [107].

---

[105] *Ibid.*, organizational questionaire. Enrique Ernesto Shaw, a founder and now president of A.C.D.E., gives a like version of Cardijn's stimulus: « ... que era tan importante un movimiento patronal católico apra que haya un recto orden social, como exista un movimiento obrero católico »; from Shaw's: « Version Grabada del Historial del Movimiento Patronal en Argentina », typewritten report, p. 1.

[106] *Ibid.*, « Informe Historia del Movimiento Patronal Catolico, Asociación de Patronos y Dirigentes Católicos de Empresa, Abril de 1959 », Typewritten report.

[107] « Communiqué de Presse », UNIAPAC Conseil central des délégués, La Haye, 5-6 février, 1960, p. 2. Cf. also, Rik Vermeire, « 10ème Rapport du voyage de M. Vermeire en Amérique du Nord. Mexique », (Décembre 1959).

Overall prospects in this immense Catholic region are closely allied to the setting up in Buenos Aires in 1958 of a quasi-branch office of UNIAPAC, a delegate-general for Latin American affairs. The post is filled by Juan Cavo, for some years a leader in the Junior Chamber of Commerce of his land [108]. In 1957 Cavo received from the Pax Christi movement a European scholarship. He elected to spend three months in the FEPAC office at Brussels, where he was received as a « stagiaire ». This experience enabled him to see at first hand the ideals and working of the Belgian organization and to establish close relations with the UNIAPAC secretariate, then seated at The Hague. In 1958 the office of delegate-general for Latin American was created, with Cavo in charge. On April 9, 1958 he presided over a meeting at Lima, Peru, attended by representatives of Chile, Uruguay, Peru and Argentina, to coordinate and re-enforce the work of the different nations and to plan approaches into other countries [109].

Rik Vermeire made an organizational and promotional tour through South America in April-June, 1960 [110].

H. UNIAPAC.

The first years of international cooperation, manifested principally by the six pre-war conferences during the 1930's have already been recorded. Secretarial needs for these European gatherings — really only France, Belgium and the Netherlands — were handled by Emile Fourmond of the French C.F.P.C., assisted by L. G. Kortenhorst, secretary general of the Dutch A.K.W.V. In 1946 Kortenhorst resigned this post to enter the Dutch parliament, and to become the year after its president (States' General), a position he still holds [111]. A. H. M. Albreghts succeded as secre-

---

[108] UNIAPAC archives, « Fiches et Personnalités ». Cavo was secretary general of the Camara Junior de Comericio, 1956-57, vice-president in 1958, and president of the Buenos Aires chapter in 1959.

[109] *Ibid.*, confidential report of Cavo. Contacts in other countries are also reported.

[110] « Communiqué de Presse », UNIACAP Conseil central des délégués, *op. cit.*, p. 2. This promotional tour and that of Vermeire three months before in North America are telling signs of UNIAPAC's determination to become truly and strongly international in character. Cf. also, Conseil central des délégués, IVB, La Haye, février 5-6, 1960.

[111] Staff members of A.K.W.V. state half-humorously that their posi-

tary general in 1946 and took on the office, also, of adminis-
trative-secretary of the international employers' affiliation,
i. e. the Conferences coalition founded in Rome in 1931.
Under his leadership preparations for the definitive establishment of UNIAPAC moved ahead, to fructify in the Rome
congress, May 7-10, 1949 [112].

During the next four years Albreghts carried major responsibility for the four extended seminars at Tilburg, Paris,
Oxford and Brussels. The Paris meet in 1950 on « L'Organisation Professionnelle » was especially noteworthy; it has
provided source material for repeated teaching on this subject which marks UNIAPAC through the past decade [113].

In 1951 Albreghts resigned from the Dutch employers'
secretariate to become minister of economic affairs in the
national cabinet, mainly charged with productivity promotion. After his service in the Dutch ministry Albreghts
returned October 1952 to fill the newly created post of secretary general of UNIAPAC, on a part-time basis. In 1955
he and Father Laureys were sent for two months to the
Americas to promote UNIAPAC's interests. They met with
numerous groups and leaders in Brazil, Uruguay, Argentina,
Chile, Venezuela and Cuba. Much of the life manifested in
the Latin Americas today results in great part from this
stimulation. In the United States they conferred with
groups and individuals, laymen and Church authorities, in
New York, Philadelphia, Washington, Louisville, Chicago
and other cities [114].

Mathew Lombaers of Holland became Albreght's full-
time assistant in 1957. Then in a decisive move of weighty

---

tions are coveted by the politically ambitious because so many of their
predecessors have found spring-boards into national ministerial posts.
Besides Kortenhorst, other A.K.W.V. secretaries to vault upward have
been C.P.M. Romme, minister of labor, 1937; A. H. M. Albreghts, minister
of economic affairs, 1951; and V.G.M. Marijnen, minister of agriculture,
1959.

[112] UNIAPAC archives, « Brief History », and « Curriculum Vitae »;
and from an interview with Albreghts, September 15, 1959, The Hague.
Since 1949 he has been professor in the faculty of economics of the
University of Tilburg.

[113] *L'Organisation Professionnelle*, 2e Session UNIAPAC, Paris, avril
1950, *passim.* This subject is a speciality of Albreghts; his doctoral
thesis at Tilburg was: « La Doctrine des formes de structures economico-
sociales ».

[114] « Voyage en Amerique du sud des délégués de l'UNIAPAC, 28
juin-29 août », *Bulletin d'information de UNIAPAC*, no. 7, Septembre
1955, p. 1-6.

import for UNIAPAC's future the secretariate was trans-
ferred to new headquarters at Brussels and a full-time
secretary general was appointed, August 1958. He is Rik
Vermeire, from 1952 to 1958 national secretary general of
the Christian Social Party of Belgium [115].

With the assistance of two full-time staff persons, Vermeire set out to systematize the organization's loose structural relations, to establish close bonds between the leaders
of the various countries, to nourish the affiliates with ideas
and projects, to open further the national groups to horizons
beyond their borders, to represent Catholic employers in
other international movements, to promote new national
associations [116]. A French language bulletin, begun in 1952,
now appears twice monthly; mimeographed « News from
the Secretariate » for internal consumption circulates as
often in French and English versions [117]. The Brussels office also services the affiliates with documentation they
request in preparation of programs, seminars and study
commissions, as well as supplying texts of more general
interest, e. g., the collective contract of Renault automotive
works of December 15, 1958, and the convention entered
into December 31, 1958 between French employers represented by the Confédération Nationale du Patronat Français
on one hand and labor unions on the other [118]. International

---

[115] This most significant move toward setting up UNIAPAC on a
solid basis and truly launching it as a world force was made financially
possible by the gift of $ 60,000 by a Belgian industrialist. More or less
these funds are to be matched by the affiliate national associations over
a period of four years, by which time it is expected that UNIAPAC will
have gained broad financial support. UNIAPAC rents office space from
the Belgian FEPAC, 71 rue de Cortenberg, Brussels. Lombaers moved
from The Hague to become Vermeire's associate with the title of secretary,
a title shared by another staff member, Manuela Regout.

[116] It must be remembered that Albreghts was only part-time. In
addition to his lectures at the University of Tilburg, he is much taken
up by work on public commissions and on the boards of directors of
several firms engaged in ship-building, textiles and container manufacture.
At most, he spent one-fifth of his time on UNIAPAC affairs.

[117] The name has been changed to *UNIAPAC Bulletin;* each issue runs
about twenty-five pages. Its contents are divided usually into activities
of international scope, documents, news from the affiliates and kindred
groups. *News from the UNIAPAC,* and *Nouvelles du Secrétariat General
de l'UNIAPAC,* mimeographed, are also from twenty to thirty pages.

[118] « Conventions collectives et accords C. » Régie nationale des
usines Renault, Annexe 1; « Convention - Le C.N.P.F., d'une part, La
C.F.T.C., La C.G.T.-F.O., La C.G.C., d'autre part », Annexe 2, to « Nouvelles », no. 10, 15 décembre 1958.

commissions meet on such issues as aid to the technically under-equipped countries. The central council of delegates, UNIAPAC's governing body, now meets thrice annually for the two to three day periods.

UNIAPAC fills a particular role vis-à-vis other international organizations. It now has consultative status with the Food and Agriculture Organization, Rome, and regular relations with the Council of Europe, Strasbourg, the International Labor Office, Geneva, and the United Nations Educational, Scientific and Cultural Organization, Paris. Through its affiliates and their members, it has influence upon the European Common Market, Nouvelles Equipes Internationales (Christian Democrat political world coalition), and Organisations Internationales Catholiques. Vermeire, the new secretary general, spends much time with the member nations, meeting leaders, speaking at reunions, promoting the world view among Christian employers. In autumn 1959 he spent five weeks in the United States, and a week each in Canada and Mexico; in April and May 1960 he made an organizational and promotional trip through South America [119].

Credit for the world view which now marks UNIAPAC is due in great part to Giuseppe Mosca, president from 1956 until his sudden death in October 1959. A past president of UCID, he brought to the international movement personal knowledge of the Americas where he has extensive business interests which required frequent visits and established there close friendships and connections.

I. *Toward a World Movement.*

No Catholic employers' association exists as yet in the United States. Since the 1955 journey there of Father Laureys and Albreghts, contacts have been increasing. Bekaert, Gormley, Mosca, Vaccari, Bona, and Burgbacher as well as others on business visits have occasionally made approaches to their colleagues and friends. A few Ameri-

---

[119] Vermeire, « Rapport du Secrétaire Général sur son voyage en Amérique du Nord », *op. cit., passim;* letters of Vermeire to writer, January 5 and February 16, 1960; and interviews already cited.

cans attended the Montreal congress in 1957, among them John Quincy Adams of New York. Under his initiative a study circle was formed in that city, a move duplicated in a dozen additional areas in 1958-59. To interchange views and develop solidarity among these groups a mimeographed « Progress Report » began appearing December 1958 [120]. A five man delegation represented the incipient movement at the Luzern congress of June 1959, among them Monsignor Dennis Coleman, appointee of Francis Cardinal Spellman as spiritual moderator of the New York branch.

At a meeting in St. Louis, Missouri, August 1959, representatives from seven cities set up a national coordinating committee of the Catholic Employers and Managers Study Groups. This action was taken while these men were attending the annual convention of the National Catholic Social Action Conference. Donald J. Thorman, president of this body, called the employers' initiative « a turning point in the history of Catholic social action in the United States » [121]. Rik Vermeire spent five weeks in the United States during November and December of 1959, meeting with groups and leaders in the East, Middle West and South.

Beginnings appear also in Asia and Africa. Through Father F. Parrel a study group has developed in South Vietnam; the missionary priest came to Europe in June 1959 at UNIAPAC's request and expense to plan with them promotion in southeast Asia [122].

In 1956 the initiative of Father Vincent Charles, S. J.,

---

[120] « Progress Report on the Activities of the Catholic Employers, Managers and Technologists Study Groups », December 1, 1958. This report is reproduced almost verbatim in Social Action Notes for Priests (NCWC), December 1958, pp. 10-11.

[121] « Catholic Employers' Organization Growing », *Work*, October 1959, p. 1. Officers of the coordination committee are: John Quincy Adams, New York, honorary chairman; Paul Tafel, Louisville, Ky., vice-chairman; Edward S. Jamieson, Chicago, president; John Regan, Montclair, N. J., secretary; George R. Donahue, New York, executive director. Headquarters address: 1066 South Michigan Ave., Chicago 5, Illinois. Also, from conversations by this writer, May 1959, with Msgr. Coleman, Donahue, and other members of the Luzern UNIAPAC congress delegation, John B. Caron, Edgar L. Freidheim and Paul Hazard, Jr., all of the Chicago group. More recent data is provided by Vermeire, « Kapport du Secrétaire Général sur son voyage en Amérique du Nord », *op. cit.*, pp. 2-8.

[122] UNIACAP archives, « Note pour le Conseil central des délégués », p. 12; *La Paix Sociale*, pp. 115-117; and from an interview by the writer with Father F. Parrel, June 6, 1959, Luzern.

strongly seconded by FEPAC, aroused sufficient interest to
launch an organization in the Belgian Congo. Jacques De
Staercke, administrative delegate of Belgium's association,
spent six weeks in the Congo invigorating the new movement in late 1958, and another FEPAC staff member, Yves
Seghen, profitted from a three month's governmental assign-
ment in the summer of 1959 to promote the group further.
Founded formally March 20, 1958, and called Association
des Cadres Dirigeants Catholiques des Entreprises au Congo
(CADICEC), this African undertaking draws some criticism
especially from French circles because it has so far only
received Belgians as members. It is not yet an UNIAPAC
affiliate. The former president of CADICEC, F. De Pooter,
became in 1959 secretary general of the newly formed secular employers' organisation, Fédération des Entreprises
au Congo. De Staercke returned to the Congo in January
1960, to consolidate the three regional sections of Leopold-
ville, Elizabethville and Luluabourg, an index to CADICECs'
advance [123].

Conferences are in progress between UNIAPAC and
superiors of the White Fathers on the possibility of an
initiative among employers of Uganda, which would be composed of Africans and directed by them.

The Holy See watches the development of UNIAPAC
with benign interest. Pope Pius XII first received the
UNIAPAC delegates during their constitutional congress,
May 7, 1949, addressing to them an allocution which has
been much quoted since. The talk states that the enterprise
is a community of work, which should unite rather than
divide labor and management, but that the enterprise is
not of its nature a true society in which relations among
participants are regulated by distributive justice. Despite
the basic as well as topical interest of this point of doctrine
— because of its implications for the cogestion (Mitbestim-

---

[123] From an interview with Jacques De Staercke, September 30, 1959,
Brussels. Also, from *Liaison*, numéro spécial, « L'Assemblée générale
statutaire de CADICEC », *passim*. Sixty-two charter members are listed.
Liaison, a preliminary lithographed bulletin published since 1957, was
replaced in 1959 by a full-size review, *CADICEC*. Approval of the organization by Church authorities, despite misgivings in some circles, is
seen from the « Message de Son Excellence Monseigneur Bruniera, Délégué apostolique en Afrique Belge », *CADICEC*, no. 1, pp. 3-4. Cf. Vermeire, letter of January 5, 1960, p. 4, regarding the Uganda plans.

mungsrecht) discussion highly current in 1949-50 — the more lasting impression upon UNIAPAC was made by Pius XII's insistent restatement of *Quadragesimo Anno* on « l'organisation professionnelle » [124]. This talk and subsequent allocutions and letters addressed to the employers' association indicate in part the role UNIAPAC and its affiliates continue to fulfill in the development and enunciation of Catholic social doctrine. Since 1957 Cardinal Siri has been named by the Holy See to guide them in this as well as other spiritual issues. Father Georges Dubois, S.J., serves UNIAPAC as priest chaplain since 1958, having succeeded Father Laureys as APIC chaplain.

This rounds out in cursory form the story of the Catholic entrepreneurial-managerial movements of sixteen nations which affiliate into the Union Internationale des Associations Patronales Catholiques.

3. CHARACTERISTICS.

Certain characteristics are already discernible in the analysis thus far given of UNIAPAC and its affiliates:

1. Catholic employers were late in associating, being the the last of the social groups to form organizations. The prior existence of workers', farmers' and middle class associations facilitated the employers' initiative in most countries.
2. In its development UNIAPAC is marked by three stages: a) between the World Wars, establishment in Holland, Belgium and France; b) after the Second War spread over Western Europe; c) and in the last four or five years, a strong effort to extend over the whole world.
3. Based upon Catholic social doctrine, the movement is primarily ideological, educational and inspirational. Economic functions are wholly absent in most national affiliates, and are on the wane in the others.

---

[124] « Discours prononcé par Sa Sainteté Pie XII à l'occasion de l'audience de l'UNIAPAC de samedi 7 Mai 1949 », (A.A.S., XXXXI, 283-286) is published in booklet form by UCID. This and ten other documents addressed especially to entrepreneur groups are reproduced in French text in *Le Chef d'Entreprise*, Marcel Clément, pp. 238-281. UNIAPAC and its affiliates were recipients of six of these.

These syndical operations are left to neutral employers' organizations.

4. While the movement is in part concerned with the class struggle and defense of employers' authority and property against the demands of labor and the state, fundamentally it is not inspired by conservative motives. The movement arose from an « inquiétude sociale » and a « prise de conscience » of certain employers, who saw the necessity of applying the social doctrine of the Church for the construction of a better society, and their own obligation as Christian employers to press for this realization.

5. The educational and inspirational purpose of UNIAPAC affiliates is addressed interiorly to their own members, and exteriorly to neutral employers' organizations and the entrepreneurial milieu in general. The scope of UNIAPAC is long-range and extremely broad, moving easily from concrete factory practices to philosophical and theological perspectives.

6. The movement openly professes its intention of exercising influence on employers', governmental and other social bodies. It is not separatist, nor ghetto, in attitude. Quite the opposite, it seeks communication with other groupings in order to promote its ideas and ideals in the socio-economic order.

7. The movement seeks where at all possible friendly relations with workers' associations. It has successfully maintained these with labor groups of Christian inspiration.

8. UNIAPAC and affiliates do not have formal relationships with political parties. They do, however, exercise *de facto* influence through those of their leaders who are also active in the political arena.

9. In its interior make-up the movement inherited certain traits of paternalism from its first antecedents, somewhat accentuated by the early dominance of family firms in its membership. Since World War II it has striven toward a re-orientation, shorn of static paternalism and aimed more at the dynamic economy of managerial big business and international scope.

10. UNIAPAC and affiliates are the entrepreneurial-managerial manifestation of Christian Democraty, defining this

concept broadly, as in the words of Michael P. Fogarty:
« that aspect of the ecumenical or catholic movement
in modern Christianity which is concerned with the
application of Christian principles in the area of political, economic, and social life for which the Christian
laity has independent responsibility [125] ».

---

[125] Fogarty, *op. cit.*, p. 435.

CHAPTER III

THE ORGANIZATIONS

The affiliates of UNIAPAC do not have uniform organizational structures and modes of operation; nor are their membership requirements identical. They do not receive their existence, format and program from above. Rather UNIAPAC is itself the creature of the relatively autonomous national groups. It would be tedious and unprofitable to delineate in detail the structure and *modus operandi* of each of the affiliates. Elements common to all the associations will be given, examples will be cited and unusual marks signalized. The number and characteristics of the memberships will be summarized and compared. These differences reflect their uneven degree of development as employers' associations — some have matured, others are in infancy; but even more they are consequences of national divergency: the varied cultural, economic, political, social and religious composition of each nation. Some advertence to these factors has already been made.

1. STRUCTURE.

The older and larger associations of Holland, Belgium and France each have several decades of tradition underlying their statutes and structure. The key body in the French C.F.P.C. is the « comité directeur », or directing committee, of twenty to thirty-five members, elected biennially by the general assembly of all members[1]. It meets monthly.

_____

[1] Information on the French association is from *Statuts, C.F.P.C.;* « Réglement intérieur », mimeographed, sixteen pages; « Directives aux Sections », mimeographed, twenty-eight pages; and from interviews with André Aumonier, délégué général, December 23, 1958, and July-August, 1959, Paris.

From its own members it elects the president and his « cabinet », called officially the bureau, of four to eight members, among whom a vice-president and treasurer are designated. Meeting often, even weekly, this bureau has wide executive powers within policy lines laid down by the directing committee. On proposal of the president the committee names the « délégué général », a full-time staff executive, responsible to the president for the over-all operation of the movement [2]. The French « délégué général », or secretary general, André Aumonier, has fourteen persons under him at Paris headquarters, of whom seven may be regarded as filling staff positions, and four others in provincial offices, these last being part-time only.

Geographically the national movement is divided into sixty-five sections, varying in size from eight hundred members in Paris, to three hundred members in Bordeaux, Nantes and Lyons, and on down to fifty or less in the smaller centers. Additionally, thirty-three other groups exist, called « correspondants », being as yet too restricted in numbers and potential to share the full activity and title of the sections. « The section is the basic cell of the life of the movement » [3]. The section can be created only on approbation of the directing committee. It has its own president, treasurer, chaplain (conseiller ecclesiastique), and several « animateurs ». Several sections can unite to form a regional union, again with approval of the directing committee, with its own officers, activity and secretariate. Thus far, such regional unions exist only in the Nord (Lille) and Normandie (Rouen); others are in formation in the Bordeaux and Toulouse areas. The national president is *ex officio* a member of the regional's directing committee and posseses the right of veto over all questions concerning the general policy of C.F.P.C. [4].

There exists also a consultative organ, the « conseil national », composed principally of the directing committee, the presidents of the regional unions and sections, and the local chaplains. They meet annually and can be called in extraordinary session by the president. Their role is to

---

[2] « Réglement intérieur », p. 3. In this study this office is rendered in English as secretary general.

[3] *Ibid.*, p. 7.

[4] *Ibid.*, p. 11.

recommend studies and orientations to be undertaken by the movement [5]. A priest becomes « conseiller ecclesiastique national » on the « proposition » of the directing committee and the « agrément » of the assembly of French cardinals and archbishops [6].

The « commission des études » is a permanent body designated by the directing committee to deepen the ideas and doctrine of the movement and to assist the president and his officers in taking positions on this or that economic or social actuality or trend. Its members can be experts outside the C.F.P.C. Temporary study commissions are also be set up when needed [7].

UCID of Italy is more decentralized than the French association. UCID is structurally a federation of ten self-sustained regional groups, each with autonomy of initiative, capable of formulating its own regulations and electing its own officers [8]. The principal national officers, the president, treasurer and secretary, are elected by representatives designated by the ten directing committees of the ten regional groups. And the national governing body, « consiglio direttivo », is composed of two delegates and the secretary of each regional group, plus the national officers. UCID's general secretariate has an administrative headquarters in Rome with six staff persons, and a study-publications center in Turin with five staff people. The ten regionals are designated as UCID Lombardia, Piemonte, Liguria, Emilia, Romagna, Campania, Toscana, Veneto, Sicilia and Marche, the first six of which have one or more full-time secretaries. Some of the groups are subdivided into provincial sections; these number eighteen in addition to the groups themselves, for a total then of twenty-eight local divisions [9].

The French and Italian organizations represent the extremes of unitary and decentralized structure. The others fall in between. All of the larger organizations divide into geographical units, Switzerland, for instance, having seven

---

[5] *Ibid.*, p. 4.

[6] *Ibid.*, p. 4-5; and from an interview with Monsignor J. Lamoot, conseiller ecclésiastique national, September 12, 1959, Lille. Referring to the action of the hierarchy in his oppointment, Lamoot translated the word « agrément » as « ratification », and not as « agreement ».

[7] *Ibid.*, p. 5.

[8] *Statuto*, art. 3 and 12.

[9] *Rubrica Soci*, pp. 19-20.

and Germany having sixteen local groupings. None of these regionals have as yet permanent secretariates. Belgium's FEPAC is a federation of two separate organizations, the Walloon APIC and the Flemish L.A.C.V.W., governed by a federal bureau appointed in paritary fashion by the two associations [10]. This federal bureau selects from its own ranks the FEPAC president and vice-president, one from each of the two language associations. Both of these have their own directing council, officers and secretariates. The Walloon APIC divides its regionals on the basis of eleven industrial areas, like Charleroi, Liège, Mons, Namur and Tournai; whereas the Flemish breakdown is according to the four dioceses of Bruges, Ghent, Malines and Limburg, each in turn subdivided into circles (kringen), sixteen in all. FEPAC has seventeen persons in the Brussels headquarters, of whom seven rate staff positions. Some six of the local groups have full or part-time secretaries.

The structure of Holland's movement is the most complex of all. This results from the presence of two Catholic employers' associations: one organization, the Katholiek Vervond van Werkgeversakverenigingen (K.V.W.), performs economic and syndical functions; the second, Algemene Katholieke Wergevers Vereniging (A.K.W.V.), is akin to other UNIAPAC affiliates, with only educational and inspirational purposes [11]. Only the latter belongs to UNIAPAC; it is set up on a diocesan basis similar to the Flemish in Belgium.

K.V.W., the economic organization, while not a member of UNIAPAC, is so closely linked to A.K.W.V. that something must be said about its structure. It is a federation of trade associations, some fifty in all. Each of these is composed of enterprises of a particular industrial branch, e. g., wool textiles, shoe manufacture, brick and tile, metal, food processing and the like. It must be insisted upon again that these industrial syndicates perform economic functions: they represent their members vis-à-vis workers'

---

[10] *Statuts*, art. 4 and 5; and from interviews with Jean Vanderstraeten, secretary general, March 26, August and September, 1959, Brussels.

[11] In addition to documentary sources cited in the preceding chapter information on Holland is from interviews with V.G.M. Marijnen, secretary general (resigned June 1959 to become minister of agriculture), March 31, 1959, The Hague; also with H. G. M. Linnebank and H. A. M. Elsen, staff secretaries, September 15-17, 1959, and with Albreghts and Spoorenberg, already frequently cited.

unions, negotiate contracts and collective agreements (often industry-wide), make representations to governmental bodies, and perform similar roles for their members. Many have their own individual secretariates; sometimes several smaller groups band together to use the same secretariate services. Each trade association appoints one representative to the « algemeem bestuur », general committee, the national governing body of the K.V.W. This general committee in turn appoints five members to the « dagelijks bestuur », executive committee, which receives also five other members from the « federatie bestuur », federation committee, of the A.K.W.V. [12]. The national staff of the general secretariate, fourteen of whom are university trained, are also the conjoint appointees of the two governing « bestuuren » of the two constituent organizations. They publish a monthly review and represent the overall Catholic employers' movement toward the public, the government, other employers' associations, the workers' movements, political parties and other bodies.

While Canada's Association Professionnelle Industrielle performs some economic functions, its structure and activity is not nearly so ramified as those of the Dutch. Canada also has regional divisions, but the great concentration of its membership is in one city, Montreal. Spain's Acción Social Patronal is the only other association sufficiently developed to need a full structure. Their organizational schema is presented here as an example [13]:

---

[12] « Katholieke Werkegevers in Nederland », illustrated organizational schema prepared by the national secretariate, presents an intelligible picture of this complex structure.

[13] « Cuestionario UNIAPAC », *op. cit.*, p. 11.

Organigrama General del Movimiento:

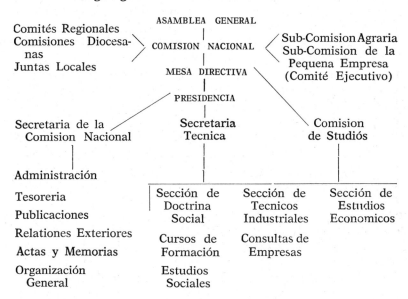

Comités Regionales
Comisiones Diocesanas
Juntas Locales

ASAMBLEA GENERAL

COMISION NACIONAL

MESA DIRECTIVA

PRESIDENCIA

Sub-Comision Agraria
Sub-Comision de la
Pequena Empresa
(Comité Ejecutivo)

Secretaria de la
Comision Nacional

Secretaria
Tecnica

Comision
de Studiós

Administración

Tesoreria

Publicaciones

Relationes Exteriores

Actas y Memorias

Organización
General

Sección de	Sección de	Sección de
Doctrina	Tecnicos	Estudios
Social	Industriales	Economicos

Cursos de
Formación

Consultas de
Empresas

Estudios
Sociales

The structures of the remaining organizations are scaled down to their more modest needs. None of them offer features worthy of note.

Coming next to the structure of the international affiliation, the principal category of membership making up UNIAPAC are « ordinary affiliated members, who are the national associations of Catholic employers, corporate persons enjoying legal personality in their country »[14]. UNIAPAC is basically a federation of sixteen such national associations. The governing body is the general assembly, also known as the central council of delegates, composed of « delegates chosen from among the members of the respective National Councils »[15]. The number of such delegates alloted each country is decided by the general assembly. Physical persons who are associate members can also participate in this assembly, which must meet at least annually, but now follows the practice of the three meetings a year.

---

[14] *Statutes*, art. 3, a.
[15] *Ibid.*, art. 9. The general assembly and the central council of delegates are the same body. The latter term is now in greater use.

« The general assembly possesses all the powers required for the realization of the aims of the Association »[16].
This assembly elects an administrative council, called also
the directing committee, which has broad powers for the
actual running of the international federation. This administrative council is composed of at least six members,
among them a president, three vice-presidents and a treasurer. « The Council has all the powers of management and
administration, except for the powers attributed to the general assembly and those of the secretary general, which are
decided upon by the general assembly »[17]. The secretary
general is the full-time staff executive of UNIAPAC. He
is named and his powers are fixed by the general assembly,
which can also entrust him with a full delegation of powers.
Ex officio he is present at meetings of the administrative
council. « He directs and administers the Permanent Secretariat as well as its subsidiary institutions, and ensures
the day-to-day management of the Association, if it is entrusted to him by the Administrative Council »[18]. UNIA-
PAC's secretary general since 1958 is Rik Vermeire. He is
assisted by two staff level secretaries, Mathew Lombaers
and Manuela Regout. As noted above, UNIAPAC established
in 1958 a Latin American delegate general, headquartered
in Buenos Aires.

In the Rome meeting of October 1959, a move was made
toward relieving in great part the central council of delegates
(C.C.D.) of its executive chores, passing these over to the
directing committee. The purpose is to enable the much
smaller latter group to meet more frequently, with powers
adequate for UNIAPAC's current management, and to enable
the central council of delegates to avoid giving its time to
administrative detail at the expense of ideology and policy[19].

This initiative toward re-assigning tasks within UNIA-
PAC's structure reflects its recent rapid growth and its
deepened determination to address itself more vigorously

---

[16] *Ibid.*, art. 7.
[17] *Ibid.*, art. 16.
[18] *Ibid.*, art. 19.
[19] « Note concernant la répartition des fonctions », L.A.J.M. van
Heijst, C.C.D., Rome, October 9-10, 1959, VI/3.

to international and long-term issues. It witnesses to the preoccupation with study, doctrine and the broad view, needs more and more felt as the ambit of the movement expands beyond Western Europe. The same session discussed at length activities in the Americas and plans for future continent-wide congresses, and received a report from the study commission on aid to underdeveloped countries. These elements are reviewed elsewhere; they are mentioned here only to indicate what pressures of broadening interests are influencing the evolution of UNIAPAC's structure.

2. MEMBERSHIP

Who can become members of the UNIAPAC affiliates? Again considerable variety is found in requirements for membership. Some associations like the French apply liberally the simply stated qualification: « To become a member of the association one must be an employer or manager of a firm, or have been one in the past » [20]. The Swiss V.C.U. distinguishes between ordinary and extraordinary members: ordinary members are independent employers, managers or persons on boards of directors, and managers of economic associations; extraordinary members are lawyers, engineers, professors, et al, who partake in economic affairs in an advisory capacity. These latter have only a consultative voice in V.C.U.[21]. Extraordinary membership is kept severely restricted, there being so far only a dozen or so in V.C.U. The Swiss association has accepted a few non-Catholics as members. So far the German B.K.U. is for Catholics only [22].

---

[20] *Statuts*, art. 6.

[21] *Statuten*, art. 3. Further information is from interviews with Prof. Willy Büchi, V.C.U. scientific advisor and delegate to UNIAPAC, September 25, Brussels, and October 3. 1959, Bad Neuenahr. Büchi is now on the faculty of the University of Freiburg, and an extraordinary member of V.C.U. He was an ordinary member when the movement was founded, being at the time secretary general of the Association suisse de l'industrie lainière et de l'association patronale des industries suisses du textile. While in this position he became one of V.C.U.'s founders and has since remained on its directing committee.

[22] « Was will der Bund Katholischer Unternehmer? » pp. 2-3. The secretary general, Wilfrid Schreiber, (interviews of September 21-22, 1959) in commenting on this characteristic insists that B.K.U. desires and maintains closest relations with Protestant friends and study centers, and that these non-Catholic colleagues understand and approve B.K.U.'s position.

5

As noted above the French C.F.P.C. also receives non-Catholics as members [23]. In 1958 they rephrased their title so that « Chrétien » now modifies « Centre » instead of « Patron ». Their declared purpose is to make an « ouverture » toward non-Catholics, welcoming them as participants in a movement which is built upon the Church's social doctrine. UCID of Italy makes no direct reference to personal religious requirements of its members [24].

Generally speaking, all the associations accept on an equal footing directors of nationalized industries. For instance, the head executive of the federal railway system of Switzerland is an active V.C.U. member [25]. Italy's UCID has many such members, e. g., Enrico Mattei, president of Ente Nazionale Idrocarburi (E.N.I.), Giuseppe Glisenti, a director of Istituto Ricostruzione Industriale (I.R.I.), and, among others, top executives of FINMECCANICA, FINELETTRICA and FINSIDER [26]. Ernesto Manuelli, president of the last named, gave one of the principal addresses at UCID's national congress, Venice 1959 [27]. The presence of these « enti statali » in UCID side by side with private entrepreneurs gives rise to certain tensions and lively discussion, the role of the state in economic affairs being a principal preoccupation of all UNIAPAC affiliates [28].

The peculiarities of Holland's organization have been sufficiently set forth; some effects of these marks on membership should already be rather clear. But to sum up: individual physical persons join the educational and inspirational movement at the diocesan level, A.K.W.V.; enterprises as legal business entities join nation-wide trade associations, each in its respective industrial branch of the K.V.W. In Holland the religious question is somewhat special as well, because of the existence of a Protestant, as well as a non-sectarian, liberal (i. e., derived of the Manchester school of economics) organization of employers.

---

[23] Cf. *supra*, Chapter II, footnote no. 48.
[24] *Statuto*, art. 4.
[25] Interview with Büchi, already cited.
[26] *Rubrica Soci*, pp. 234, 230, 227, 218, 233 respectively.
[27] Ernesto Manuelli, « Le Scelte Economico-Sociali nell'Industria », IX Congresso Nazionale UCID, Venezia, 8 Maggio 1959.
[28] The writer attended such a discussion at a regular meeting of UCID's Circolo di Roma, April 23, 1959. A paper on state participation in industry was read by Giuseppe Glisenti of I.R.I.

Whereas many of the business firms of small and medium category can be called Catholic to the extent that the family or principal owners are Catholic, in the case of larger scale stock companies such a denomination is usually impossible or meaningless. Often no one really knows who own the shares, and of course they can change hands rapidly. Further, it is the practice of the largest Dutch corporations to give their membership equally to the Protestant, liberal and Catholic employers' associations. Such is the case with Royal Dutch Shell (petroleum), Philips (electronics, appliances), KLM airlines and Unilever (chemicals). None of these is truly committed to the ideology or policy line of any of the three movements. This adherance, however, does give some channel for communication of social principles particularly through personal contacts with the corporation managers. Such a situation makes it difficult, as will be seen shortly, to make a true estimate of the numerical strength of the Dutch movement. The same is true to a large degree of all UNIAPAC affiliates. The presence of one top manager of a large corporation in a Catholic association may engender an overall influence equivalent to having hundreds of smaller entrepreneurs as members, or it may be only a formality of public relations.

The current success story of one member of Holland's K.V.W. exemplifies the changes effected by « growing big ». Hubert and Willem van Doorne are brothers, technical and commercial « geniuses » respectively, who were three decades back auto repair mechanics. After the last War they began assembling a few lorries for the Dutch army, there being no automotive industry in Holland. Their production grew. They began experimenting with an automobile, and launched in 1958 the DAF (from Doorne Auto Fabriek), a small machine of imaginative design. In 1959 thousands of DAFs were manufactured, by 1961 about ten thousand workers will be employed. The Doornes are now in the metal industry group of K.V.W., but will probably feel the necessity for financial and public opinion reasons to associate with the liberal, and maybe the Protestant, groups as well, in the same way that Shell, KLM, Philips and Unilever do.

In short, once an enterprise reaches national and international status, it appears to outgrow the separatist confessional framework of the Dutch employers' syndical association.

Another force is now operative on the Dutch scene, pressing against the three-fold division. The necessity of having the whole of Dutch industry represented in the European Common Market favors a unitary rather than a tri-partite formula. The liberal, Protestant and Catholic groups must reach common agreement on who will be their delegates to the numerous commissions and sessions on the international plane and what policies will be pursued. Further, the respective industrial associations of the six Common Market nations formed in 1958 the Union des Industries de la Communauté Européenne (UNICE), a neutral federation with headquarters in Brussels — whose president happens to be Léon Bekaert, the president of FEPAC as well. All nations except Holland are represented by their neutral bodies: Bundesverband der Deutschen Industrie (B.D.I.) and Bundesvereinigung der Deutschen Arbeitgeververbande (B.D.A.), Fédération des Industries Belges (FIB) — of which Bekaert is also president, Conseil National du Patronat Français (C.N.P.F.), Confederazione Generale dell'Industria Italiana (CONFINDUSTRIA), and Fédération des Industriels Luxembourgeois (FIL). Holland is in the awkward position of having four adherents, the Protestant and Catholic, and two liberal associations, one concerning economic issues, the other dealing with social and workers' affairs. Many Dutch feel this division of their national position is weakening and that a unitary front is desirable. So talk is heard to the effect that on this score also the confessional trade associations with syndical functions are probably passé, and that in consequence, Catholics should allow K.V.W. to fade away in favor of a combined economic organization of all the nation's employers. Simultaneously, this view posits a great strengthening of A.K.W.V.'s educational and inspirational influence, so that the ideas and ideals of Catholic social doctrine would penetrate the broadest embrace in employers' circles. However, the inherited system still has its defenders who cannot countenance relinquishing direct participation on boards and commissions, official and otherwise, the seats of which are often allotted to the confessional employers' trade associations through an established formula which assures to the Catholic employers governmental and public acknowledgement and direct voice in socio-economic affairs. The Protestants are faced with the same dilemma [29].

Another question arises: Who is an entrepreneur, or a manager? So long as the firm is small and owned by one or a few persons, these are clearly the employers — the classical « patronat », or in the expressive Dutch, the « werkgevers », charged with directive responsibility, policy and decision making. But in the larger enterprises, and especially in the greater « sociétés anonymes », there exists a chain of command, with a sloping gradient of responsibility. The organizational schema differs not only from country to country, but from industry to industry, varying also with the individual firm's history, workers' syndicates and other factors. For instance, the breakdown of the managerial command in the FIAT and RIV industries of Turin is about as follows [30]:

TITLE	U. S. TITLE EQUIVALENT	No. OF DEPENDENT WORKERS
Direttore Officina	Plant Manager	1000 to 5000 men.
Capo Officina	Supervisor	200 to 1000 men.
Capo Reparto	Superintendent	50 to 200 men.
Capo Squadra	Foreman	10 to 50 men.

Who in this table qualifies as a member of UCID, or of other UNIAPAC affiliates? The plant manager, certainly; the supervisor, maybe; the superintendent, probably not; the foreman, no. Managers themselves disagree as to who they are.

The editors of *Fortune* magazine published a recent study which attempts to distinguish top-managers by designating them as executives. But from questionaires they found that « many corporation presidents hold that all men

[29] From interviews with Spoorenberg and Albreghts, and at the A.K.W.V.-K.V.W. secretariate, and the Protestant employers' secretariate, already cited. Also, interview with Beatrice Verschueren, conseiller of UNICE, September 10, 1950, Brussels; and *Statuts*, Union des Industries de la Communauté Européenne, p. 1.

[30] Interview with Giuseppe Prever, direttore centrale of RIV, Turin, March 21, 1959. The direttore centrale oversees the operations of several factories. RIV manufactures business machines and ball-bearings, especially for FIAT. Prever is a founder and officer of the Gruppo Piemonte of UCID.

in management are executives, and by management they
mean everybody who supervises the work of others, right
down to the foreman in the shop »[31].   Peter F. Drucker
reports a similar lack of precision in the meaning of the
word:

> What then is management: What does it do?   There are
> two popular answers.   One is that management is the people
> at the top — the term « management » being little more than
> euphemism for « the boss ».   The other one defines a ma-
> nager as someone who directs the work of others and who,
> as a slogan puts it, « does his work by getting other people
> to do theirs »[32].

Non-owning management at some level is certainly qual-
ified to membership in all UNIAPAC affiliates.   In the earlier
years most leaders of the French, Belgian and Dutch movements were themselves proprietors as individuals or in family firms.   A change in the composition of the associations
is now in progress.   They show a growing anxiety for receiving managers gladly and for adjusting programs to this rising proportion of non-proprietors.   In March 1958 the French
group added « Dirigeants » to its title.   The newer associations of Italy, Argentina, Peru, Portugal and Uruguay have
included « Dirigenti » and « Dirigentes » in their titles from
the beginning.   The Walloon section of FERAC has since
its founding called itself Association des Patrons et Ingénieurs Catholiques (APIC).   « Ingénieurs » is not to be translated into the English as « engineers ».   The word here covers
a much broader concept: e. g., technologists who direct a
chemical or manufacturing process and its task force, and
non-technicians as well, lawyers, for instance, or accoun-
tants, business administrators, sales managers, marketing
and public relations directors, et al, who have a certain
minimum of personnel under them and some latitude in the
conduct of their operation.   These latter are also called
« cadres supérieurs », about equivalent to « staff ».   Belgium's APIC and its Flemish L.A.C.V.W. both accept these
as members:

---

[31] *The Executive Life*, editors of *Fortune*, p. 16.
[32] Peter Drucker, *The Practice of Management*, p. 6.   Both these
books make, of course, greater precisions in the course of their development.   These citations indicate the initial confusion, which is, in fact,
never completely clarified.

Technologists and staff men are very often invested with managerial responsibilities in the firm. FEPAC cannot attain its goal of christianizing social and economic life without the collaboration of all who exercise management functions.

From the first years of its existence the Catholic employers' movement grouped together heads of firms, technologists and staff personnel.

For several years the last two have organized into specific circles, in order to guarantee the effectiveness of their action [33].

Within APIC this level of management forms a perceptible strata which is becoming more structured and is developing a life of its own. They have set up a Conseil Général des Ingénieurs et Cadres Supérieurs, which is divided into regional units and study groups [34]. They publish a monthly news-sheet, *Promotion,* and have their own national institutes and seminars. The format and initiative of this current within APIC is heavily inspired by two French groups which are specifically for the « cadres et ingénieurs »: Union Sociale d'Ingénieurs Catholiques (USIC) and Mouvement des Ingénieurs et Chefs d'Industrie d'Action Catholique (MICIAC) [35]. Because of the existence of these two groups in France the C.F.P.C. does not have a similar staff-level stratum in its midst and thus remains more expressly entrepreneur in composition. APIC is undergoing readjustment as this middle-management category increases and asserts its individuality. Probably coming constitutional changes will make mandatory a proportioned participation of these « ingénieurs-cadres » in the governing council, and the election of one of their number to the office of national vice-president.

Beyond question, the advent in increasingly greater numbers of non-owning managers into European industrial

---

[33] « Rapport Annuel 1957 » p. 16. In France and Belgium the « ingénieur » normally holds a diploma as a graduate of a school of higher study, usually in a technical field as chemistry, geology, mechanical engineering, etc.

[34] Interview with Jean Gondry, « responsable » of Brussels group, September 30, 1959; and information from interviews and meetings already cited.

[35] Interviews with Father Joseph Thomas, S. J., Louis Hibon and Claude La Grange, officials of USIC and MICIAC, December 23 and 30, 1958, Paris. Italy has a similar organization for this professional group, Unione Cristiana Italiana Technici (UCIT). The German and Swiss affiliates seem to be less concerned with this phenomenon, probably because of the « akademiker Verband » which absorbs many of the middle-management group.

circles, and the fact that UNIAPAC generally speaking has
now surpassed the family firm stage to address itself to big
industry, will cause pressures and needs that will call for
a new response in structure, program and orientation.

What is the numerical strength of UNIAPAC? How
many members has each of the sixteen affiliates? The following table gives an estimate [36].

COUNTRY	TITLE INITIALS	NUMBER OF MEMBERS
Holland	A.K.W.V.	1836
Belgium	APIC	1500
	L.A.C.V.W.	1900
France	C.F.P.C.	4832
Great Britain	C.I.C.	100
Italy	UCID	1950
Germany	B.K.U.	500, with 170 additional junior members.
Switzerland	V.C.U.	280 ordinary, 12 extraordinary, 40 candidates.
Spain	A.S.P	2500
Portugal	UCIDT	500
Canada	A.P.I.	582 firms represented by over 1000 persons.
Chile	USEC	134
Argentina	ACDE	184
Uruguay	A.P.D.C.E.	270
Peru	UNDEC	24
Cuba	ANEC	20
Mexico	USEM	50

Any attempt at adding these figures to arrive at a sum
total is of doubtful value because of the different meaning
given to member as seen above. Nonetheless, additions
shows about 18,500 members in the overall UNIAPAC. These
numbers in turn should be interpreted in terms of size of
firm in which the member has entrepreneurial or managerial influence. Actually data necessary for careful analysis of this nature is offered by none of the affiliates. Hol-

-----

[36] These figures are from UNIAPAC files, brought up to date, 1959,
in the interviews already cited. Exceptions are Canada, Cuba, and Peru,
which are figures of 1956, 1957 and 1958 respectively.

land's syndical K.V.W. affords some comparison with other associations in the organized national economy: [37]

EMPLOYERS' ASSOCIATION	ESTIMATED PERCENTAGES OF:		
	Output of Nation	Capitalization	Workers
V.N.W. and C.S.W.V. - liberal	68 %	70 %	65 %
K.V.W. - Catholic	25 %	20-23 %	27 %
V.P.C.W. - Protestant	7 %	5-7 %	8 %
	100 %	100 %	100 %

No other national affiliate except Canada attempts such a comparison with other employer's associations. Canada claims simply to be the largest employers' organization in the Province of Quebec. That Holland's K.V.W. and Canada's A.P.I. can make such estimates at relative numerical strength arises again from their peculiar nature: their members are firms, not persons. The other UNIAPAC affiliates in no way consider themselves as parallels and equals with the other expressly economic bodies. They are consequently not comparable entities. The neutral employers' associations are not then competitors, but rather the object of influence from the Christian groups. The secretary general of France's C.F.P.C. openly declares:

> The employers' organization (secular) of France, the Confédération Nationale du Patronat Francais, is not a totalitarian and monolithic block. Influences are at work within it and our own influence is gaining; we intend to be the living proof of the pluralism of its positions ...
> Perhaps we have in our sections lost sight of the role of C.F.P.C. as an element of influence in the midst of the employers' syndical associations [38].

This expresses the viewpoint of the whole movement, as will be seen below in the treatment of purposes and exterior influence.

---

[37] From Linnebank, and supported as a good estimate by Elsen and Albreghts. DeKlerk of the Protestant association estimated that members of his group directed 9 % of the national economy. Interviews already cited.

[38] André Aumonier, « Rapport fédéral présenté aux Assises nationales du C.F.P.C. », June 19, 1953, *Documents et Commentaires*, no. 4, août-septembre-octobre 1953, p. 36.

Granting that the UNIAPAC affiliates are so unique in nature and purpose as to preclude accurate quantitative comparison with other groups, the next step is to look into the composition of their own membership. What are the sizes of the enterprises over which they exercise managerial functions? The national secretariates have not sought such information from their membership. France and Belgium (at the writer's insistence) tentatively break down the size of firms with which their members are connected according to number of workers employed. These are classified as large, medium and small firms and are expressed in percentages of the total national association's membership as follows [39]:

FIRM SIZE, by number employed:	France C.F.P.C.		Belgium FEPAC	
Large - 500 or more employed	10 % of members		3 % of members	
Medium - 50 to 500 employed	70 %	»	50 %	»
Small - 10 to 50 employed	15 %	»	47 %	»
Agriculturists	5 %	»	0 %	»
	100 %		100 %	

Applying these estimated percentages to the membership of each association as given above at the following breakdown results:

FIRM SIZE, by number employed:	France C.F.P.C.		Belgium FEPAC	
Large - 500 or more employed	483 members		102 members	
Medium - 50 to 500 employed	3382	»	1700	»
Small - 10 to 50 employed	725	»	1598	»
Agriculturists	242	»	0	»
Total membership	4832 members		3400 members	

The tentative nature of these statistics must be again insisted upon. The diversity of the members must be again adverted to. These figures include the director general of France's Union des Industries Textiles, J. de Calan, as well as the owner of a small textile mill of a few score looms employing a dozen workers. The Belgian figures include a mechanical engineer supervising a hundred men in a wire

---

[39] These estimates are from Jean Vanderstraeten, FEPAC secretary general, and Mlle. Lecour Grandmaison, of the C.F.P.C. secretariate.

making process, as well as Emmanuel Vaes, of the « College de Commissaires » and management supervisor for the Société Générale de Belgique, capitalized at three billion Belgian francs and exercising authority over 20 % of the country's production, and 40 % of that of the Belgian Congo. The inclination then to count these members as identical units becomes obviously more and more questionable. Furthermore, the degree of conviction of the members, their activity within the movement and the influence they exercise exteriorly varies greatly. This variation is expected by C.F.P.C. leaders. Father B. M. Boyer, O. P., chaplain of the Paris section, ranges the members of the different sections in concentric circles: a small really convinced nucleus of 3 or 4 men; a second ring of 12 to 15 militants; a next circle of the active members, who pay their dues and attend sessions, perhaps a hundred or so on the average; and finally a much larger sphere of sympathizers, « the influenced »[40]. Father Boyer insists on the formula: « Attract and draw along the others through men of top quality ». C.F.P.C. does not then see itself as a mass movement, seeking an indefinitely large membership. Another thousand or two thousand adherents would be desirable, but great numbers are not their goal.

B.K.U. of Germany does want to treble or quadruple its membership[41]. They want an increase from today's five hundred to some fifteen hnndred or two thousand members. That number would be considered ideal provided they are well dispersed geographically and industry-wise. But again they do not want a mass movement of great proportions. While deliberately avoiding the word « élite » as sounding presumptuous, they do emphasize their search for leaders who will commit themselves actively to the employers' apostolate. It seems that both B.K.U. of Germany and UCID of Italy have in their organizations a greater proportion of larger entrepreneurs and top managers than do France

---

[40] Interviews with Father B. M. Boyer, O. P., December 23, 1958 and June 30, 1959, Paris.
[41] Interviews with Schreiber, already cited. B.K.U. membership is concentrated in the Rhineland, Ruhr and Münster areas. Bavaria has almost no members due to special difficulties: Bavaria's traditional separatist regionalism, and the establishment after World War II of a general Catholic association for the professional-managerial class on a fraternal lodge basis.

and Belgium [42].   But perhaps because of their relative organizational youth, the first two do not stress leadership
formation and dedication as intensely and successfully as
do the older associations.   It might also be that it is more
difficult to interest top executives in such efforts at formation: they husband their time more sparingly and are in-
clined to feel that having already « arrived », they are pas-
sably influential.   Many other factors proper to these nations
could be explored as affecting stress on formational efforts:
recent economico-political history, religious and intellectual
life, initiatives of chaplains (recall Father Laureys), the favorable atmosphere of the small group formational approach
among other strata in Belgium and France, as the Jocist
and « foyer » movements.

It will be noted in the last two tables that whereas
France's C.F.P.C. estimates five percent of its members to
be agriculturists, Belgium's FEPAC claims none.   Farmers
of the latter country have their own Catholic organization,
as do the Dutch.   The French members are very large opera-
tors, really agricultural-industrialists in the rationalization
and mechanization of their enterprise, and the number of
non-propertied workers they employ.   Germany's B.K.U. has
very few agriculturists, ten to be exact [43].   UCID of Italy has
a much higher portion of its membership in agriculture,
about fifteen percent [44].   It has a special commission to

---

[42] Both B.K.U. and UCID publish confidential directories, *Mitgliederverzeichnis B.K.U.* and *Rubrica Soci UCID*, alphabetically listing all their
members, the firms with which they are connected, addresses and
telephone numbers.   The German directory gives also residential address
and telephone, and a second listing classifying all their members according to industrial branch, e. g., Chemische industrie, Eisen-und Stahlin-
industrie, Energie and Wasser, Lederwaren, Milch und Milchprodukte,
and so forth.   They give a third listing of all members according to
regional section, and add an alphabetical roll of their « Juniorengruppe ».
The Italian directory's main section is by regional group only, with
an alphabetical index at the back covering the whole nation.

[43] *Mitgliederverzeichnis B.K.U.*, p. 85.   These are under a special
classification: « Land-und Forstwirtschaft ».   Of the ten, seven members
are of titled families, including three counts (Graf) and two princes.

[44] *Rubrica Soci, passim*.   The number of agriculturists varies considerably with the region: Gruppo Emiliano Romagnolo (Bologna) lists
fifty-five of its two hundred fifty-two members as « agricoltori »; Gruppo
Campano (Naples) lists only seven as « agricoltori », of whom three are
also industrial « dirigenti », in its total of ninety-seven members.   The
percentages are then over 20 % of the first Gruppo in agriculture, and
only 7 % of the latter.

develop the interests of its agricultural adherents and to work on the issues of that sector of the economy. The associations of Spain, Chile, Argentina and Uruguay also have goodly numbers of landed proprietors among their memberships.

In summary, the membership of UNIAPAC is not at all numerous. And while most affiliates seek to increase their numbers, none of them foresee indefinite growth into a mass movement as likely or desirable. Whereas historically the Catholic employers' associations began among private entrepreneurs, managers of nationalized industries and services are now welcomed as members. In a shift from the smaller family firm, they are anxious to receive non-owning managers into their midst. In some affiliates this presents the problem of determining what level down the managerial gradient still qualifies for admittance, and what re-orientation is needed in view of this change.

3. METHOD OF OPERATION

The analysis of the structure of the UNIAPAC affiliates gives a preview of its manner of operation, again following national divergencies. Much fuller detail will be given in coming chapters on education, influence, and formation; the brief points made here are introductory to this later treatment.

To grasp their organizational method, the national office of the various affiliates affords the best point of departure. The life of the organization flows out from headquarters in three directions: downward to its component regional sections and groups; upward and outward into the other employers' associations, governmental departments, workers' and other socio-economic bodies; and through these outward into general society. It must be immediately emphasized, however, that headquarters is not intended here to mean only the permanent staff of the secretariate. Indispensable as they are, this life from the central heart wells up as much from the kernel of dedicated employers who are the national leaders. But they would be relatively stagnant were it not for the collaboration of the professional organizational executives whom they employ as their staff.

It is not only a question of the employer-leader lacking
time from his workaday duties to give more than a few
hours a week to his association. The full-time staff bring
much more than their time: they bring organizational know-
how to the art of affecting men and institutions, of marshall-
ing the scattered currents of influence into an effective
force, a blunt or a subtle force, as the circumstances might
require. Often too, the staffmen bring an outsider's approach, detached criticism and a sense of dedication which
reach the minds and pierce the consciences of the entrepreneur group. The entrepreneurs in fact are seeking this
stimulus.

Headquarters is then the active fusion of these two
elements: the national employer-leaders and the full-time
staff. The writer visited headquarters of six UNIAPAC
affiliates and interviewed leaders of seven others [45]. The
intra-organizational relations at the top correspond to this
general pattern, although variations do occur. UCID of
Italy is very decentralized as already noted. It is a federation of ten regional groups. Six of these have their own
full-time salaried secretariates, the others are likely to
acquire them in time. In consequence, the activity of the
group is in great part animated by their regional headquarters. UCID does, however, have a strong national
bureau of study, located at Turin, which supplies the regional secretariates with information, ideas, and program
material. UCID national does not then direct the annual
program of UCID regionals. The latter decide their own
annual calendar of events. This usually takes the form of
a monthly lecture and discussion, sometimes following a
year-long theme. The more powerful regionals present
several offering. In spring 1958, for instance, the groups
of Genoa, Milan and Turin sponsored courses on « Problemi
della Comunità Economica Europea » [46]. These ran simul-

---

[45] The writer visited, in their headquarter cities and in several regional sections, the UNIAPAC affiliates of Switzerland, Holland, Belgium,
France, Italy and Germany. Interviews were made on the occasion of
congresses and other meetings with leaders of Spain, Portugal, Canada,
Great Britain, Argentina, Uruguay and Chile. In addition, five weeks
were spent at UNIAPAC headquarters, Brussels, during March, April,
August, September and October, 1959. Interviews were also held with
leaders of the embryo groups of Vietnam and the United States.

[46] « Ciclo di Riunioni sui Problemi della Comunità Economica Europea », promotional folder; and from an interview with Giulio Barana,

taneously in the three cities, meeting twice a week for nine weeks from March to May. The eighteen lecturers were all well-known men in their fields, some of them enjoiying national or international stature, such as Giuseppe Pella, former prime minister and currently foreign minister, and Vincenzo Cazzaniga, national director of ESSO Standard Italiana. They spoke respectively on, « L'Avvenire dell'Economia Europea », the opening lecture, and « Il Problema della Energia nella Economia Europea Integrata ».

C.F.P.C. of France attempts to a much greater degree than UCID to stimulate and direct the activities of its sixty-five sections. Annually, « Directives aux Sections » and a « Programme de Travail » are sent out [47]. These are not hard and fast obligations, but considerable moral suasion is exercised to develop uniform local methods and programs. Monthly « Fiches de Travail » are sent out from the Paris office, either by direct mail or via the publication, *Professions*. Among the subjects submitted for study and discussion during 1959 were [48]: Property's Bases, Justice in Wage Differentials, Public Opinion, Labor-Management Committees, Justice in the Formation of Profits, Investment Planning as a Major Problem in Conscience and in Fact. The central office however does not want to suppress local initiatives :

> The purpose of these outlines must be well understood: they can in no way dispense our members, and especially not the section presidents and « animateurs », from a serious personal study of the questions treated in the sections. The outlines aim at supplying a common framework for discussion to which all can readily refer. They will usually indicate a short bibliography.
> The intention of headquarters is to employ these outlines as a practical means of conducting meetings and for giving members a formation which is common to all the movement. They should become a teaching instrument, a type of in-

secretary of UCID Lombardia, March 20, 1959, Milan. Sixty-three persons attended the Milan course; the fee was thirty thousand lire each, about forty-nine American dollars. The participants were mostly managers of 35 to 50 years of age. Sixty more managers attended the Turin series.

[47] « Directives aux Sections » is mimeographed and runs twenty-eight pages. « Programme de Travail » is printed and runs thirty to forty pages annually.

[48] « Fiches du Travail », *Professions*, January through June 1959, pp. 5, 5, 5, 5, 7, and 6 respectively.

tellectual discipline and a common language, which are necessary so that C.F.P.C. can acquire its own work method in keeping with its own mission [49].

The instruction goes on to state that before each meeting all participants should read the outline and reflect upon its content. And most importantly, after each discussion, the section should send their reflections back to the Paris center's commission of studies. This is because the material is worked out in view of the next biennial national study session, called « Les Assises », and the sections make their contribution to its planning by their own local analyses, which are returned to headquarters in resumé form. By this means the national center invites stimulation from below.

The above quote mentions « animateurs » of the local sections. These are key persons in the French operation. They transform the dead letter into the living spirit:

> An « animateur » is a member who, having participated in a C.F.P.C. training session, dedicates afterward part of his time to the activity of the section, under the authority of its president.
> More especially, the « animateur » strives to apply to conduct of meetings techniques which help to keep them alive and beneficial [50].

The « animateurs » are formed in semi-annual training sessions extending three days, to which some twelve to fifteen men are invited: « those who, by their personal convictions, apostolic forcefulness, and professional and social connections, can most effectively penetrate the employers' milieu » [51]. These sessions are semi-retreat in character; conferences are given on the role of the entrepreneur, his intellectual and spiritual life, and his Christian vocation as expressed through C.F.P.C. Much time is reserved between conferences for private reflection. Their professed goal is: « to give these men techniques which have proven successful in industrial, commercial and social circles » [52]. The

---

[49] « Directives aux Sections », pp. 15-16.
[50] *Ibid.*, p. 8.
[51] « Sessions d'Animateurs des Sections », mimeographed insert accompanying letter of invitation sent out by C.F.P.C., August 1959 for session of October 21-24, 1959.
[52] *Ibid.*

« animateurs » are very highly esteemed in the French association; the life of the movement in its local extremities depends upon them. Plans are afoot to develop this phase of the operation further. Belgium's FEPAC has begun a similar program of quasi-retreat sessions following the French model.

The « animateur » returns to his section charged especially with animating the meetings, of intensifying their impact upon the members and locality. These meetings are combined social, religious, educational and economic experiences. *Professions* carries regular brief reports, from a score of sections; typical subjects during a given month were profit-sharing, the acquisition of property by workers, unemployment, Christian basics on property and authority, and industrial organization [53].

Similar subjects are treated in a like manner in most sections of the other national associations. FEPAC of Belgium, for instance, reported the following among the activities of its sections during March 1958: Malines, conferences on « Relations between Trade Union and Management Organizations »; Antwerp, lunch, conference of Father N. M. Wilders, O.F.M., on « Teilhard de Chardin »; Louvain, continuation of the course on professional morals by Father De Clerq, S. J.; Tournai, conference of Father Vincent Charles, S.J., on « Le Congo 1959 »; Antwerp, Conference, « What Can the Small Firm Expect from the Market Expert? »; Charleroi, « The Objectives of the Christian Trade Unions »; Turnhout, « Panel: Our Attitude toward Property »; Antwerp, conference, « The Management of Small Firms in the United States » [54]. Some of the larger sections, e. g., Antwerp and Paris, meet weekly. Furthermore, some regionals have smaller groups of ten to fifteen who meet weekly or fortnightly independently of the public meetings cited above.

B.K.U. of Germany likewise reports in its montly *Rundbrief* local activities of a similar nature [55]. The Cologne

---

[53] « La Vie du C.F.P.C. » *Professions*, no. 436, mai 1959, pp. 13-15.

[54] *Bulletin de Contact*, no. 108, 15 mars 1958, pp. 5-6.

[55] *Rundbrief* is mimeographed and issued monthly, the only regular publication of B.K.U. In view of its present membership, potential among Catholic employers and the nation's position in the economic world, the German association has so far the smallest number of staff personnel, as compared with other UNIAPAC affiliates. Schreiber, secretary general, is only part-time, he being a well-charged professor at

headquarters supplies less directive material than does the
French national office.   Switzerland's V.C.U. on the other
hand followed a uniform program for all its sections in
1959-60, on the subject of development assistance to the
under-equipped countries [56].   This topic was due to the inspiration of the world congress which V.C.U. hosted in
June 1959 and to the stimulus of UNIAPAC, which is urging
its affiliates to interest themselves in this world economic-
political problem.   The Spanish associations, A.S.P., is organized more on the Italian model: it has strong regionals
with local paid staff and they work out their own program,
sometimes including ambitious courses and institutes.

Back at the national level the secretariates serve not
only as administrators, but more importantly as study centers for their movements.   Commissions of study meet for
periods varying from two months to several years, seeking
to deepen understanding of topics of immediate or of long-
term interest.   These groups are developers of the Catholic
social doctrine within the entrepreneurial-managerial ambit.
Such current commissions in France are on industrial organization, the exercise of authority in the firm, and profit-
sharing [57].   Eight to twelve men compose these groups;
among them a strong majority are always themselves employers and managers.   It is not merely a team of experts.
They meet weekly or fortnightly, depending upon the press
of the subject.   Material for the section programs of the
future, for national institutes and public declarations are
prepared in this way.

More attention will be given below to these elements
and to the doctrine formulated and disseminated interiorly
and *ad extra*.   Likewise later chapters will be devoted to
the means through which influence is exerted and formation
is given for christianizing the entrepreneurial milieu.

---

the University of Bonn. His assistant, Bernard Kulp, is the only full-
time staffman. B.K.U. has as yet no regional secretaries.

[56] Interview with Büchi, already cited. V.C.U. publishes a printed
monthly, *Bulletin: Interne Mitteilungen der Vereinigung an die Mitglieder*,
which reports on local activities.

[57] Interviews, already cited. Father B. M. Boyer, O. P., is director
of the « Bureau des Etudes » of C.F.P.C. *Documents et Commentaires*,
a quarterly publication, gives voluminous reports on these study commissions.

4. Relation to the Church

In their relation to the Catholic Church UNIAPAC and affiliates are not branches of official Catholic Action. The French association is very specific on this point: « C.F.P.C. is not a movement of Catholic Action. It is a movement of temporal action » [58]. The French go on to recall the 1955 declaration of the cardinals and archbishops of France on the necessity of marking well and preserving carefully the distinction between Catholic Action and temporal action. The hierarchy states that the first is essentially an apostolate of the laity in the sense that this apostolate has for its proximate end the extension of the Mystical Body and the rule of Christ. Temporal action, on the other hand, is not in and of itself an apostolate, but has rather as its proximate end the construction and administration of the earthly city through a direct action of the social and political order on institutions and structures. While they eschew any predilection for vain and subtle precisions, the hierarchy insist on this distinction in order to avoid grave confusions of a practical nature which could compromise the Church and give strength to the charge, already exploited in several countries, that Catholic Action is nought but a new clericalism, or camouflaged political activity [59].

FEPAC endorses a like concept of its mission. Frequent recourse is made in recent statements to the address of Pope Pius XII to the Second Congress of the Lay Apostolate, October 1957 in Rome. The Belgians also deny any claim or desire to be counted as official Catholic Action. They regard themselves as participants in the apostolate of the laity in the wider sense, with the characteristic role of « the consecration of the world », in keeping with Pius' statement that this « consecratio mundi » is the essential work of laymen as laymen. The employers view themselves as filling preeminently the Holy Father's requirement that those who would consecrate the world should be « men who are in the very midst of economic and social life, who participate in the government and in legislative assemblies » [60].

---

[58] « Directives aux Sections », p. 11.
[59] *Ibid., passim.*
[60] Pope Pius XII, Allocution to the Second World Congress on the Lay Apostolate, October 5-13, 1957, Rome (A.A.S., XXXXIX, 922). This

In their effort at finding their orientation vis-à-vis the
Church the UNIAPAC affiliates cite such papal statements
made to general groups [61], but by now they have themselves
received numerous addresses and letters from which to formulate their position as lay apostles [62]. One of these to
France's C.F.P.C. summarizes particularly well the role of
the Catholic employers' associations from the Church's point
of view:

> Members of C.F.P.C. must aim at being present in organi-
> zations of employers and industrialists, to which they ought
> to bring the ferment and Christian spirit that shall have
> permeated them through study and prayer. Especially during
> these difficult hours, they ought to contribute to the matur-
> ing of healthy orientations, with just and courageous stands
> and policies, upon which the economic vitality and social
> peace of the nation can thrive. An authentic apostolate is
> to be exercised in this their world, and a deepened knowledge
> of Catholic social doctrine will be for them not only a precious
> light, but also the justification and source of their zeal [63].

---

is quoted by R. P. Thiefry, S. J., « L'Apostolat des laïcs dans l'Eglise
et le discours de SS. Pie XII en octobre 1957 », *Bulletin Social des Industriels*, no. 248, juin 1958, p. 211.

[61] *Ibid.*, « L'appel que Nous lancions l'année dernière aux catholiques
allemands s'addresse aussi aux apôtres laïcs du monde entier, partout
où règnent la technique et l'industrie: 'Une tâche importante vous in-
combe, leur disions-Nous, celle de donner à ce monde de l'industrie, une
forme et une structure chrétienne ... Le Christ par qui tout a été créé,
le Maître du monde demeure aussi Maître du monde actuel, car celui-ci
également est appelé à être un monde chrétien. Il vous appartient de
lui conférer l'empreinte du Christ'. (Message radiophonique au Kölner
Katholikentag, 2 septembre 1956, A.A.S., XXXXVIII, 626). Telle est bien
la plus lourde, mai saussi la plus grande tâche de l'apostolat du laïcat
catholique ». (A.A.S., XXXXIX, 934-935). This likewise is quoted by Thiefry,
ibid., p. 212, as applicable to FEPAC. The address of Father Georges
Dubois, S. J., to the national congress of FEPAC, April 1959, entitled
« Dirigeants et Cadres: Leur Mission Chrétienne », is an excellent treatment of the subject, *Bulletin Social des Industriels*, no. 256, avril 1959,
pp. 145-154.

[62] Marcel Clément, *Le Chef d'Entreprise*, pp. 238-281, gives in French
the full text of the following statements of the Holy See to UNIAPAC
and affiliates: Allocutions of Pope Pius XII to UNIAPAC, May 7, 1949
(A.A.S., XXXXI, 283-286); to UCID, January 31, 1952 (*Discorsi e Radiomessaggi di Sua Santità Pio XII*, XIII, 463-466); to UCID, June 5, 1955
(*Discorsi*, XVII, 117-123); and letters of Msgr. G. B. Montini to the
Second Hispanic-Portuguese Congress of Catholic Employers, June 11,
1954; of Mons. A. Dell'Acqua to UNIAPAC, May 9, 1955; and to C.F.P.C.,
March 8, 1956.

Pius XII gave another allocution to UCID, March 7, 1957, *Discorsi*,
XIX, 25-31; and Pope John XXIII gave a short talk to UCID, January
30, 1959, *L'Osservatore Romano*, XCIX, 25 (29, 992), 31 gennaio 1959, p. 1.

[63] Letter of Msgr. Dell'Acqua to C.F.P.C., March 8, 1956, quoted by

In his 1952 address to UCID Pius XII called attention to the role of entrepreneurs and managers on a scale wider than the enterprise. Their responsibilities extend beyond the merely economic as leaders of society:

> ... in social and public life, by means of legislation and educa- tion of the people, you must strive to transform the mass, which remains amorphous, inert, unconscious, and at the mercy of selfish agitators, into a true society whose members, while distinct from one another, constitute, each in keeping with his function, the unity of a single body[64].

These papal addresses set forth the relation of the Cath- olic employers' associations in language and formulation ac- ceptable to the members themselves. No strict or formal definition of this relationship is thought to be necessary. Referring to the last quoted address, the secretary general of UCID, Vittorio Viccari, five years later called it a most clear confirmation of the orientation, character, competence and means actually embraced by the « social movement of Christian employers and managers »[65].

Spain and Portugal, as mentioned earlier, are exceptions to the rule in their relation to the Church. Due to govern- mental impediments to independent associations of citizens they have organized purposely within the framework of of- ficial Catholic Action[66].

As already seen from the history of UNIAPAC, at the national, diocesan and local levels hierarchy and clergy have been very close to the movement from its origins despite its non-official character. Priests like Fathers Laureys, Van Overbeke, Alet, Bouvier, Arnou, Höffner, David and many others were prime movers in their respectives areas, and

---

Dubois, *op. cit.*, p. 153. The entire text is given by Clément, *op. cit.*, pp. 278-279.

[64] Pope Pius XII, « La Impresa Cristiana », *Avanzate e Lavorate,* pp. 12-14 (*Discorsi,* XIII, 463-466). This UICD booklet reproduces three addresses given by Pius XII to UCID in 1952, 1955 and 1957, and his 1949 talk to UNIAPAC. The manuscript of the first talk was given to UCID by the Pontiff.

[65] Vittorio Vaccari, « UCID Dieci Anni », January 31, 1957, p. 6.

[66] UNIAPAC archives, « Cuestionario », question 6, p. 1. The Spanish organization states: « Forma juridica: Asociación de Apostolado Seglar, que forma parte, como organizacion autónoma en lo específico que le es proprio, de la Asociación de los Hombres de Acción Católica ». The Portuguese report says: « Estatuto aprovade a face da concordata com a Santa Sé ».

often founders.   Today the role of the priest in UNIAPAC
affiliates causes some quiet discussion, as does his very title.
The title « aumonier » or « chaplain » is often avoided in
favor of « conseiller ecclésiastique » or « consulente morale ». The leaders seem anxious to assert the lay nature of
their movement.   This may be a delayed reaction to the
weighty role played by priests in the earlier years, as well
as an expression of today's reality [67].   The priests seem quite
satisfied with withdrawal from the obviously temporal order.
They see their role as being the doctrinal and spiritual
spheres.   Besides approving and appointing chaplains, or
moral councillors, at the national and local levels, members
of the hierarchy are themselves often present at congresses
and institutes, and frequently they deliver principal addresses.

The international movement was from its earliest conception in 1930 preoccupied with the naming of a chaplain
or ecclesiastical councillor.   The preliminary « projet »
brought to Rome by Steenberghe, Fourmond, Zamanski, et
al, in 1931, included the proposition, « The chaplain is named by the Pope » [68].   When the « Conférences Internationales » were transformed in 1949 into a true « Union Internationale », UNIAPAC, the question of the chaplain became more important.   The Holy See requested « that the
presence of a 'Conseiller Ecclésiastique' be determined more
strictly » [69].   However, no one was appointed to this office
until 1957.   In the interim the chaplain of the nation in
which an international gathering occurred filled the role,
while Father Laureys of Belgium performed many of the
functions without bearing the title.   In 1956 it was proposed
to the Holy See by UNIAPAC that he be named officially [70].

---

[67] These are undocumented observations by the writer.
[68] *Waar Voor Wij Staan*, p. 88.
[69] *Ibid.*, quotes Monsignor Montini to this effect as words addressed
to Vaccari.
[70] A. H. M. Albreghts, « Le Père Laureys — Aumônier depuis 25 Ans »,
Bulletin d'Information de l'UNIAPAC, no. 3, mars 1956, p. 28: « ... je désire
manifester en ce bulletin la joie que nous causa à tous la décision una-
nime du Conseil Central des Délégués à Lucerne par laquelle Père Laureys fut proposé comme candidat à la place d'aumônier général de
l'UNIAPAC.
« Cette organisation, sur le plan international, n'avait pas encore
d'aumônier général. Jusqu'à présent cette charge était assumée par
l'aumônier où se tenait l'assemblée.

A few months later, before action was taken, Father Laureys died.

In March 1957 Giuseppe Cardinal Siri of Genoa, who had been for several years « consulente morale » of Italy's UCID, was appointed by the Holy See to the spiritual charge of UNIAPAC. The letter of appointment gives him no title; Monsignor A. Dell'Acqua, substitute secretary of state, writes: « I have the honor of communicating to your Most Reverend Eminence that the Holy Father has deigned to confide to you the charge of developing in favor of UNIAPAC the same activity with which you have with such wisdom occupied yourself for UCID » [71]. Father Georges Dubois, S. J., successor of Laureys as chaplain of Belgium's APIC, became « aumônier-conseil de l'UNIAPAC » in 1958, in day to day charge of spiritual and doctrinal matters under Cardinal Siri.

The first message of Cardinal Siri to UNIAPAC is a good resumé of the relation of the hierarchy and clergy with this lay movement of temporal and social action:

> We have requested a message of His Eminence: it is very simple, and in the phrases of His Eminence himself:
> « I must pray for UNIAPAC. That is my first duty. I must help you intellectually and as a friend. I must remind you that your Faith sometimes demands sacrifices, that we must work for a more human and Christian order, that we must seek not only at safeguarding our rights but also at fulfilling our great obligations » [72].

« Quand la candidature du Père Laureys, à laquelle son Général a déjà donné son approbation, sera agréée par le Secrétariat d'Etat du Vatican, la nomination sera définitive.

« En fait, cela ne changera pas beaucoup, car le Père Laureys a déjà prêté une telle assistance au développement et à l'épanouissement de l'UNIAPAC, que promu en qualité d'aumônier général, il ne lui sera guère possible de faire plus ».

[71] *Bulletin d'Information de l'UNIAPAC*, no. 1, mai 1957, p. 9, from letter no. 370037/SI, Segreteria di Stato di Sua Santità. Occasionally, Cardinal Siri is referred to as « Protecteur » of UNIAPAC. Since he is to do for UNIAPAC what he does for UCID, it is well to quote the latter's *Statuto*, art. 11: « Il Consulente Morale è nominato dall'Autorità Ecclesiastica ed ha l'incarico specifico di consulenza, in materia morale e religiosa, a tutte le iniziative della Unione ».

[72] *Ibid.*, p. 10.

CHAPTER IV

PURPOSES AND POLICIES

Having seen something of the general concept and history, structure and membership of UNIAPAC and affiliates, attention must next be focussed on purpose. Why do associations of Catholic employers exist? What *raison d'être* justifies a « centre chrétien » for entrepreneurs and managers, distinct from their neutral organizations? What is the finality of the UNIAPAC movement?

The Catholic employers' associations themselves manifest deep preoccupation over the meaning of their presence in the socio-economic world. Their documents, addresses and programs frequently express these self-same questions. Seldom is a major assembly called without an analysis of the movement's purpose by one of their leaders. In consequence, the answers are voluminous, and of striking consistency [1].

---

[1] Besides those of Léon Bekaert cited below, some of the best statements are from the following: Joseph Zamanski, « Enfin les Patrons », *Nous, Catholiques Sociaux*, pp. 147-160; *L'Avenir de l'entreprise, Un patronat qui s'engage*, pp. 9-29, and *passim*; « Introduction », *L'Organisation Professionnelle, op. cit.*, pp. 9-20; Charles Harmel, « Introduction », *L'Entreprise Privée*, Ire Session UNIAPAC, Tilburg, mars 1948, pp. 11-18; « Une grande association patronale », *Revue Générale Belge*, no. 14, décembre 1946, pp. 207-219; A. H. M. Albregts, « Avant-Propos », *Aspects sociaux de la coopération économique*, Conférence Européenne UNIAPAC, Knokke-Bruxelles, 12-14 juin 1958, pp. 5-10; « La vocation de l'UNIAPAC », *Bulletin d'Information de l'UNIAPAC*, no. 6, mai-juin 1953, p. 1; « Le Temps et Nous », *ibid.*, no. 1, janvier 1955, p. 1; « De la responsabilité internationale de l'UNIAPAC », *ibid.*, no. 2, février 1956, p. 1; *Waar Voor Wij Staan, passim*, especially pp. 7-11; Bernard Jousset, « Qu'est-ce que l'UNIAPAC? », *Documents et Commentaires*, no. 8, décembre 1954, pp. 5-11; André Aumonier, « Rapport Général aux Assises Nationales », *ibid.*, no. 4, août-septembre-octobre 1953, pp. 25-37; « Pour un ' Patronat de Conquête ' », *ibid.*, no. 9, avril 1955, pp. 3-6; « L'influence des mouvements patronaux catholiques dans le milieu professionnel », *ibid.*, (Congrès International UNIAPAC, Montréal, 1957), no. 20 décembre 1957, pp. 39-48; Jacques De Staercke, « Le rôle de l'UNIAPAC », *ibid.*, (Journées

Today's most authoritative interpreter of the UNIAPAC
mission is Léon A. Bekaert of Belgium. Back in the 1920's
he was a prime mover in launching the Flemish organization, and a close-worker with Father Laureys through
twenty-five years. He was instrumental in forming FEPAC
and UNIAPAC, and has brought to both his ardent support
and high prestige as one of Europe's leading industrialists,
known too in Africa and both Americas. Since 1952 Bekaert
has served as president of the neutral, secular manufacturers' association of his nation, Fédération des Industries
Belges (FIB), and was a founder with other industrialists
of the six Common Market nations of the Union des Industries de la Communauté Européenne (UNICE). Since
the formation of this latter employers' federation in 1958,
Bekaert has served as its president. He is likewise honorary president of his own industry's national association, Fédération des Industries des Fabrications Métalliques de Belgique (FABRI-METAL), and holds office in several top economic and financial institutions, being, for instance, regent
of the Banque Nationale de Belgique, and president of the
Fondation Industrie-Université [2]. For his distinctive service
to his profession and nation he received in May 1959 from

UNIAPAC, Porto, Portugal, 1956), no. 16, décembre 1956, pp. 21-35; « Le
mouvement patronal catholiques, ses tâches et ses moyens d'action »,
Bulletin Social des Industriels, (Congrès International UNIAPAC, Montreal,
1957), no. 243, janvier 1958, pp. 6-13; Vittorio Vaccari, *7 anni di Azione
Sociale UCID, passim*, especially pp. 5-24; *UCID Dieci anni, passim; Una
Dirigenza Cristiana per un progresso sicuro, passim;* « Una filosofia per
la nuova dirigenza », *Operare*, xii, 5, settembre-ottobre 1957, pp. 28-32;
Msgr. Joseph Lamoot, « Les chefs d'entreprise et la mission apostoli-
que de l'Eglise », *Documents et Commentaires*, no. 18, juin 1957, pp. 7-
27; Georges Dubois, S.J., « Dirigeants et Cadres: Leur mission chrétienne », *Bulletin social des Industriels*, no. 256, avril 1959, pp. 145-154;
Emile Decré, « L'UNIAPAC et la Paix Sociale », *La Paix Sociale, op. cit.*,
pp. 129-150; Rik Vermeire, Address to B.K.U. Tagung, Bad Neuenahr,
October 2, 1959, UNIAPAC Archives ; « The Aims of UNIAPAC », *passim;*
L. Brouwers, S.J., *Le Problème Social, passim;* « La doctrine sociale
de l'Eglise et l'Entreprise », *Bulletin Social des Industries*, no. 177, mai
1951, pp. 220-235; Franz Greiss, *Das Zeitalter des Menschen, Die Zweite
Phase der Industriellen Aera, passim;* Msgr. Joseph Höffner, *Das Ethos
des Unternehmers, passim;* Fritz Burgbacher, « La Paix sociale sur le
plan national et international », *La Paix Sociale, op. cit.*, pp. 77-96; Willy
Büchi, « Die Einstellung des Christlichen Unternehmers zum Gewerkschaftsproblem », *VCU Bulletin*, no. 19, September 1952, pp. 134-135; *VCU
und der Arbeit*, (Tagungsergebnisse 1949-1956), *passim;* « La paix sociale
et la profession », *La Paix Sociale, op. cit.*, pp. 59-74.

  [2] UNIAPAC Archives, « Fiches et Personnalités », *passim.*

the Belgian king the high designation of « Grand-Officier de l'Ordre de la Couronne » [3].

Currently Bekaert is president of FEPAC, a post he has occupied for fifteen years, and vice-president of UNIAPAC. And most remarkably, this man who is so thoroughly immersed in the active direction of his own firms which employ over ten thousand workers spread over several countries, and in the economic affairs of his nation and of Europe at the highest echelon, a man then of the empirical workaday world of business and commerce, is capable of enunciating the great ideas and broad visions and Christian motives which animate UNIAPAC and affiliates. Repeatedly he has been requested to express these at national and world assemblies; his is the most authoritative single voice in UNIAPAC circles. Consequently, this writer will draw principally from a few of Bekaert's statements in this first formulation of an answer to the question: What is the purpose of the Catholic employers' movement? [4]

1. Education, Presence and Influence, Formation.

Speaking in Paris to the French C.F.P.C. on the « Rôle et Responsabilités d'un Centre du Patronat Chrétien », Léon Bekaert sets forth the purposes which motivated himself and the other founders of FEPAC in these phrases:

> They (the Belgian founders) had for their purposes the spreading amidst the employers' world of knowledge of the social doctrine of the Church, to enable the industrialist members (of FEPAC) to fulfill more perfectly their professional responsibilities of justice and charity, and to prepare them, through the elaboration of a coherent and constructive

---

[3] *Bulletin social des Industriels*, no. 258, juin 1959, page 226.

[4] Some of his addresses are the following: Léon A. Bekreat, « La mission du patronat chrétien », *Rapports du Congrès de Rome du 7 au 10 mai 1949*, UNIAPAC, pp. 116-127; « Esprit chrétien et humanisme économique », *Progrès Economique et Progrès Social*, 4e Session UNIAPAC Bruxelles, février 1952, pp. 121-123; « Rôle et Responsabilités d'un Centre du Patronat Chrétien », *Documents et Commentaires*, no. 3 juillet 1953, pp. 1-10; « Le comportement du chef d'entreprise devant l'évolution économique et sociale », *ibid.*, no. 21, mars 1958, pp. 23-39; « Les devoirs du dirigeant chrétien », Congrès National FEPAC, *Bulletin social des Industriels*, no. 256, avril 1959, pp. 181-186; « Les perspectives du patronat chrétien », *ibid.*, no. 258, juin 1959, pp. 243-245; « La paix sociale et l'entreprise », *La Paix Sociale, op. cit.*, pp. 39-55.

entrepreneurial doctrine, to accomplish adequately and in felicitous collaboration with their non-Christian colleagues the functions to which they would be called within the neutral employers' organizations of the different industrial sectors to which they belonged [5].

During the first years of its existence, Bekaert admits, the Catholic organization was regarded with suspicion by the neutral employers' association, now known as the Fédération des Industries Belges (FIB). The neutral group feared that the Catholics would behave as mere dissidents, or the partisans of overly progressive views. In any case the utility of a Christian movement separate from the all-embracive FIB was gravely doubted. Still many non-Catholic industrialists readily granted the necessity of a social doctrine for employers — « for while many industrialists did not share our philosophical opinions, they did admit the necessity of having a *social doctrine* for entrepreneurs » [6].

Bekaert explains that at bottom it was this conviction, that the entrepreneur needed a positive social doctrine, which bit by bit relieved the original suspicion. Also, collaboration by FEPAC members in the solving of grave problems of national and industry-wide scope resulted in time in the selection of FEPAC members as leaders of various neutral and branch organizations. So it came about that Bekaert himself became president of his own industrial sector, FABRIMETAL, and then stepped up in 1952 to the presidency of the nation-wide industrialists' association, FIB, while still remaining president of the FEPAC.

The constant confrontation of these two employers' organizations, each deploying its activity on such different levels, gives rise in Bekaert's mind and through his daily life to the pressing question of the opportuneness of the existence of an employers' movement based upon ideological and religious affinities [7]. He sees this questioning of the

---

[5] Bekaert, « Rôle et Responsabilités », *op. cit.*, p. 2. This particular address presents an excellent synthesis and will be the principal source in the following treatment. For sake of simplicity only the first two or three words of Bekaert's titles will be cited hereafter, all having been fully listed in footnote 4 above.

[6] *Ibid.*, the emphasis is Bekaert's.

[7] Some of these points were discussed with the UNIAPAC industrialist by the writer in an interview at his residence in Zwevegem, September

seeming divisiveness of UNIAPAC and affiliates as more legitimate today than in the past, because today more than
ever entrepreneurs must unite, must impose upon themselves a rigorous discipline, and must cordinate their means
of persuasion and of action, all to compensate for their nu-
meric weakness by cohesion and the force of convictions.
The reality of tensions and tests of strength is not denied
by the Catholic movement. Their particular plea is that
the combat be not conceived primarily as a narrow defense
of selfish interests, that the entrepreneur should perceive
something of his mission toward the continuity and perfection of the free society and of Christian civilization.

Employer's associations posit that the entrepreneurial-
managerial function is necessary to and inherent in all life
in society. Regardless of the social organization adopted
by a human community, those central units of human activity called economic enterprises will always require leaders,
Bekaert goes on to recount. Such leaders are found today
as well in collectivist and communist society as in the so-
called capitalist nations. Men with authority to direct production are needed in both systems [8]. The great difference
in Western society is the postulate of free enterprise, the
freedom of economic initiative. This form of economic and
social organization is in the eyes of the employers' movement the only one reconcilable with the Western concept
of civilization; it is the system which best assures, in an
institutional manner, two essential prerogatives of man:
« Freedom to work, that is, the faculty of choosing his trade
and of exercising it freely under rule of law and morals;
and the right of property, that is, the faculty of utilizing
to his personal advantage, and within the framework of
the common good, the goods legitimately acquired » [9].

Bekaert believes that in general the entrepreneur grasps
with growing clarity this relation between fredom of economic initiative and socio-political freedom. He comes to see
that his role is not merely economic, that in the great turmoil of this generation the entrepreneur is a keystone in
the edifice of free society. But granted that employers per-

13, 1959, but the documentary sources are closely followed throughout
this section.
    [8] Cf. Milovan Djilas, *The New Class*, *passim*, especially pp. 37-69.
    [9] Bekaert, « Rôle et Responsabilités », *op. cit.*, pp. 3-4.

ceive theoretically some of the broader consequences of their
function as artisans of a free economy, to Bekaert's mind
they often identify the work of employers' organizations with
the narrow defense of their own interests. Concretely they
think principally of banding together to oppose the claims
of labor or the intervention of the state; they make concerted appeals to public opinion and apply joint pressure
to governmental bodies. Such negative tactics are bound
to fail, in Bekaert's judgement, because the entrepreneur's
power is extremely weak in face of universal suffrage and
of the contemporary current of egalitarian and communitarian ideas. Today the only way that an employers' organization can make sense is if it is itself based upon ideas, on
a doctrine of the entrepreneurial-managerial mission [10].

The neutral employers' movement must come face to
face with various ideological currents. Their so-called neu-
trality is an illusion. They cannot claim to defend their
members' rights and interests without any notion of whence
these derive and without any concepts regarding the economic system in which are to operate.

But most fundamental of all, doctrine is required in
the realm of action. Bekaert insists that entrepreneurs must
have recourse to doctrine to guide and justify their conduct
in the enterprise vis-à-vis the government and society. This
doctrine must derive from philosophic, moral and social
roots sufficiently deep not only to withstand the shocks of
controversy and public attacks, but also, and most importantly, of such solidity and consistency that this doctrine
does not give the appearance of being merely an adroit
camouflage of organized self-interest. Usually employers
have found only a negative unanimity against the claims
of labor and government: « Entrepreneur action so conceived is bound to fail in advance. Christian or non-Christian,
the employers' organization makes no sense unless it reposes
on a doctrine of the employers' mission » [11].

More than ever, ideas rule the world. And parroting
the worn ideas of nineteenth century *laissez-faire* liberalism
the neutral employers' movements find it impossible to forge
a unity of conviction and a conception of man and society
to justify his claims and his acts, and to point the way for

---

[10] *Ibid.*, p. 5; and Bekaert, « Le Comportement », *op. cit.*, pp. 31-36.
[11] Bekaert, « Rôle et Responsabilités », *op. cit.*, pp. 5.

his leadership. Bekaert discerns here a major weakness of
the neutral movements: « But the weakness, I could almost
say the tragic drama, of the neutral employer world, is
that, in this our epoch when more than ever *ideas govern
the world*, they find it nearly impossible to create a unity
of thought and a conception of social life which justify its
action in an irrefutable manner and which indicate the goal
toward which it must strive » [12].

Bekaert's thesis, as he goes on to his climax, is that in
the immense confusion of multifarious ideas and systems
proper to our age, the employer-managerial milieu is likewise subjected to incertitudes and the gravest dissensions.
More than other groups, because more under attack, employers need the stability and light of natural law and Christian social doctrine. And this deep need can be supplied
to the neutral movement only by the employer who is a Christian, a Christian convinced by and formed in the Church's
social teaching.

Such a Christian has a special mission to the world of
the entrepreneur: because he alone knows profoundly *why*
Marxism in all its manifestations offers no solution to the
problems of the worker and society. As he likewise knows
why liberal theory, with its suppression through forgetfulness or through ignorance of the social and moral character
of economic affairs, and its fuzzy identity of private interests
with the common good, is impotent for begetting a human
society of basic harmony. To Bekaert's mind such a formed
Christian employer knows with certitude the moral sources
of his authority, his right of initiative and of property.
And he possesses as well the measure for delimiting his
rights and the responsibilities they impose. In presence of
never-ending tensions resulting from the wage-worker system and the human dependencies it creates, the Christian
employer learns from this social teaching why he must and
how he can temper this potentially explosive relationship,
by a just division of profits and by the creation of a true

---

[12] *Ibid.*, p. 7. Emphasis is in original. It is obvious, of course, that
liberalism and liberal are used here in the older European, and not in
the present American, meaning of the terms. The concept intended
here, and throughout this study, is derived from the Manchester school
of economics. By liberal, then, Bekaert does not signify progressive or
radical; rather he means conservative and *laissez-faire*.

community of work, of interests and of aspirations in the enterprise. To the Christian employer, says Bekaert, the economy acquires its true significance in the overall structure of creation; the economy is measured and governed by a creativity greater than the economic, so the Christian is never measured and governed and enslaved by the merely economic. Risk itself, an element so innate to the entrepreneurial ethos, conveys to the Christian spiritual values a creative admission of man's insufficiency, coupled with a confidence in his providential role.

The UNIAPAC leader states that the Christian concept enhances human work with a special surcharge of value. This conceives work in all its forms and levels as a continuation of the work of God. Work then can confer neither distinctive privilege nor degradation. The boss and the manual laborer can meet in all equality and like dignity, because both fulfill the plan of Providence, and if they work conscientiously they are equals in the eyes of God. From all this it results that not only relations, but the very tensions and oppositions in society must be dominated and illumined by this magnificent consciousness of human dignity, of respect of man for his fellowman, and of simple love for one's neighbor.

Bekaert realizes that, « for a world given up to doubt and scepticism », such claims can appear arrogant or simplicist. He defends them nevertheless as postulates of the Catholic Faith, adhered to by hundreds of millions over the world: « that is our strength, our wealth and our meaning »[13]. Leaders acting from this Faith must bring out the fact that in social life the *efficacious* solution of a problem is none other than the *just and equitable* solution. (His emphasis.) The fact is that human conscience is not only a guide toward eternal rest in heaven, but offers as well often enough the key for settling the bitter daily conflicts on earth. It is precisely these solutions, just, honest, equitable, and at the same time effective socially and economically sound, which the Christian social organizations must help the employer to find by joint study and collaboration.

By now the purpose of the Catholic employers' associations become clear and precise to Bekaert:

---

[13] *Ibid.*, p. 8.

They have for their first and principal mission to con-
front the social and economic actuality with the doctrine of
the Church and Christian morals, through a sincere and profound study.

Their principal task is to determine each day the exact
impact of that doctrine and to strive to apply it in all
spheres ...

Seen from this angle the mission of a Christian employers'
center is immense. It extends to all domains, the public as
well as the private, the social as well as the economic domain,
and to education, to public finance, to construction, to
health [14].

Still to the Belgian industrialist leader, this is not
enough. Entrusted with this doctrinal formation on current issues Christian employers must seek constant and living communication with their peers in the neutral organizations. This is the second imperative. Because if the Christian idea, which has been and remains today the great ideological reservoir of our civilization, does not inspire apostles
among those who, willy-nilly, constitute the managerial
class, then our society will no longer uncover the forces
requisite for resisting disintegration and decay.

Bekaert decries the lassitude and apathy of employers
toward the great social issues. « How can you expect a society to be balanced and healthy, if only representatives of
the worker class are dynamic and active? » He disclaims
any attempt at detracting from the immense merit of the
pioneers and militants of the worker's movement. But he
objects, « Too often we identify social action with labor
action » [15]. Whereas true social action aims not at promoting the welfare of one social category, however numerous
it might be, but at the progress and harmony of all groups,
at the creation of a better society in its integrity. Bekaert
affirms further that the unionization of the workers has
proven a powerful instrument for emancipating the worker,
for raising his low standard of living, for his spiritual en-
richment, and for making him, in the full sense of the term,
a man. A century's experience has demonstrated that where
workers were organized by Marxist forces, they became in
tendency materialist and collectivist; whereas those to
whom Christian organizations addressed themselves re-

---

[14] *Ibid.*, p. 9.
[15] *Ibid.*

mained Christian. In view of such results the Christian
employers' movement has no right to become moribund and
pass away.

A commonplace affirmation proclaims the existence today of only two forces in the world which propose a logical,
realistic and all-embracing solution to the human predica-
ment: Communism and Christianity. Between these lie no
intermediaries, Bekaert asserts; they alone are the irrecon-
ciliables of our age, the two poles around which all mankind
gradually group themselves. All stand in awe of the psy-
chology and propaganda Communism employs in order to
capture the masses. Most fortunately the Holy Fathers have
with telling perspicacity reiterated the necessity of organizing the Christian forces by group and profession, and from
the Church employers have a rich doctrinal base for action,
rooted in the natural law, and embracing the whole man
in all his weakness, strength and glory of his supernatural
destiny. Finally Bekaert concludes:

> The response which Christianity offers to the agony of
> man is much more complete and satisfying than that which
> Communism proposes to the human being, and if the latter
> has won out it is because we have not affirmed with sufficient
> force and conviction the Christian alternative, consecrated by
> twenty centuries of experience.
> We, Christian employers, are somewhat the pawn of these
> two ideological powers of humanity, but we can equally be
> the lever which will move one side of the scale.
> Would that history can one day record that in this tor-
> mented century we have done honor to the privilege of hav-
> ing belonged to the Christian employers' movement [16].

A first impression created by this synthetic view of the
role of the Christian employers' movement, enunciated by
its top leader, is its well-nigh unlimited scope. It addresses
itself to society with a sweeping all-embraciveness of Olym-
pian proportions, claiming that this very quality is one much
needed by employers as a group. It offers an antidote to
balance the old liberal emphasis on the individual and the
motive of self-interest. Employers must overcome this in-
ward-regarding attitude, and develop an outward orientation, a view of the whole society. The only deep-rooted,
well-rounded and fully human ideology derives from Chris-

---

[16] *Ibid.*, p. 10.

7

tian social doctrine. The Christian movements must interpret this doctrine in terms of economic actualities to their own members; but far from stopping there, they must penetrate the whole entrepreneurial-managerial world.

Still much room remains for disagreement and discussion. Starting from one common doctrine members do not necessarily nor usually concur on its application to a concrete reality. The Christian association must not behave as the monolithic partisan of a hard and fast « party-line ». As André Aumonier, secretary general of France's C.F.P.C., expressed it: « We are not a sect which has fixed in detail the comportment of its initiates; we are a *center*, a place of encounter, a place of research and confrontation of diverse experiences »[17]. Consequently, the association is open to every initiative or tendency so long as it measures up to the tests of Christian doctrine. It collaborates with other like-minded groups. And it makes no effort to conceal its declared intention of exercising influence in the very heart of the neutral employer's movement. Aumonier observes that such secular organizations as the Confédération Nationale du Patronat Français are not totalitarian blocs; influences are at play within them. The Christian movement directs its initiative at proving these neutral groupings to be truly pluralistic, by bringing its own doctrine and views to bear constantly on the policies of these employers' associations. Jacques De Staercke of FEPAC also insists on this objective: « The presence of the Christian employers in their respective lands at the different levels: nation, industry, enterprise. This policy of presence is an important element of re-Christianization, or, at least, of seeking to orient solutions within the Christian perspective. The Christian employer performs the role of catalytic agent »[18].

Thus far two purposes of the Christian employers' organizations stand out clearly: 1) education, the development and imparting of Catholic social doctrine; 2) presence and influence, penetrating the employer milieu with these Christian convictions in order to put that doctrine to work. The *modus operandi* as well as the stated aims of most UNIAPAC affiliates set forth another purpose: 3) for-

---

[17] Aumonier, « Rapport Général », *op. cit.*, p. 32.
[18] Jacques De Staercke, « Le Rôle de l'UNIAPAC », *op. cit.*, p. 25.

mation of militants who become committed to the employers' mission at an ever-deepening level.

The necessity of selecting and forming entrepreneurs in the secular sense of management development is also a definite preoccupation of UNIAPAC. Its 1953 world congress at Cologne was devoted to this subject. But the specific reference here, as this third purpose, is to the selection of already functioning and proven entrepreneurs, or promising young ones, for formation as bearers of the Christian message within their own ranks, among their fellow employers. Concerning this goal, the Holy See said in a message to C.F.P.C.:

> May your members take seriously the duty of being present in employer and industrial organizations: that they will bring into these the true ferment of the Christian spirit with which they will have filled themselves through study and prayer.
> May they bring to these organizations assistance for the maturing of healthy policies — especially during these difficult hours which we now traverse — positions which are just and courageous, upon which economic vitality and social peace for the nation can find support. There is an authentic apostolate to be exercised in this employers' world, proper to themselves, and a deepened knowledge of Catholic social doctrine will be for them not only a precious light, but also the justification and source of their zeal [19].

The degree to which spiritual apostolic formation figures in their actual programs varies considerably among the UNIAPAC affiliates. The small group approach has long been current in France especially. The statutes of Italy's UCID place formation as the first of its goals: « The purposes of UCID are: the spiritual and moral formation of the members and particularly the development in them of professional morals » [20]. Father Laureys demonstrated by his close attention to a selected circle of leaders his conviction of such a need. FEPAC centered its national congress of 1959 on the theme of employers' and managers' spirituality in view of their apostolic mission. The distillate of their ninefold conclusion is that development of an employer-

---

[19] Msgr. A. Dell'Acqua, « Lettre aux assises nationales » C.F.P.C., 8 mars 1956, M. Clément, *Le Chef d'entreprise*, pp. 279-280.
[20] *Statuto UCID*, art. 5.

managerial spirituality is a primordial task of their movement, which can be realized only by a theological study of
terrestrial realities; and that this spirituality must bind together the spheres of the life of ideas, the managerial life,
and the interior life, all aiming at becoming witnesses of
Christ and preparation for the coming of His Kingdom,
amidst their employer and manager colleagues in the economic milieu [21].

UNIAPAC itself fully embraces this third purpose. In
concluding a 1959 statement of aims the international body
echoes its national affiliates: « To accomplish those tasks
and face those employer responsibilities it is undeniable
that the employer must have an adequate formation » [22].
And the formation results not only from privately received
theoretical doctrine, but also from personal effort and action
induced by daily responsibilities. The final report of the
1959 UNIAPAC congress concludes to the need for going
beyond economic and social solutions, beyond doctrine and
exterior action: « The Christian employer has a spiritual
conception of his role which animates his technical knowledge and moral reflexes: he is an instrument of the peace
of Christ » [23]. From this interior peace does social peace
proceed, continues the report. There follows then the responsibility of praying — with the prayer of the Christian
who is also an employer, prayer for the men with whom
he works, prayer with a ready heart, open to welcome the
seeds of spiritual advance.

Besides these three common purposes of education,
presence and influence, and formation, there appears now
and again discussions of such insistency upon the need for
« humanization » of work and the economic arena that this
is sometimes elevated into a fourth purpose [24]. Such a goal
is, however, so implicit in the Christian social doctrine that
it is not treated separately in this study. Other aims sometimes expressed seem likewise either a rephrasing of these

---

[21] « Conclusions: Dirigeants chrétiens et Progression humaine », Congrès national FEPAC, *Bulletin social des industriels*, no. 256, pp. 178-180.
[22] « The Aims of UNIAPAC », p. 10.
[23] Decré, « UNIAPAC et la Paix Sociale », *op. cit.*, p. 144; also, Vermeire, address to B.K.U., *op. cit.*, pp. 6-9.
[24] Sergio Ossa Pretot, « Le rôle des organisations patronales catholiques », (report on discussion group), *La Paix Sociale*, *op. cit.*, pp. 107-
108; also, Vermeire, *Address to B.K.U.*, *op. cit.*, pp. 12-13.

three, or the accentuation of some subdivision thereof. These three seem then sufficient for the structure and scope of this study.

2. Social Order for Social Peace

Education, presence and influence, and formation have themselves, however, a common goal: the upbuilding of a just social order. Here lies the great goal of all Catholic social movements. The employers are one current in the whole stream: UNIAPAC's national and world-wide initiatives seek by education, influence and formation the promotion of a just social order as the basis for social peace.

« Social Peace » was the theme of the 1959 UNIAPAC congress. Preparatory to this conclave each of the affiliates was requested to draw up a current analysis of the social order in their perspective nations, something of a barometric reading of the degree to which this order, or the lack of it, generates social peace, or social tension. This was an extremely ambitious effort, netting voluminous results of uneven quality [25]. But withal, consideration of the questionnaire and the answers helps considerably in understanding further the outlook, methods and goals of UNIAPAC and affiliates. These reports will be frequently cited in the remainder of this study.

For now it suffices to profit but briefly from these questionnaires in order to see what further light they throw on the purposes and policies of these employers' associations.

The lengthy definition, or better, description, of social peace given in the original UNIAPAC questionnaire characterized it as follows:

1. Social peace is a situation in which the natural opposition of interests permanently existing between management and labor as social partners — each group tending to affirm their own interests and aims — does not result in an unbridgeable chasm from struggle, suppression and or-

---

[25] The responses of France, Belgium, Holland, Germany, Switzerland and Italy are mimeographed and bear non-uniform, descriptive titles. Other responses are in UNIAPAC archives in typed form only. The FEPAC report runs to twenty-nine pages, single spaced, an estimated twelve thousand words. And mere excerpts from the Swiss answer come to thirty-seven pages, single space type.

ganized force, but which situation finds rather a basic balance through pacific means and reciprocal understanding.

2. This situation recognizes that the opposition of interests cannot be entirely eliminated but only diminished to a certain degree.

3. Social peace can therefore be attained only in a measure of more or less; it can exist but in a relative and not absolute degree.

4. Nor is social peace permanent; constant and active effort must be exerted to maintain even relative social pacification.

5. It is then not sufficient to examine a given situation, « but the instruments which could give the means for social peace should be examined continuously, which could help us to reach the new situation we want » [26].

The German affiliate, B.K.U., in commenting on this concept of social peace, adds that wherever men live together conflicts of interest can be expected. In consequence, « ... the problem of social peace concerns the whole of life in society. It is not then a question of a special problem of relations between the social partners (employers and labor) ». They re-stress the « more or less » nature of this ideal, « that in general all interests can never be completely satisfied. From a certain angle social peace will always be a compromise » [27]. Further, this compromise cannot be forced by sheer power, for instance, by the state; B.K.U. wants this harmonization of interests to come about in all possible freedom.

V.C.U. of Switzerland sees the necessity of a similar broad view: « *Social peace is a sociologically interdependent phenomenon.* It cannot be isolated to one single level, like, for example, the level of the enterprise » [28]. It is impossible, they continue, to promote labor-management peace in the factory while carrying on a society-wide class struggle. Harmony within the local work-community and harmony among the various levels of economico-political life — city,

---

[26] « Social Peace and Employers' Responsibilities », (List of questions of UNIAPAC to the national associations), pp. 1-2.

[27] « Observations relatives au questionnaire UNIAPAC, commentaire allemand », juin 1959, p. 1.

[28] « Extraits de la réponse suisse au questionnaire UNIAPAC sur la paix sociale », pp. 35-36.

regional, national and supernational — are all interdependent. V.C.U. declares further that the statement so often cited by J. Messner, « The social question must be resolved in the enterprise or else it will not be resolved at all », does not in any way mean that social peace is the exclusive problem of the enterprise. Still harmony in the local work-community is essential: « Still social peace cannot be realized at a higher level, in the industry and in the state and in the international sphere, unless there exists at the same time a peaceful atmosphere of work in the enterprise. These different spheres live together, in a sort of sociological symbiosis » [29].

A similar position taken by FEPAC of Belgium, on the inter-relatedness of all areas of society in striving for social peace, leads them to the more basic issue of the institutional structure of society [30]. To their mind UNIAPAC must go beyond limited objectives. Because a true social peace should result from a sufficiently general accord on economic and social structures and on the objectives of human progress. So long as a great part of the people lack confidence in the institutions in which they must daily participate and from which they must depend for their necessities of life and advancement, then social peace is inherently impossible to realize. And such in fact is the case, in the judgment of FEPAC. Rather than social peace, there reigns a constant state of tension more likened to a succession of armistices of indeterminate duration. More precisely, as FEPAC sees it, the Belgian labor unions, both socialist and Christian, even if they participate in these institutions and procedures (described in the response) for reconciling, avoiding and moderating social conflicts, nevertheless, consider the actual structure of society as needing profound modification, or even replacement by another structure. The positions of Belgian trade unions, however, are graduated, FEPAC notes, being different among the Christian unions as compared with the socialists. And even among the latter in the present period the principal emphasis is on improving the lot of the worker in and through existing institutions, rather than insistence on doctrinaire reforms of structure [31].

---

[29] *Ibid.*
[30] « La paix sociale et les responsabilités patronales », juin 1959, p. 1.
[31] *Ibid.*, pp. 1-2.

The content of the UNIAPAC questionnaire reflects a parallel over-all concern with the institutions conducive to the social order which must underlie social peace. Adhering to this outline the responses report on the existence and evaluate the operation of these institutions: in the work-community (the local enterprise), at the level of professional groups and industry branches, and on the national and international planes.

Much of the literature and programming of the national associations reflects an identical preoccupation. What new organs should be created? How can the present ones be changed and made to work better? These are the recurring themes: « comités d'entreprise », collective agreements, workers' and employers' syndicates, professional organization at the industry-wide level, national economic councils, the new intermediate institutions of « droit public ». The employers' formerly sovereign property and unrestrained authority are memories of the past, often nightmares still haunting the present. The evolutions in structure come about with these changes from the absolutism of property and authority.

In today's evolving economy UNIAPAC seeks then a social order conducive to and creative of social peace. UNIAPAC affiliates are not simplicists; they realize the complex inter-relatedness of the elements and institutions of society; of the various spheres: political, social, familial, and economic; of the different planes: local, professional, regional, national and supernational. They know that up-building a peaceful social order is a long, arduous process. First, they seek to educate their own members, developing and imparting doctrine on these issues; second, they strive to bring this doctrine to bear upon managerial policy at all levels, to be present in the employers' milieu and to influence their entrepreneurial colleagues at large; third, they try to form apostolic employer-leaders to carry out this vocation within the business world.

Such then are the ultimate objectives of UNIAPAC and affiliates. Some details of this three-fold program of education, presence and influence, and formation must next be investigated.

Chapter V

EDUCATION AND DOCTRINE

From the body of Catholic social doctrine UNIAPAC affiliates elaborate principles and practices reflecting their own employer-manager point of view, with emphases and precisions proper to their own right and responsibility, light and vocation. They perform within the Catholic social movement a role which no other group can fulfill, and into the broad circle of business affairs and management they bring the unique impact of the Christian message phrased in the employers' idiom.

This chapter will give a brief resumé of UNIAPAC doctrine, divided into seven sections: 1) Property, 2) Workers and Their Rights, 3) Class Struggle and the Comunity-of-work, 4) The Human Person and Family, 5) Industrial Organization, 6) The National and International Communities, 7) The Role of the Entrepreneur and Enterprise.

This exposition of doctrine will be very schematic; detailed analyses of these large issues are impossible in this or any single study. The introductory chapter expressed a modest aim: to uncover and review the approach of the UNIAPAC associations to, or at least to register their awareness of, these issues, with some modicum of evaluation. UNIAPAC and its national affiliates do not offer a neatly packaged statement of their doctrine. They have no hard and fast party line or set creed. Even were they to desire this, national and continental divergencies would render it unattainable. They seek rather a current and recurring interpretation of Christian principles applied to concrete reality. The present writer attempts to distill the content of numerous declarations and resolutions, editorials, interviews and study outlines into a representative synthesis.

Before entering into the positions of UNIAPAC, something must be said about certain over-all concepts of employers in general. Prior to the advent of today's non-owning managerial system, the entrepreneurial position in its starkest simplification revolved around two concepts: property and authority. Private possession of productive property, together with the exercise of non-governmental authority over its use, have been the twin pillars of the Western « free enterprise » system. Sharing the fruit of property resulting from work was a consequent question, secondary to and heavily dependent upon the two prior central issues. As a man's prime concern is his own continued self-existence, so employers have sought first to safeguard their existence as possessors of productive property and of authority in the productive operation. Losing these attributes the employer ceases to exist. Likewise employers' organizations make defense of their members' property and authority central goals. Industrial relations of the past century have seen the sovereign property and absolute authority of employers progressively restricted by labor unions and political action, and taken over in varying formulae by workers and government.

Productive property and authority are today still undergoing dynamic change, change deeply complicated by the increasing power of non-owning managers, « the managerial revolution ». The profundity of these changes is reflected by the current attempt to find a new basis for the « legitimacy » of management's *de facto* control. This study cannot stray afield to explore these dynamics. It can merely witness that UNIAPAC shows a growing awareness of them, and, in the opinion of this writer, UNIAPAC's most forward looking leaders feel the inherited burden of an overly static concept of property and proprietary authority, and are striving to re-think and re-interpret and re-formulate these traditional notions in keeping with demands of a new membership, actual and potential, composed increasingly of non-owing managers. When UNIAPAC speaks today of « employers » — patronat, Unternehmer, werkgevers, imprenditori, empresarios — it must be well understood that this means non-owning management as well as actual proprietors. On the other hand, it does not mean non-responsible and non-powerwielding stockholders. Employers and managers, then, are today still concerned, as were yesterday's individual and family proprietor, with preserving private title to productive property and the exercise of non-governmental authority over its use [1].

While UNIAPAC and affiliates also defend private property and authority, they do so in the context of an over-all philosophy of man and life and society, Christian in inspiration, and with the goal of enabling the enterprise and economy to make their own indispensable contribution toward a Christian and human world social order. So UNIAPAC concepts of property and authority must be constantly seen not in isolation, but in relation to the greater whole of human society.

1. PROPERTY.

In Catholic social teaching the right to property is not the mere result of *de jure* contracts and statutes, nor of the *de facto* power it confers, but is derived rather from the very nature of the human person. An UNIAPAC expression of this doctrine has been phrased by Father L. Brouwers, S. J., national chaplain of Belgium's FEPAC, in this manner:

> — against socialism: that property, including means of production, has an inviolable personal character, founded in natural law.
> — against liberalism: that private property has an equally social character, bearing social obligations which owners cannot avoid.
> — that the economic system, to function in healthy fashion, must be based on private ownership, but in such a manner that property fulfills its social purpose willed by God: that all can live a life worthy of man.
> — that private property, to overcome obstacles to the attainment of its social destiny willed by God, can be submitted by the state to certain restrictions, but these must not lead to its simple disappearance [2].

---

[1] Reference to the change in UNIAPAC's membership was made in chapter III, section 2, above. Concerning the « legitimacy » of management, cf. Peter F. Drucker, *The New Society*, pp. 99-105, and *passim;* A. A. Berle, Jr., *The Twentieth Century Capitalist Revolution, passim.*

[2] L. Brouwers, S. J., *Le problème social*, p. 43. The author is national chaplain of Belgium's FEPAC, which published this 134 page booklet expressly for use of its members. Again, liberalism as used here denotes the Manchester or *laissez-faire* concept, not the more recent American usage meaning radical, progressive, or the opposite of conservative.

In this schematic statement both socialism and old
liberalism are opposed as untenable extremes. Opposition
to collectivism is characteristic of all exponents of Western
free enterprise; UNIAPAC literature reflects abundantly this
same view [3]. What is more noteworthy is the direct opposition to *laissez-faire* liberalism and insistence on the
social character of property. A distinguishing mark of
Catholic employers' organizations is here expressed in their
avowal that the healthy economic system must function « in
such a manner that property fulfills its social purpose willed
by God: that all can live a life worthy of man ».

Father Brouwers' arguments against collectivism rephrase the usual Catholic position, drawn from the nature
of man endowed with reason. Man enters the world im-
perfect and weak, not possessing in himself the elements
indispensable for his maintenance and development. He
seeks these necessities in the abundance of nature. Contrary to the mere animal who seeks but the needs for immediate consumption, man through his reason foresees the
future return of these needs and husbands not only goods
for later consumption, but devises means of production
which can continue and increase consumptive goods without
themselves being destroyed at the first usage. In this
manner man provides for the necessities of his nature and
assures a stable development of his human powers. To the
objection that the state could exercise a similar providence,
Brouwers responds that the state is posterior to man, that
man had already received from nature the right to protect
his existence through property before the formation of the
political order, and that dependence upon the state would
impair man's dignity in reducing him to animal level by
preoccupation only with consumptive goods. Further, collectivism would accord to the state a dangerously prepon-
derant power and would weaken the effectiveness and zeal
of the worker who is spurred on and buoyed up by the hope
of improving his situation by acquiring property of his own.
Workers themselves, Brouwers maintains, in their claims
against capital do not want the abolition of private prop-

---

[3] *L'entreprise privée*, 1er Session UNIAPAC, Tiburg, mars 1948, *passim;*
Les nationalisations, FEPAC, *passim*, (août 1955); « Un moyen inattendu
de pénétration communiste », *Professions*, no. 432, janvier 1959, p. 7.

erty, but rather combat a regime which renders accession to property impossible:

> This is so true that socialist leaders have had to moderate their ardor on this point, and to acknowledge the inviolability of savings and the legality of modest rural and craft possessions, so as to oppose only a certain social domination usurped by capitalist property. Moderated in this manner, Socialism on this point is not much different from Catholic doctrine [4].

A French C.F.P.C. study outline shows similar concern for the worker participation in private property: « A *human* life implies not only immediate subsistence, but the further presence around each person of a certain safety-zone of property without which, in our modern civilization, one cannot feel himself truly a man » [5]. That is why the wage question ties in directly to the problem of accession to property, the statement continues, and especially to ownership of housing.

Because the modern capitalist system first evolved under the aegis of liberalism the points on which Catholic employers contravene old liberal tenets are of especial interest to this study. Condemnations of unmitigated liberalism are as firm in UNIAPAC writings as are condemnations of socialism. The attacks of Leo XIII, Pius XI and Pius XII against the liberal extremes are heartily seconded by the Catholic employers' movement [6]. Brouwers rejects bluntly the liberal definition of property as « the right to use and to abuse a thing as one's own ». He invokes the Catholic distinction between right of possession and right of usage, and develops the matter in summary as follows: *laissez-*

---

[4] Brouwers, *op. cit.*, p. 46.

[5] « Fiche de Travail no. 6; La propriété », *Professions*, no. 432, janvier 1939, p. 11. This three thousand word treatment is study circle material directed to the local sections of C.F.P.C. It is in consequence neither profound nor exhaustive. It is cited precisely because it contains that formulation of Catholic doctrine which the French employers on the average study and embrace. The same motive applies to full use made here of Brouwers' booklet, *Le problème social*. The goal here is not a treatment of Catholic doctrine as such, but as taught, nuanced and accepted by UNIAPAC affiliates and their members.

[6] Brouwers, *op. cit.*, pp. 23 ff. Recall the pioneering position of Léon Harmel on state action for the common good, and of course Bekaert's more recent analysis.

faire liberalism says, « This belongs to me alone, so this is for me alone ». Socialism counters, « This is for all, and so belongs to all ». Christian social doctrine says, « This belongs to me, but is for us all ». The goods of the earth have been destined by God for the welfare of all men. But their equitable distribution has not been determined by God. He leaves to human wisdom to set up freely the system by which the world's goods attain their goal: an existence of human dignity for all men. Private property best assures these values of the human person, especially the exercise of his potencies, his liberty and his responsibility [7].

Accession to property by workers is currently a principal preoccupation of UNIAPAC leaders, occasioning many articles, discussions and exchanges of experience. The October 1959 meeting of the central council of delegates, UNIAPAC's governing body, devoted much time to this subject, both on the principles involved and on methods of application and dissemination [8]. A preliminary motion by B.K.U. of Germany observed that the worker is the dominant social type of our industrial era. In the political sphere the worker has the same rights and responsibilities as other citizens. But in the economic sphere he is generally limited to his function as a worker. His participation in the two other economic functions is grossly insufficient: he shares but slightly in the spiritual and creative element of the enterprise (now proper to the entrepreneur), and he has but little participation in the possession, conserving and increase of durable productive goods, especially in the form of industrial capital. To perfect that free society which fosters the development of man in the Christian sense, the B.K.U. statement goes on, man must exercise to the maximum all three functions, including the possession of capital goods [9].

---

[7] Brouwers, *op. cit.*, pp. 48-57.

[8] « Le Problème de l'accès à la propriété », conseil central des délégués, Rome, 9-10 octobre 1959, *passim*. The B.K.U. motion is subtitled: « L'accession à la propriété des masses ouvrières — l'alternative positive de la nationalisation des capitaux, revendiquée par le socialisme ». This material and discussion reported here are unpublished and confidential. The present writer, who was present as an invited guest at the closed session, has obtained permission of the UNIAPAC secretariate to report them in this form.

[9] The subject will be given more thorough attention in section 3, below.

While reacting against the wave favoring nationalization in the post-World War II years, UNIAPAC leaders and doctrine admit the right of the state to nationalize certain enterprises. But they insist that the principal role of the state is to regulate and supervise private enterprise to prevent it from harming the collectivity and to direct it toward the common good. The cases in which the state itself is justified in entering the economy are by way of exception and only when demanded by the common good. These are particularly as follows, according to Bouwers: 1) The state can organize services for which private initiative lacks the means and power. 2) The state can forbid or even nationalize monopolies which really harm the collectivity through excessive concentration of power or exploitation of the people. 3) Certain industries can be reserved to the state because they exercise such economic power that leaving them in private hands imperils the common good; examples of such are railways, banking, mines, water and electricity. That the state *can* enter or reserve these sectors to itself does not mean that it *ought* to do so, because the extensions of political dominance may only increase the harm and danger to the collectivity [10].

---

[10] Brouwers, *op. cit.*, pp. 58-67, gives a good resumé of this matter. The present writer sat in on a private and very preliminary discussion by UNIAPAC leaders on nationalization which revealed a broad spectrum of opinion. German members were in general more opposed to state ownership, and French leaders more permissive toward it. One of the latter seemed favorable to nationalization of French coal mines and even insurance companies, because so many of the first were heavily subsidized to the benefit of individuals, and the latter because they exert financial and familial power affecting the whole nation. A German participant had no objection to state owned railroads, but balked at further concessions. The same French leader observed that collectivization in Russia permits them to circle the moon, and that this is made possible by concentration and control over the economy. Obviously, UNIAPAC does not dictate a monolithic party line; national and regional differences on this and other issues are expected. The presence of directors of nationalized industries as members of UNIAPAC affiliates was adverted to already in chapter III, section 2, above. It was noted there that the « enti statali » of Italy are fully represented in Italy's UCID. Cf. Ettore Soave, « Due idee e molti personaggi nel dibattito per le participazioni statali », *Operare*, xiv, 1, gennaio-febbraio 1958, pp. 35-50.

Rik Vermeire has commented to the present writer: « You will note that discussions on nationalization concern public services, which in Europe are already largely nationalized (postal and telegraph systems, railroads, etc.), and basic sources of energy (coal, electricity, nuclear energy). There is not at present — and I have never known on the

UNIAPAC believes that this danger of nationalization can best be countered by the spread of property on a broader base. Meanwhile, nationalization continues to menace the employers. The B.K.U. motion of October 1959 cites the constant pressure of the « Marxist heresy » toward nationalization as the only way to social justice:

> One example among many others: recently, the economic expert of the German Socialist Party (SPD), Dr. Deist, who has the reputation of representing the very moderate, and even anti-Marxist, group of the party, demanded nationalization of coal mines of all the nations of the European Community. This clearly demonstrates that the danger menaces not only an individual country, but presses as well upon the other nations of Europe [11].

The motion concludes that the struggle against nationalization would gain much more dynamism if UNIAPAC could successfully promote a policy of wide property distribution, avowing by this that the lack of property among the masses is an ephemeral phenomenon in the course of the natural development of the free industrial society, in no way conforming to its intrinsic nature. « We can state: the wide distribution of property is as necessary for the free economy system as the right of universal suffrage is necessary for our political system » [12].

Having briefly seen UNIAPAC principles on property, proposals must next be considered for countering, modify-

----

Continent — any current which aims at nationalizing steel, for instance, nor any other branch of industry ». From letter of February 19, 1960, p. 3.

[11] « Le problème de l'accès à la propriété », *op. cit.*, p. 2. Consequent to this preliminary motion a commission has been set up by UNIAPAC to develop the matter at some depth. It begins meeting at the time of this writing. UNIAPAC circulated in February 1960 a first draft of the points to be considered, prepared by Schreiber. A few sentences might be indicative of orientation: « Generalized accession to property by workers will not resolve the problem of co-management (cogestion) ... Generalized accession to property by workers will not resolve the problem of concentration of economic power, since power is not attached to property, but to the function of management, so often exercised by non-owning managers ... (Accession to property) will never displace old-age pensions which form part of social security. Revenue from property can but supplement annual income, never replace it ». The outline then comments on ways and means, citing among others the plans of Haussler, Dittmar and Gleitze: « Accès des travailleurs à la propriété », UNIAPAC Commission de programme, pp. 2-3, and *passim*.

[12] « Le Problème de l'Accès à la Propriété », *op. cit.*, p. 5.

ing and collaborating with the power of property, especially through workers' syndicates, collective bargaining, social security, promotion of the work-community, profit-sharing, industrial organization and similar means.

2. WORKERS AND THEIR RIGHTS.

A. *Labor Unions.*

UNIAPAC doctrine conforms fully to papal teaching on the dignity of the worker as a human person, his right to a just wage meeting the needs of himself and his family, the necessity of social security and legislation protecting these and other rights. Since historically the principal means through which workers have defended their interests and advanced their claims have been by collective action through labor syndicates, this section will concentrate on the position of UNIAPAC and affiliates in this regard. This is an essential element in the study of Catholic employers' organizations, particularly since so many employers' groups have often made opposition to trade unions a general policy[13]. Recalling UNIAPAC history already reviewed, from their very birth the associations not only admitted the prerogatives of workers' syndicates, but frequently collaborat-

---

13 A Belgian observer of the industrial scene in the United States, Albert Verschueren, *Les relations industrielles aux Etats-Unis, passim,* especially pp. 18 and 69, considers that labor unions are more accepted among Belgian employers than they are in American business circles: « But we feel the N.A.M. (National Association of Manufacturers) to be against unions ... Management, and, we can say equally, the government of the United States, have not integrated labor unions within national life ». Verschueren is director of the Fédération des Industries Belges (FIB); the writer interviewed him October 1, 1959, Brussels.

An American writing on the French « patronat » judges them to be definitely inimical to syndicalism: Henry W. Ehrmann, *La politique du patronat français, passim* especially pp. 359 ff.: « In the factories the majority of employers consider union activities as harmful. Even in large enterprises union delegates are often treated with 'cold intransigence' ».

The Swiss V.C.U. observes that their nation's principal organization of employers, Zentralverband Schweizerischer Arbeitgeber-Organizationen, « was created originally *to combat the syndicates and syndical action* ». (Their emphasis). By now, however, they are admitted as part of economic life: « Réponse suisse au questionnaire UNIAPAC sur la paix sociale, 1959 », p. 17.

8

ed actively with them, and even contributed to their founding and strengthening. The work of Léon Harmel, the Dutch leaders and Joseph Zamanski set the early pattern in this direction which is still followed today.

The director of the commission of studies of France's C.F.P.C., Father B. M. Boyer, O. P., broaches the question directly in a doctrinal acticle on the question : « Can a Christian employer be against labor unions? » [14]. He avows that at times a Christian employer of top quality is heard to say : « I am against the unions ». This statement might be the consequence of bitter personal experiences or a global judgment of the role of labor unions in the national economy. But as such, and minus the distinctions a longer discussion might bring out, this statement is not in accord with Catholic social doctrine. Boyer then goes on to outline the proper attitude which the Catholic employer should have toward unions, abstracting from particular conflicts.

He traces the clear expression by the Church of the worker's right to associate, citing principally the letter of the Sacred Congregation of the Council to Bishop A. Lienart of Lille, June 5, 1929. This is a very apt reference not only because of its content, but further because, as Boyer points out, it was in answer to a complaint of the « Consortium du Textile de Roubaix-Tourcoing », an employers' group whose members were in great part Catholic, in the very region where Léon Harmel first launched UNIAPAC's antecedents. This assertion of the right of labor to form syndicates was addressed directly to Catholic employers themselves, in truth a rebuke to their effort at impeding the progress of the unions. Boyer cites further papal documents supporting labor syndicates as a solid support of today's economic structure, as legitimate, laudable means of defending workers' interests, and as indispensable to assure to workers their due place in society. He concludes with an exhortation to the members of C.F.P.C. to seek frequent contacts with the syndicates over and above those necessary for contracts and settlement of disputes.

Another article in C.F.P.C.'s official organ, « Autorité

---

[14] B. M. Boyer, O. P., « Un chef d'entreprise chrétien peut-il être contre les syndicats? », *Professions*, no. 421, janvier 1958, pp. 3-4. Father Boyer also serves as chaplain of the Paris section of C.F.P.C. and edits *Documents et Commentaires*, the association's quarterly review.

Patronale et Syndicalisme Ouvrier », by Father Philippe Laurent, S. J., reminds C.F.P.C. members that the hierarchy in France has asserted the duty of the worker to belong to a union. « And if the Church imposes membership in a syndicate as a moral obligation on workers, any employers opposing the development of unions, directly or indirectly, would go counter to the directives of the Church »[15]. Laurent proceeds to the main point of his treatment: that employers should cooperate with union leaders in their enterprise committees (comités d'entreprise), even if these men are Communist (C.G.T.); otherwise, « ... systematic opposition to the C.G.T. runs the risk of confirming the Communist doctrine that no accord is possible between the social classes. There exists for employers », Laurent avers, « a moral duty of making the enterprise committee successful in spite of C.G.T. ».

UCID of Italy devoted its 1954 congress to the theme of collaboration in the enterprise. The kernel of the congress' concluding resolution is that closer collaboration is possible only on condition that paternalism is renounced and that the functions of workers' organizations freely chosen by the workers are recognized and are allowed to play their full role[16].

Emile Decré, UNIAPAC vice-president and president of the French affiliate, as the concluding rapporteur of the 1959 UNIAPAC congress reviewing the consensus of the assembly, stated that social peace depends upon a willing dialogue between the social classes. This dialogue, he explained, supposes mutual esteem and respect for the forms in which these classes are organized, and: « In social history, labor syndicates have been the means which permitted workers to obtain acknowledgment of certain of their rights. In today's industrial society consideration of the role, opportuneness and value of union representation is a pre-condition for social peace »[17]. One of the five formal resolutions

[15] Philippe Laurent, S. J., « Autorité patronale et syndicalisme ouvrier », *Professions*, no. 384, 18 février 1956, p. 9.

[16] « Mozione Generale », *La Collaborazione nella Impresa*, Atti del VI Congresso Nazionale UCID, Rapallo, 29-31 gennaio 1954, pp. 295-296.

[17] Emile Decré « L'UNIAPAC et la Paix Sociale », *La paix sociale*, Congrès mondial UNIAPAC, Lucerne, 4-7 juin 1959, p. 140. The same report goes on the justify workers' unions from papal documents, and also stresses the obligation of syndicates to collaborate sincerely with

adopted by this UNIAPAC congress repeats that social peace can result only from loyal cooperation of the different social categories with: « this legitimacy of labor union action, the conclusion of collective contracts, the development of paritary organisms and of all that leads to a more organic unity among those who collaborate in productive work » [18].

As will be seen below in some detail, the long-term institutional goal of UNIAPAC is the gradual structuring of the economy into professional, or industrial, organization. Workers' syndicates are seen as necessary elements for this future realization and should be supported for this additional reason. The secretary general of C.F.P.C., André Aumonier, developes this line of thought. In some enterprises all employees and workers are not union members, and sometimes it even happens that none at all are. « Should we conclude that the labor syndicate is a heterogenous element in the enterprise, a bit of dust blocking the carburetor? ». Beyond a doubt, Aumonier agrees, at present many feel that way. That is why it is opportune « to recall all that trade unionism has done for the worker by way of material, intellectual and spiritual advance these past seventy-five years ». He agrees that some union functionaries seek selfish expansion of their influence and make ever higher demands which render peaceable solutions most difficult. But rather than fruitless jousting with the force of unionism, Aumonier asserts it is more intelligent to understand and acknowledge it, and to associate with workers' unions for the construction together of the industrial organization of the economy [19]:

> Any professional industrial organization which would establish itself through a break with the trade union tradition and which would not give to constituted syndicates participation

---

other social classes without aiming at exclusive domination of the state and society.

[18] « Résolutions », *ibid.*, p. 153.

[19] André Aumonier, « Ce qui dépend de nous », *Professions*, no. 431, décembre 1958, p. 7. It must be noted here that « l'organisation professionnelle » is a term having special and determined import in UNIAPAC circles. It denotes their proposed elaboration of the papal doctrine of « ordines », and its closest approximation is usually rendered in the United States as « the industry council plan ». Section 5 below treats this subject expressly. Aumonier is here refuting the corporatist concept of certain rightists who would do away with labor unions.

in the economic and social management of each industry,
would be destined to enevitable failure.

And what is true of the workers' syndicate is likewise
true of the employers' syndicate, and we do not see how a
professional organization could do without one or the other,
even though the legislative text — as some might wish —
passed over the organizations (syndicates) already existing.

FEPAC of Belgium devoted its 1951 national congress
to the theme, « Le Patronat devant le Syndicalisme ».   A
few titles of addresses at the two day meet will convey best
the scope and depth of treatment: « The Origin and Growth
of Syndicalism, Syndicalism as a Political Force, Church
Doctrine on the Nature and Mission of Syndicalism, Evolution of Syndicalism and Employers' Attitudes ».   Excerpts
from the concluding motions of the congress state [20]:

> The Congress esteems that:
>
> 1 - The trade union is a necessary and permanent organ
> in professional (industrial) life. It is freely constituted for
> the defense and promotion of the professional interests of
> dependent workers, and for the development of their per-
> sonality in every way that this development is determined
> by industrial life. It is in the social system of a private
> economy that the union finds its character as a necessary in-
> stitution and the possibility of its organization and operation.
> 2 - Employers have the duty of cooperating loyally with
> trade unions despite the difficulties usual to human affairs,
> in the sincere desire to discover and to promote together
> modes of action most favorable to the industrial common
> good, with the consciousness that each one fulfills a social
> function, and with the intention of contributing to the progres-
> sive structuring of those professional (industrial) institutions
> which the Sovereign Pontiffs have counseled with such in-
> sistence, and repeated most recently by His Holiness Pius XII
> in his discourse of June 3, 1950. That cooperation appears
> as the guarantee of social peace, that is, the tranquility of
> good order.

L'Organisation Professionnelle, a volume reporting in
detail the 1950 UNIAPAC session of the subject, lends full
support to this same thesis: that far from condemning
trade unions, the Catholic employers' movement sees in them
an indispensable organ for constructing a truly human free

---

[20] *Le patronat devant le syndicalisme. Bulletin social des industriels,*
XIIème Congrès de FEPAC, Liège, 15-16 décembre 1951, no. 183, janvier 1952.

society. The workers' associations must continue « their essential purpose of representing and defending the interests of the workers », but further they should combine with employers' groups in the organization of each sector of production [21].

B. *Collective Agreements.*

Having seen the clear admission by UNIAPAC and affiliates of the right of workers to unionize, it is well to note next their position concerning collective agreements, or collective bargaining, (conventions collectives) which determine and enforce wages, benefits and conditions of work so vital to labor, and the strike, the ultimate weapon of the workers unions in defense of their claims [22].

In its questionnaire on social peace, already alluded to as preparatory to its 1959 congress, UNIAPAC asks its national affiliates for a survey of the use of collective agreements in their nation and a judgment on its efficacy as a factor for social peace.

In 1950 C.F.P.C. issued a manifesto on the « Positions du Patronat Chrétien ». A third of the text is devoted to « Les Conventions Collectives ». They assert that sooner or later, and better sooner than later, collective agreements will become the order of the day. For the present it is most necessary to prepare an atmosphere favorable to their elaboration : « by human contacts within the firm ; by frank

---

[21] Alberto Zanelli Quarantini, « La représentation professionnelle », *L'Organisation Professionnelle*, 2e Session UNIAPAC, Paris, avril 1950, pp. 170-171, and *passim*. The desire of UNIAPAC affiliates for contact and cooperation with labor unions is already well realized. Interchanges, personal and official, are very common. Cf., for instance, report of a talk by Georges Levard, secretary general of Confédération française de travailleurs chrétiens, to C.F.P.C., « perspectives d'avenir du syndicalisme français », *Professions*, no. 423, mars 1958, pp. 4 ff. ; and report of a taped interview of Gerard Picard, president of Confédération des Travailleurs Catholiques du Canada, « Le syndicalisme ouvrier », *Les Dossiers de l'A.P.I.*, no. 4, pp. 10-16.

[22] For American readers it is well to note that in Europe a collective agreement generally covers a whole industry or region. The contracting parties are often the employers' association and the labor unions of the industry or region, even of the nation. Seldom is the collective agreement between a single employer and the workers' organization of that single plant or firm.

and loyal cooperation in the entreprise committee, neutralizing as far as possible those who strive to make it an instrument of class struggle; and by collaboration in the co-managed organisms of social security, housing, training, and the like » [23]. C.F.P.C. states that collective agreements have always appeared to employers of Christian inspiration as demanded by the reciprocal interdependence of employer and labor, wanting to discuss between themselves in full freedom the conditions of work. These agreements are of great importance as the first stage toward professional organization, in that they call upon the different parties to regulate the domain of work by their own common accord, and after reviewing the history and some marks of the collective contract, C.F.P.C. asks its members « to take an immediate and especial interest in the study, drawing up and conclusion of collective agreements, and to arouse the interest of as many of their colleagues as possible ». If used properly, « Positions du Patronat Chrétien » concludes, collective contracts can be an instrument of social progress, and — it repeats — a first and important step toward professional organization.

V.C.U. of Switzerland, in answering the UNIAPAC questionnaire on social peace, credits the sixteen hundred collective agreements in that country with promotion of employer-labor rapprochement: « It is undeniable that collective contracts and their development have contributed in considerable measure to the pacification of relations between employers and workers. Thanks to these agreements, the foundation and conditions for productive cooperation have been created ». Germany's B.K.U. makes a similar judgment [24].

The Catholic Industrialists' Conference of Great Britain is mose reserved in its opinion of these contracts:

> Most wage agreements are arrived at by collective bargaining. As a system it works reasonably well. Such agreements are not for a specific period, but go on until superseded by fresh agreements. It is doubtful if they make for social peace, because there is now a tendency to put in a claim for increased wages once a year, whether there is any justification for it or not; and there is a tendency on the part of employers' organizations to seek a compromise solution to

---

[23] « Positions du patronat chrétien », p. 3.
[24] « Réponse suisse », *op. cit.*, p. 18.
« Observations relatives au questionnaire UNIAPAC, Commentaire allemand, juin 1959, pp. 9-11.

an unjustified demand, instead of resisting it and making a
fight. Certainly there is no conscious aim of social peace in
collective agreements — they are regarded simply as a method
of settling a particular question [25].

FEPAC of Belgium states that on the whole collective
contracts fix wages and conditions in their country, and:
« The parties (employers and labor) find in them a real advantage and generally they are respected, with this reserva-
tion that the unions always consider the contract as a mere
milestone along the road of social progress. They reserve
the privilege of demanding sooner or later its modification
or the drawing up of a new contract ». But on the whole
the collective agreement does contribute to social peace,
in the judgment of the Belgian employers [26]. In like vein
C.F.P.C. of France reports that while « ... collective contracts
have incontestably favored social peace, they have been at
times unable to prevent serious conflicts ... » [27]. And finally,
Italy's UCID concludes: « The collective contract is a rule
of negotiation habitually accepted and, despite its limits, is
recognized as an instrument of social peace » [28].

These general judgments may be appropriated as expressing those of UNIAPAC as a whole.

C. *The Strike.*

Turning next to the position of the Catholic employers'
associations on the strike, Brouwers defines the strike as
the concerted and collective suspension of work with the
intention of creating difficulties for the enterprise and of
obtaining through these accordance of formulated demands [29]. In effect, the FEPAC chaplain explains, the worker

---

[25] « Reply of the Catholic Industrialists' Conference to the Questionnaire on Social Peace », June 1959, n. 8.

[26] « La paix sociale et les responsabilités patronales », Fédération des
patrons catholiques de Belgique, Juin 1959, pp. 17-19.

[27] « Réponse du Centre français du Patronat Chrétien (C.F.P.C.) au
Questionnaire de l'UNIAPAC sur la Paix Sociale et les Responsabilités
Patronales », p. 9-10.

[28] « Observations relatives au questionnaire UNIAPAC », juin 1959,
p. 4.

[29] Brouwers, *op. cit.*, pp. 95-100. His doctrine on the right to strike
as summarized here is admittedly much simplified, and even primitive.
Still it contains the basic elements to portray the position taught UNIAPAC
members.

who refuses to offer himself for work exercises his right of ownership, similar to the vendor who refuses to sell his merchandise to buyers who do not accept his conditions. Just as the isolated worker can refuse to work, so several can do so together; multiplication of the act does not modify its nature. The fact, Brouwers continues, that the suspension of work is a concerted act does not render illicit an act which is good in itself, provided that a just end is pursued, as for example, the demand of a right, and provided too that honest means are employed. Beyond a doubt, the FEPAC priest concedes, the collectively planned suspension of work is an extreme resort: it is economic war. « But since under certain conditions, the strike is the sole efficacious means at the disposal of the workers to obtain justice from recalcitrant employers, we cannot deny them the use of this weapon » [30].

However, in view of the grave difficulties inevitably resulting from the strike, it is highly desirable that the state should be capable of preventing it. In a civilized society vengeance and repression of injustice are removed from individual initiative and are reserved to the public authority. In like fashion, to Brouwers' mind, in a developed society public authority should extend its protection to workers and employers with special juridic powers permitting the state to solve such conflicts. « Nevertheless », he concludes, « so long as such does not exist, Catholic moral recognizes for workers the right of legitimate defense by the unique efficacious means: the concerted and collective suspension of work » [31]. The chaplain goes on to expose requisite conditions for a legitimate strike, and some aspects of different types, as the political and general strike, that against public services, of solidarity and of protestation, and against private sectors vital to the health of the people.

The 1959 UNIAPAC questionnaire on social peace requests of the national associations an analysis of the recent history of strikes and lockouts in their respective countries, and for such details and observations as the number of factories and workers involved, working days and wages lost, and, « What was the result of the strikes on social

---

[30] *Ibid.*, p. 96.
[31] *Ibid.*, p. 97.

peace? » [32].   FEPAC's response to the last point reflects the
dominant opinion: strikes spoil the psychological climate
in which paritary negotiations normally proceed, a local
strike confined to a single firm damages relations between
management of that enterprise and the workers much more
radically than does an industry-wide strike; and most importantly: « A system of collective contracts and of regulation of the right to strike as described above (in FEPAC's
reply) would bring remedy to the problems posed by the
strike » [33].   The sole dissenter to this response common
among UNIAPAC affiliates is Great Britain's C.I.C.   They
seem to take for granted that strikes and lockouts will occur
occasionally, and see them as not only legitimate but even
at times the best way to settle a dispute:

> The definition (by UNIAPAC's questionnaire, of social
> peace) seems to exclude the resolution of differences by
> struggle, constraint and the use of organized force such as
> strikes and lockouts.   But these may be a perfectly legitimate
> and proper way of resolving differences and sometimes it may
> be best to fight out a dispute and settle it once and for all
> rather than to escape the responsibility of the question in
> trying to arrange a compromise.   In British eyes the fact
> that there are hard fought disputes need not of necessity
> disturb essentially friendly relations [34].

D. *Job Security and Unemployment.*

Many other precisions of the doctrine of UNIAPAC affiliates could be exposed, for instance, on family wage, housing, social security, leisure, training and advancement.   All
of these could properly come under this section on « Workers

---

[32] « Social Peace and Employers' Responsibilities », p. 8.
[33] « La paix sociale et les responsabilités patronales », *op. cit.*, p. 11.
FEPAC deplores that legal regulation of the right to strike is almost
non-existent in Belgium; pp. 6-10.
[34] « Reply of the Catholic Industrialists' Conference », *op. cit.*, p. 1.
This British minority view may be in part explained by these further
quotes: « There is no Trade Union in England which has as its avowed
object the perpetuation of the class struggle ... Almost all employers
in England have an outlook and ideas toward Industrial Peace that are
in accord with natural law and therefore imbued with Christian principles ...   The old idea of *laissez-faire* is quite dead.   The employers'
outlook, by and large, is shared by the majority of the executive leaders
of trade unions »; pp. 1-2.

and Their Rights ». Let it be sufficient to repeat that UNIA-PAC policy and practice on each of these conform and adapt to Catholic social teaching, interpreting it as fitting to a region or nation or industry at a given time under concrete circumstances [35].

Before closing this section, however, brief mention must be made of job security and unemployment, an issue highly current in UNIAPAC circles. A joint statement was made on the subject in February 1959, by Achille Cardinal Lienart of Lille, and Archbishop Emile Guerry of Cambrai; and a second analysis was put forth on the question by Paul Cardinal Richaud of Bordeaux, at the same date [36]. The local section of C.F.P.C. at Roubaix-Tourcoing issued a public declaration in which they draw from the bishops' statement three principal conclusions, « ... which solicit our reflexion and make demands of our duties as employers anxious to realize in the concrete the social doctrine of the Church ».

This C.F.P.C. group cites, firstly, the recent national accord on indemnities for complete unemployment, and the agreement just signed by the textile syndicate of Roubaix-Tourcoing covering partial unemployment, as testifying to the concern felt by the employers for alleviating the material effects of forced loss of work and for obtaining the prompt reclassification of unemployed workers. « We thank Cardinals Lienart and Richaud for having strongly emphasized the moral disorder which unemployment constitutes in itself, as well as the sad psychological conseguences to the victim, and the unbalancing effect on the welfare of his home and family, and on their temporal and spiritual destiny. Everything should be done to spare men such suffering ».

Secondly, they admit that in light of these facts, it is indispensable that all plans involving unemployment be attentively and jointly studied by management and by personnel representatives, together with the proper syndicates,

---

[35] The concern of UNIAPAC affiliates for some of these issues will be seen in part below in sections 3 and 4.

[36] S. Em. Cardinal Lienart et S. Exc. Mgr. Guerry, « Les licenciements ouvriers et le chômage dans le Nord », *Bulletin social des industriels*, no. 255, mars 1959, pp. 91-92; S. Em. Cardinal Richaud, « Comment répondre en chrétiens aux problèmes économiques et sociaux actuels? », *Professions*, no. 433, février 1959, p. 3.

taking into account the concrete economic situation of the firm and also the human situation of the workers and the possibility of their reclassification.

Finally, the C.F.P.C. of Roubaix-Tourcoing attaches highest importance to the concluding part of the episcopal declarations, which treat of the urgency of reinforcing and establishing anew inter-syndical relations and of orienting them toward an authentic professional (industrial) organization. At least to a partial degree unemployment is due to default of foresight, of discipline and of collaboration within the industry and the economy as a whole, the statement concludes [37].

When the present writer interviewed leaders of C.F.P.C. in the Roubaix-Tourcoing region, September 1959, he was told that following the episcopal statements, in consequence of initiatives by C.F.P.C. members, confidential gatherings had been held which resulted in pledges among employers of the area assuring that in view of the moral and socio-political issue raised by unemployment, no worker group would be discharged by an individual enterprise without prior consultation with the employers' organizations in order to plan reclassification and re-hiring of the men affected.

The declarations of the hierarchy served to re-direct current concern on the problem of unemployment which has received close prior attention from UNIAPAC and affiliates. In 1952 C.F.P.C. published a fifty-five page booklet entitled, *Le chômage et l'équilibre production-consummation.* This reported the findings of a long-term study commission and concentrated on having employer and government circles understand the necessity of adopting measures to augment consumption to absorb increased production, and the relation of this equilibrium on unemployment. FEPAC of Belgium devoted its 1953 congress to the theme, « La politique de l'emploi et le chômage », and another study is reported by FEPAC in a hundred page booklet, *Le chômage structurel et la politique regionale,* published in 1958. They emphasize the need of industrial diversification, adaptation and development of new industries, and principally, the national in-

---

[37] « Le Groupe de Patrons Chrétiens du C.F.P.C. de Roubaix-Tourcoing prend position », *ibid.,* p. 12.

dustrial solidarity necessary to cope with unemployment, which is not to be left to the individual firm, much less to the affected workers, alone [38].

UNIAPAC devoted its 1955 world congress to the theme, « Full Employment and the Employers' Mission » [39]. The three days of lectures and discussions covered the economic and political, human and technical aspects of the issue. Bernard Jousset, then UNIAPAC president, summarized the organization's position in his concluding address. He first stresses the necessity of maintaining full employment: « It is of direct import, for the future of our form of civilization, that the specter of massive unemployment, as the result of a major economic crisis, must be definitely avoided » [40]. He warns, too, that labor will refuse an economic structure which does not assure the workers a regular wage, and that neither will unemployment consequent to sudden rises of production within a firm or an industry be accepted by labor. Further, endemic under-employment in countries weak in raw materials, capital and equipment, and whose populations are rising, is also of grave concern to UNIAPAC.

Jousset then reviews the discussions of the congress concerning the ideal of full employment in a free economy, technological unemployment, and the role of the state. Regarding the last he surveys methods found, or in consideration, in various nations: the first Beveridge plan to vary rate of social security payments according to economic actuality, pre-planned public works to be executed only when depression approaches, budgets extending over several years, control of money markets, and others, all following the general principal of reducing excess buying power in

---

[38] *Le chômage et l'équilibre production-consommation*, Commission des Etudes du C.F.P.C., *passim; La politique de l'emploi et le chômage*, XIVe Congrès de la FEPAC, Gand, 21-22 février 1953, *Bulletin social des industriels*, no. 195, mars 1953; *Le chômage structurel et la politique régionale*, FEPAC, *passim.* Cf. also, « Au delà des allocations-chômage un effort en faveur du meilleur emploi », *Professions*, no. 434, avril 1959, p. 16; « La lutte contre le chômage, vers des solutions concrètes », *Documents et Commentaires*, no. 12, décembre 1955, pp. 31-86. UCID of Italy devoted its 1951 national congress to the theme: « La disoccupazione nella vita economica e sociale italiana ».

[39] B. Jousset, « Le discours de clôture du Président: Un inventaire des moyens d'action pratique », *Plein emploi et missions des chefs d'entreprise*, XII Congrès de l'UNIAPAC, Paris, 18-21 mai 1955, *Documents et Commentaires*, no. 11, octobre 1955, pp. 73-80.

[40] *Ibid.*, p. 73.

boom times, and of raising it during depressed periods, attentive always to inflationist tendencies and to the increase of production.

Jousset concludes with a warning that the continuance of our free civilization depends upon « ... justice built upon love of our less favored brothers, of whom the Lord has given us charge, and whom we have no right to condemn to death in refusing them the right to work *without a compensation* which permits them to *consume the products of that machine which shall have suppressed their jobs* »[41]. He exhorts his colleagues to engage themselves in concretizing in their respective spheres the convictions resulting from this congress on full employment.

Concerning workers and their rights the guiding principles are by now well formulated: the Catholic employers' associations recognize the right of workers to associate in syndicates and through these to bargain collectively and to defend their just claims in last resort by a concerted strike. They realize that unemployment is a moral evil and not a mere economic inevitability; they agree to collaborate as a whole with colleagues, government and labor groups to assure job security. And most importantly, UNIAPAC emphasizes that labor unions are an essential element in the structure of the Christian social order which must be built up by professional, or industrial, organization.

3. CLASS STRUGGLE AND THE COMMUNITY-OF-WORK

A recurring theme of UNIAPAC is the necessity of overcoming class struggle by transforming the local enterprise into a community-of-work (communauté de travail), in which employer and workers feel themselves to be partners in a common undertaking, finding solidarity in its success as redounding to their mutual benefit, as well as that of the general society[43]. This goal, observes FEPAC, is closely

---

[41] *Ibid.*, p. 79.

[43] *Ibid.*, p. 5: « Dans l'entreprise la paix sociale dépend de tous les membres qui la constituent. Celui qui dirige doit s'efforcer d'unir les intelligences et les volontés en vue non seulement de produire des biens, mais encore de constituer une véritable communauté de travail ». Cf. Georges Henry, « L'Intégration du travailleur à l'entreprise », *Progrès économique et progrès social*, 4e Session UNIAPAC, Bruxelles, 1952, pp. 85-

allied to the promotion of human dignity of the workers, and is, in consequence, very close to the heart of Pope Pius XII. « It is the inverse of the class struggle! They (employers and workers) eat, one might say, at the same table, and have parallel interests; why shouldn't they be animated by a truly communitarian sense? Granted that all Catholic employers recognized the value of this community feeling they know too how difficult it is to realize it in practice » [44].

UNIAPAC's questionnaire on social peace naturally explores the means pursued in this regard by the national affiliates [45]. The responses cite several methods and institutions proper to their respective countries, often passing judgment of praise or doubt upon them, e. g., sharing of information, orally or by plant news-sheets and bulletin boards; the selection of personnel delegates; making available social workers and assistance, especially helpful with security benefits, subsidies, pensions, etc.; creation, with worker participation, of credit unions, pension and sick funds supplementary to those required by law; special attention to the family of the workers (gifts at birth, Christmas, etc.); sporting and cultural activities; and others. All of these vary greatly according to the size of the firm, the mentality of the employer, social history of the region and the general class atmosphere. Specific treatment will not be made in this study of each of these widespread means of developing among workers identification with and attachment for their firm [46]. UNIAPAC affiliates regard these

---

108. Regarding the class struggle, cf. Anacleto Benedetti, « Le classi e la evoluzione sociale », *Operare*, settembre-ottobre 1958, pp. 60-68; also, Philippe Laurent, S. J., « L'Intégration des travailleurs à l'entreprise », *Professions*, no. 430, novembre 1958, p. 16.

[44] « Collaboration dans l'entreprise », *Rapport annuel de 1956*, FEPAC, mai 1957, pp. 7-8.

[45] « Social Peace and Employers Responsibilities », *op. cit.*, pp. 5-6.

[46] Supplementary insurance, familial and pension funds of many types are encouraged and exist under auspices of individual UNIAPAC employers, e. g., Société ouvrière de prévoyance et d'épargne, Société parisienne de cémentation, Argenteuil, S-&-O; and these are also organized collectively by national affiliates, e g., by the Flemish association, L.A.C.V.W. C.F.P.C. outlines some of these efforts in its response to the UNIAPAC questionnaire, « Réponse du D.F.P.C. », *op cit.*, pp. 3-6. Concerning help for families, Britain's C.I.C. says, « Any idea of direct contact with workers' families would be extremely unpopular on both sides in England, where Paternalism is not accepted as good »; from

means as obviously important, but they devote much more effort currently to promotion of institutions more directly contributory to the community-of-work. These are especially enterprise committees (comité, or conseil, or commission d'entreprise), profit-sharing and the spread of ownership. Some attention must be given to each of these, and to the further issue of co-management (Mitbestimmungsrecht, cogestion).

Again, this thesis can merely give the briefest summary of the UNIAPAC position of these broad and complex realities. The Catholic employers' associations are extremely alive to these issues, and to attempt an immediate generalization;

1. They support heartily, and even enthusiastically, enterprise or labor-management committees (comité, conseil, or commission d'entreprise) and make constant appeals to their members to do their utmost to make them work successfully, and to give their fellow employers a good model to follow.

2. They endorse profit-sharing in principle, particularly when the profit results from higher productivity, and they exchange experiences on how the various plans operate.

3. They see the spread of property as a principal answer to the class struggle and nationalization, and grant that this property should be not only housing, but productive industrial property (shares) as well. They find difficulty however in formulating plans for achieving this, exchanging experiences by literature, study meetings and conversations; and, importantly, they are chagrined that workers are not more interested in obtaining industrial shares and holding on to them.

4. They are adamant against co-management in so far as it would touch the economic direction of the local plant. They favor co-direction of social and welfare organs, and promote ultimate co-direction of the economy at the industry-wide and national levels through paritary professional organization (industry councils, « ordines »).

« Reply of the Catholic Industrialists' Conference », *op. cit.*, p. 2. B.K.U., in its « Observations relative au questionnaire », *op. cit.*, p. 4. states « Many employers refuse personal contact (with workers) as being outmoded ».

A. *The Enterprise Committee.*

C.F.P.C. of France designated « comités d'entreprise » as the subject for study by its local sections during April 1959. The work outline sent out from the national secretariate gives an excellent summary of this institution, which came into existence officially in France in 1945 [47]. By law these committees must be established in industrial or commercial firms employing more than fifty men. Other countries have varying determinations of firm size, e. g., Holland, twenty-five employees; Germany, a hundred workers; Belgium, one hundred fifty [48]. In France the enterprise committee is composed of the head of the firm, delegates of the personnel who are elected for two years, and representatives of the trade unions present in the enterprise. Rules of election and *modus agendi* are laid down by law. The committee meets at least once a month, generally during work hours. Wages for time spent in meeting are paid by the firm to a maximum of twenty hours a month. The attributes of the enterprise committee are as follows:

1. In cooperation with the management, it sets up regulations applicable inside the factory or plant.

2. In the economic sphere of plant operation, and with solely consultative role, the committee makes studies and suggestions for improved production organization and worker utilization; examines the annual overall report and suggests ways of handling benefits; in stock companies (société anonyme) it examines also the financial report and certain accounting practices.

3. On the social plane, and with power of decision, it

---

[47] « Comités d'entreprise, Fiche de travail no. 9 », *Professions*, no. 435, avril 1959, pp. 5-6. In 1947 C.F.P.C. adopted a resolution stressing the importance of enterprise committees and the necessity of making them work: « Que le comité d'entreprise ne soit pas une arme de lutte de classes et une étape vers l'expropriation des entreprises, il nous appartient d'y travailler ». From « Résolution adoptée par la C.F.P. à la suite des journées de mai 1947 », Joseph Zamanski, *L'Avenir de l'entreprise*, pp. 168-172. For American readers probably « Comité d'entreprise » could be better translated « labor-management committee ».

[48] These data are from the associations of Holland, « Réponse A.K.W.V. au Questionnaire », p 1; Germany, « Observations », *op. cit.*, p. 3; Belgium, « La paix sociale », *op. cit.*, p. 26. Cf. also, « Les Conseils d'entreprise », *Bulletin d'Informations sociales*, FEPAC, juin 1958, pp. 1-2.

directs some of the social endeavors established to benefit the workers and their families, e. g., canteens, vacation colonies, sport and leisure clubs, educational projects, credit unions, medical service, etc. [49]

C.F.P.C. sees in the enterprise committee an important step toward the gradual participation by workers in the responsibilities of the enterprise and their better integration therein. It notes that this offers the manager a chance to know what goes on in his firm and to exchange viewpoints with the workers on a periodic, regular basis rather only at time of dispute or negotiation. And more often than one thinks, C.F.P.C. states, « Harsh, but frank discussions, have been able to create a spirit of mutual comprehension, which, without doing away with conflicts, led to an understanding of their causes and which enabled the workers to grasp more fully the motives for managerial decisions » [50]. C.F.P.C. exhorts its members to patient, indefatigable explanation to the workers of the real concrete situation of the enterprise, giving them maximum information, to lead them to a concept of and an attachment for the common good of the firm. The employer must also strive to understand the sufferings and needs which underlie labor demands. All these attentions by the enterprise committee to the operation of the firm, C.F.P.C. concludes, must be tied in with just wages, a fair allotting of posts, provisions for hygiene and safety, and the careful choice of foremen. Because the enterprise is a whole, these many factors together make it a community-of-work.

In its response to the UNIAPAC questionnaire in 1959, C.F.P.C. reports that after fourteen years of experience the enterprise committees have given good results: « Thanks to the personnel delegates, regular contacts have been established, problems have been solved before they arose, the difficulties and aspirations of the worker class have been better appreciated ... The committees are an excellent means for the education of the worker delegates and are undoubtedly very useful for safeguarding social peace ... » [51].

---

[49] « Comités d'entreprise », *op. cit.*, p. 5.

[50] *Ibid.*, p. 6.

[51] « Réponse du C.F.P.C. », *op. cit.*, p. 4. Cf. « A propos des Comités d'entreprise », *Professions*, no. 434, mars. 1959, p. 12. This reports an

A similar institution, the enterprise council (conseil d'entreprise), has been defended and encouraged by FEPAC in Belgium despite « a climate of mistrust on the part of a large fraction of employers and the skepticism of many labor leaders »[52]. FEPAC in 1954 launched a campaign to make the enterprise councils understood and to develop among employers the disposition and skills needed to make them successful. Day-long study days were held: « More than nine hundred heads of firms had occasion to compare their experiences with those of their colleagues. Actual cases were studied and examined in order to discover the reason for success or failure ». This FEPAC report of 1954 stresses again the necessity that Catholic employers humanize the structures of their firms and eliminate the class struggle. It holds that the enterprise council offers a rare means toward these pressing goals, and « for putting an end to the situation of those who feel themselves ' as strangers ' in the very firm where they spend their whole existence ».

By 1958 the enterprise council had attained such status in Belgium that FEPAC published a hundred page *Vade-Mecum des Conseils d'entreprise*, containing all necessary data on the burgeoning institutions[53]. The volume is intended to supply new members of the councils with ready documentation. The material is written by company heads, directors of personnel and other active managers. A correlation of several pertinent laws is given. FEPAC expresses the hope that this synthesis on the operation of enterprise councils will stimulate the adaptation of methods and institutions in the world of work for the further evolution of society.

Other national affiliates attach like importance to promotion of the community-of-work. UCID of Italy devoted its 1954 congress to the theme of collaboration in the enter-

---

inquiry concerning actual working of the enterprise committee made in forty-eight firms by the Bordeaux section of C.F.P.C.

[52] « Les Conseils d'entreprise », *Rapport d'Activité, Année 1954.* FEPAC, avril 1955, pp. 7 ff. In Belgium the workers may designate an expert accountant to go over the firm's financial report with them in the enterprise council.

[53] This was in the form of a special issue of FEPAC's review, *Bulletin social des industriels, Le Vade-Mecum des Conseils d'entreprise,* no. 250, septembre-octobre 1958, *passim.*

prise[54]. V.C.U. of Switzerland in its response on social
peace reports with approval notable voluntary efforts by
employers to create social institutions within the firms,
which « have most certainly contributed toward cleaning
up the makings of social conflict ... toward the positive position now shown by the workers for the firm and the enterprise community »[55]. Among several practices and institutions given, the principal Swiss organ in this field is the
workers' commission or the enterprise commission (commission d'ouvriers, or, de l'entreprise). These are not
founded nor regulated by law; voluntarily 63 % of Swiss
firms with more than fifty workers have set up these commissions. Their purposes are similar to the obligatory
French and Belgian organs just described: consultation by
management of the workers on managerial decisions affecting worker interests, the hearing of labor propositions and
complaints, joint administration of social and welfare institutions, the receiving from management of general data
on the plant operation, productivity and measures planned
for the future, etc. V.C.U. recounts the ups and downs of
these commissions, the mistrust and optimism variously
centered upon them. However, V.C.U. is hopeful; on the
whole the experiment has worked out well: « All things
considered, the idea and conviction of the necessity of a
constitutional cooperation between workers and employers
in the enterprise has gained much headway ».

B. *Sharing Profits and Spreading Property.*

Passing from the enterprise council, or committee, two
other means of overcoming class struggle and of developing
the community-of-work must be briefly considered. These
are the sharing of profits and the spread of property ownership. The latter includes, of course, the acquisition by
workers of their own homes. Over the decades UNIAPAC
affiliates have constantly stressed Catholic social doctrine on

---

[54] *La Collaborazione nella Impresa*, VI Congresso Nazionale UCID,
Rapallo, 29-31 gennaio 1954. Cf. also, Giuseppe Prever, « Le relazioni
umane nella Impresa », *passim*; Prever is an officer of UCID Piemonte;
this is a talk given by him to the XXV Settimana sociale, 1952.
[55] « Réponse Suisse », *op. cit.*, pp. 2-10.

the primacy of the family. In keeping with this position the employers' associations have proposed, supported and activated many methods for purchase by workers of their own housing [56]. But this section will not review these particulars; it will pass on directly to the very current issue of profit-sharing and the acquiring by workers of interest in productive property, especially as a partaking in the increased productivity of the enterprise. These are aims common to most UNIAPAC affiliates, with varying degrees of emphasis. The French word « l'intéressement » is used to denote this concept, and for the sake of brevity as well as precision this term will be adopted here.

Numerous plans of « intéressement » are followed by individual firms in diverse nations, and numerous, too, are the articles and statements by UNIAPAC affiliates reporting and evaluating these, and proposing others. Even a schematic review of the field would go far beyond the limits of this study. Consequently, concentration will be devoted here to the position and development of C.F.P.C. regarding « intéressement ». In 1959 a new law on the matter went into effect in France, a law which was framed in keeping with general recommendations made by C.F.P.C. and heartily aproved by it. In general UNIAPAC affiliates teach that the class struggle is not germane to modern Western capitalist or mixed economy, that to develop a sense of the community-of-work integration of worker and employer are necessary, and that « intéressement » is a major means of accomplishing these goals. The French C.F.P.C. teaches this doctrine in the abstract, and also in the concrete by assisting in the preparation of this noteworthy plan for its implementation. In consequence, this plan will be discussed as a type of what UNIAPAC stands for in this field.

An ordinance, dated January 7, 1959, sets up regulations for formation of contracts between employers and workers for the « intéressement » of workers [57]. According to the

---

[56] Cf. section 4, below.

[57] « Ordonnance no. 59-126 du 7 janvier 1939 tendant a favoriser l'association ou l'intéressement des travailleurs à l'entreprise », (*Journal Officiel* du 9 janvier 1959). The ordinance is signed by C. De Gaulle. A copy of it, used here, is attached to a « Déclaration du C.F.P.C. sur l'intéressement des travailleurs à l'entreprise », Communiqué de Presse (January 23, 1959).

French ministry of labor, these contracts have two objectives: first, to promote better relations between employers and workers, and second, to enable workers to participate in the development of the enterprise. Concretely, these contracts could have the following effects for the worker:

1) To assure them part of the profits of the firm.

2) To enable workers to acquire some degree of capital. When the firm's capitalization is augmented, a certain number of shares would go to the workers. Eventually, they, the workers, would be able to designate one of their number on the firm's board of directors.

3) To have workers share in the increase of productivity.

These contracts are to be entered into freely by employers and workers. C.F.P.C. rejoices that they are not obligatory, nor of a set pattern. Rather various modalities can be tried out according to the needs and situation of each enterprise. They are to be drawn up either by joint discussion by management and union delegates together, or to be prepared beforehand by the employer and submitted to the workers for ratification. In the latter case a two-thirds majority approval by the workers in required. The maximum duration of each contract is three years. The ordinance requires that each contract establish precise rules for calculating the division of profits and for enabling workers to oversee records of the firm to verify that what is theirs is truly accorded them. Very importantly, this financial control will be made either by the enterprise committee, or by a commission designated by the enterprise committee, or, as a third alternative, by delegates especially elected by the workers. All the accounts of the firm are to be communicated to these comptrollers at least twice a year, and each worker is also to receive detailed information when he receives the amount due him.

An employer who enters into a « contrat d'intéressement » receives certain specified reductions of taxes on income and capital gains. The ministry of labor emphasizes that such a contract leaves intact to the employer all powers of management and direction with the personnel having right only to the accounting of the results of the firm's operation, and leaves to labor unions all freedom of action and syndical rights unimpaired.

In 1947 C.F.P.C. had proposed a law similar in essentials. In their « Déclaration du C.F.P.C. sur l'Intéressement des Travailleurs à l'Entreprise » [58], they recalled this 1947 initiative and quote Pius XI from *Quadragesimo Anno*, who advises « ... that, so far as possible, the work-contract be somewhat modified by a partnership-contract, as is already being done in various ways and with no small advantage to workers and owners. Workers and other employees thus become sharers in ownership or management or participate in some fashion in the profits received » [59]. Consequently, the declaration goes on, C.F.P.C. supports the effort of the government and invites its members to undertake with courage the actualization of the ordinance. An article in their monthly organ says further:

> C.F.P.C. fervently desires that this ordinance will be for Christian employers a new occasion for affirming — in a most concrete way — their solidarity with their collaborators of every rank.
> This « material solidarity » can take on quite diverse aspects and in coming numbers (of *Professions*) we will publish actual accounts of employers who, having already initiated a system of « intéressement », are able to specify the consequences.
> But « material intéressement » can in no case be separated from « psychological intéressement » of workers in the enterprise, which always presupposes information to and formation of the personnel [60].

The two subsequent issues of the C.F.P.C. organ report in some detail the experience of « intéressement » of a large firm of five thousand workers and of two smaller firms. Two further issues give reflections and discussions based on case studies. Both emphasize that besides the financial advantage to the worker, another most important result is that the worker has motive to become personally interested in the firm's operation, because his share of profit and stock

---

[58] *Ibid.*, p. 1. The earlier initiative is reproduced in « Résolution adoptée par la C.F.P.C. à la suite des journées de mai 1947 », Joseph Zamanski, *L'Avenir de l'entreprise*, pp. 168-172.

[59] Pope Pius XI, *Quadragesimo Anno*, par. 65, *Sixteen Encyclicals of His Holiness Pope Pius XI*, N.C.W.C. translation, p. 26 (A.A.S., XXIII [1931], 199).

[60] « A propos de l'intéressement du Personnel », *Professions*, no. 433, février 1959, p. 7.

from productivity depend upon output, sales, budgets, etc.
So « intéressement » satisfies, too, a deep need and right of
the worker: « When he works man has a vital need of know-
ing the purpose of his work and of making that goal his
own ... 'Intéressement' is important for the assurance
which it gives to workers that they have been socially regarded as having taken a personal part in the life of the
enterprise, and treated as a complete man »[61].

Back in 1947 the French association had organized
study days which concluded to the necessity of « intéressement » and led to the publication by Joseph Zamanski,
co-founder of C.F.P.C. and first president of UNIAPAC, of
a book, *L'Avenir de l'Entreprise, Un Patronat qui s'engage*.
This volume reports the plans for « intéressement » of
thirty-five employers who were C.F.P.C. members, offering
these as pioneer examples from which the other members
could learn and devise their own systems[62]. C.F.P.C. made
another public declaration on the subject in 1952, this time
conjointly with three other ideological movements[63]. The
Christian trade unions, responding to this declaration, formed with employers — many of them C.F.P.C. members —
a joint action body to collaborate in fostering « intéresse-

---

[61] Maurice Cliquet, « Trois sujets de réflexions sur les expériences
d'intéressement des travailleurs à la vie des entreprises », *Professions*,
no. 436, mai 1959, p. 5. The quote is credited to B. M. Boyer, O. P. Cf. also:
« A propos de l'intéressement du personnel deux entreprises du bâtiment Nantais font part de leurs réalisations », *Professions*, no. 434, mars
1959, p. 7; « A propos de l'intéressement du personnel le cas d'une
importante société de la région parisienne », *ibid.*, no. 435, avril 1959,
p. 7; Maurice Cliquet, « Discussions autour de l'intéressement », *ibid.*,
no. 437, juin 1959, pp. 5-6; « Restauration de la propriété », *Bulletin d'information de l'UNIAPAC*, no. ii, août 1957, pp. 82-86. This last is a
report from the general assembly of Holland's A.K.W.V., 1957, on « Les
divers aspects de la propriété privée ».

[62] Joseph Zamanski, *L'Avenir de l'Entreprise*, pp. 56-135.

[63] André Aumonier, « L'Influence des mouvements patronaux catholiques dans le milieu professionnel », *Documents et Commentaires*, no. 20,
décembre 1957, p. 44. The three other associations were Centre des
Jeunes Patrons (C.J.P.), Association de Cadres Dirigeants de l'Industrie
(ACADI), and Union des Chefs d'Entreprise pour l'Association du Capital
et du Travail (U.C.E.-A.C.T.). C.F.P.C. shares with these groups many
doctrinal and policy positions, and quite often the three collaborate.
A good explanation of U.C.E.-A.C.T. is given by Joseph Daniel, René
Théry, « Projet d'Association du Capital et du Travail », *Revue de l'Action
Populaire*, no. 34, novembre 1949, pp. 650-678. Since 1958 U.C.E.-A.C.T.
has changed its title: « pour l'Association du Capital et du Travail »
has been replaced by « Action pour des structures humaines », and the
call initials are re-written as UCE-ACT.

ment ». This is called « Comité d'Action pour le Développement de l'Intéressement du Personnel à la Productivité des Entreprises (CADIPPE) » [64]. It is clear then that the 1959 ordinance was part of a gradual evolution of C.F.P.C.'s position on profit-sharing and the acquiring of property, a concept which by 1959 had penetrated a broad sector of French employer circles.

Other UNIAPAC affiliates have given much attention to « intéressement » and its relation to the community-of-work. In 1948-49 the Brussels regional of APIC held a series of studies and conferences on the subject, two of which are especially *ad rem* : « L'Entreprise, Communauté du Travail », and « Le Sort du profit dans le debat Salariat et Association » [65]. And FEPAC devoted its entire congress of 1954 to the theme, « Productivité et rémunération du travail ». In its conclusion the congress distinguishes between *indirect* participation in increased productivity on the part of consumers by the lowering of prices, and *direct* participation on the part of those who have actually contributed to the gain in productivity, the workers among them. FEPAC advises that a « protocolle de productivité » be settled beforehand : « This method alone is satisfying : a) it constitutes for all the participants an efficacious stimulus for bettering their productive activity; b) it fortifies their sense of personal responsibility; c) it creates the conditions necessary for the will to cooperate » [66]. The method best suited to each firm is to be decided according to particular cases and set up in institutional formulae. And FEPAC states further : « These institutions of direct participation will depend certainly on the social relations proper to each enterprise,

[64] André Aumonier, « L'Influence des mouvements patronaux catholiques dans le milieu professionnel », *op. cit.*, p. 44. Cf. also « Après la déclaration commune, quelques précisions », *Professions*, no. 312, février 1953. The writer interviewed officers of CADIPPE, Roland Renard and M. Dumont, at their center, 58 rue du Faubourg-Poissonnière, Paris August 25, 1959.

[65] Pierre Louveaux, « L'Entreprise, Commuauté du Travail », and Jean Michiels, « Le sort du profit dans le debat ' Salariat et Association ' », *L'Entreprise et son destin*, APIC, pp. 49-76, 77-92 respectively. It is to be noted here that, as often happens in UNIAPAC circles, authors of both these reports are employers directly concerned with day-to-day management of sizable firms.

[66] *Productivité et rémunération de travail*, XVe Congrès de la FEPAC, Charleroi, 11-12 décembre 1954, *Bulletin social des Industriels*, no. 213. janvier 1955, p. 58 and *passim*.

but they will also of themselves create ... conditions favorable to a profound transformation of that human community which is the enterprise ».

The German, British and Swiss associations manifest a similar concern for profit and property sharing. V.C.U. of Switzerland published a brochure in 1958 covering much of the ground already touched upon, entitled « Création de propriété de la part des travailleurs », and their response to the UNIAPAC questionnaire on social peace reports that the great mistrust among workers concerning property acquisition has been more and more abandoned [67]. C.I.C. of Britain records a similar change : « Profit sharing has in the past been a cause rather of discord than of peace. Many employers who used it did so as a weapon against trade unionism. The trade unions are still suspicious of the schemes but not so hostile as they were » [68].

Attention was given to the subject of broadening the base of property owners in the German B.K.U. congresses of 1957 and 1958. Excerpts of these discussions have been published in booklet form [69]. In its response to the UNIAPAC questionnaire B.K.U. cites some well-known firms which are carrying out programs of « intéressement ». While admitting that profit-sharing and property acquisition stimulate the individual activity of many workers and their responsibility as well, both redounding to social peace, the German association warns that new problems and tensions will arise with the spread of property among the many. The nature of these difficulties were discussed by the present writer with Wilfred Schreiber, who is secretary general of B.K.U. and author of the booklet referred to above [70]. In the first place, workers tend to choose security rather than property. They are more interested in being certain of a

---

[67] Otto Meyer, « Création de propriété de la part des travailleurs », V. C. U.; « Réponse Suisse », *op. cit.*, pp. 11; the latter adds the following quote: « C'étaient les syndicats chrétiens qui étaient pour la propriété privée et en même temps pour une généralisation aussi grande que possible de la propriété ». (Secrétaire syndical A. Heil dans: *Le travailleur suisse de la métallurgie*, 1958 no. 5.).

[68] « Reply of the Catholic Industrialists' Conference, » *op. cit.*, p. 4.

[69] Wilfrid Schreiber, *Vermöbehsbildung in Breiten*, B. K. U., *passim. passim.*

[70] « Observations relatives au Questionnaire », *op. cit.*, p. 6; and interview in Cologne, September 21, 1959; also, further conversations in Rome, October 9, 1959.

set income than in the holding of the source of that income in the quasi invisibile form of shares. Also, when they do obtain shares, workers are counselled, often by employers themselves, not to leave their accumulating capital in one firm and thus risk the loss of both their property and job in the case of the firm's failure. Rather they should scatter their investment in several enterprises [71]. Since workers generally have not the knowledge needed to handle investments, and to cut down fees and service costs, workers' investors' trusts are developing [72]. Over the years these will acquire great financial power.

Schreiber cited a plan advanced by German socialist circles which would require that half the capital credit acquired by each worker be re-invested by law outside the firm in which he works, and that this be done by a state-operated investment trust. With dismay the B.K.U. leader pointed out that the board of directors of this trust would within a few decades control the financial destiny of the great corporations of the land.

Such are some of the problems raised by the effort to spread ownership of productive property. Despite difficulties UNIAPAC affiliates continue to espouse that ideal and to experiment with ways and means. B.K.U. in its motion presented to UNIAPAC on the subject, already cited in section 1 on property, states:

> The combat against nationalization would gain much headway if we could succeed in actualizing a policy of wider distribution of property, avowing that the lack of property among the masses is only an ephemeral phenomenon in the course of the natural development of the free industrial society, not conforming to its intrinsic nature. We could say:

---

[71] Bernard Jousset, past president of UNIAPAC, stated in a discussion that part of the capital acquired by workers in his own factory is re-invested in selected large corporations to give them security against losing both wages and savings; Rome, October 9, 1959.

[72] C. I. C. of Britain confirms this B. K. U. point: « The normal or employees' shareholding scheme has the disadvantage that a man is being asked to invest in the company where he is being employed instead of spreading the risk; so in the last two years there has been a great growth of unit trusts which allow small investors to take a financial interest in first class companies other than their own. One firm has lately undertaken to sell unit trust shares to its employees on a hire purchase basis ». From « Reply of Catholic Industrialists' Conference », *op. cit.*, p. 5 FE-PAC makes quite identical points, « La Paix sociale », *op. cit.*, pp. 27-28.

the broad distribution of property is as necessary for the free economy system as the right of universal suffrage is necessary for the political system of democracy[73].

C. Co-management.

Of necessity the Catholic employers' associations were very attentive to the discussions of the past decade over co-management (Mitbestimmungsrecht, cogestion), and were understandably in hearty agreement when Pope Pius XII contradicted the concept that right of economic co-management within the enterprise derives from natural law. While this teaching, rigorously adhered to by UNIAPAC, seems quite clear, a short exposition of the question is appropriate in view of the momentous effect co-management would have upon the wage system. Further, the subjects continues to come up for discussion.

In November 1957, seven years after Pius XII's definite condemnation of co-management as deriving from natural law, a doctrinal study of the issue appeared in the monthly organ of C.F.P.C., *Professions*. Brouwers also treats it in some detail in his presentation of Catholic doctrine published in 1958 by FEPAC[74]. He considers the subject under the heading of restriction of employer authority on the part of workers. Brouwers notes an increasing desire by the worker to cease feeling himself a stranger in the enterprise where he works and of seeing himself more really integrated

---

[73] « Le problème de l'accès à la propriété ». Conseil central des Délégués, Rome, 9-10 octobre 1959, p. 5. An international UNIAPAC commission began meeting on the subject, February 1960.

[74] B. M. Boyer, O. P., « Doctrine: Réfuser la co-gestion n'est pas bloquer le progrès social », *Professions*, no. 419, novembre 1957, pp. 3-6; L. Brouwers, S. J., *Le Problème social*, pp. 109-116. Other sources on the question are: R. Clemens, « L'Organisation de l'économie et la nature juridique de l'entreprise dans l'Allocution Pontificale du 7 mai 1949, *Bulletin social des Industriels*, novembre 1949, pp. 383-390; R. Goris, « Het Medebeheer », *De Christelijke Werkgever*, July 1951, pp. 242-251, and, August 1951, pp. 257-282; P. Bayart, « Analyse du discours de S. S. Pie XII du 3 juin 1950 », *Bulletin social des Industriels*, juillet-août 1950, pp. 290-299, and, septembre-octobre 1950, pp. 345-352. For a most recent non-employer Catholic discussion of co-management cf. J. Y. Calvez, J. Perrin, « Le problème de la co-gestion », *Eglise et Société économique*, pp. 359-365. Cf. also, Oswald von Nell-Breuning, S. J., *Wirtschaft und Gesellschaft Heute*, especially chapter two entitled « Mitbestimmung », pp. 91-161; and Jeremiah Newman, *Co-Responsibility in Industry, passim.*

into it by some participation in its management and responsabilities. He quotes *Quadragesimo Anno* as having touched
this point: « We consider it more advisable, however, in
the present condition of human society that, so far as possible, the work-contract be somewhat modified by a partnership-contract (contrat de société) ... Workers and other
employees thus become sharers in ownership or management (gestion) or participate in some fashion in the profits
received » [75].

Immediately following this quote Brouwers states:
« There is every evidence that in this text there is no question of a *right* on the part of the workers, or of an *obligation* on the part of the employer. It is a counsel, prudently
formulated, a counsel which Pius XII accentuated in 1944 » [76].
Brouwers recognizes the fact that of late the aspirations of
workers have moved along these lines to the point where
they begin to claim co-management, « ... this being understood in a sense much broader than shareholding (action-
nariat) or participation in profits, as a right founded in
nature, and which cannot be refused them » [77].

A resolution passed by the Katholikentag of Germany,
Bochum, September 4, 1949, declared that Catholic workers
and employers agreed to acknowledge that the participation
of all collaborators in decisions concerning social, economic and personnel questions is a natural right in conformity
with the order willed by God, having as its corollary that
all share in responsibility. The assembly went on to ask
that this right be legally recognized. This formulation of
« Mitbestimmungsrecht » or « droit de cogestion » became
the object of much discussion [78].

Brouwers notes that Pius XII some months before in
his allocution to UNIAPAC had counseled the attribution of
economic responsibility to workers at the industry and national level [79]. The FEPAC chaplain then presents the teach-

---

[75] Pope Pius XI, *Quadragesimo Anno*, par. 65, *op. cit.*, p. 26 (A.A.S.,
XXIII (1931), 199).

[76] Brouwers, *op. cit.*, p. 110. The reference to Pope Pius XII is to
his radio message of September 1, 1944. (A. A. S., XXXVI, 252-254).

[77] *Ibid.*

[78] Calvez, Perrin, *op. cit.*, p. 360, give this resumé.

[79] Pope Pius XII, « Allocution du 7 mai 149 aux membres de l'Union
Internationale des Associations Patronales Catholiques », Marcel Clément,
Le Chef d'Entreprise, p. 238, (A. A. S., XXXXI, 284-285). The key words of

ing of Pius XII, June 3, 1950, on « cogestion » by workers
within the enterprise, and concludes: « In a most formal
fashion he (Pius XII) affirms that the right of *economic co-
management* (*cogestion économique*) is not founded in natural law, that it is neither a necessity intrinsic to the nature
of the work-contract, nor to the nature of the enterprise.
And the Pope adds the reason: opposition to the right of
property, danger of collectivization »[80].

Another FEPAC authority, writing in their monthly review a few months after the Pope's allocution, enlarges on
these reasons:

> In effect, economic co-management by wage earners belong-
> ing to the personnel of the enterprise — i. e., the participa-
> tion by the wage earners in decisions of the economic order,
> in all those decisions which concern the nature and quantity
> of the product, the nature and quantity of the different
> means of production to be put in motion to produce them —
> this right of economic co-management amounts to separa-
> tion of the initiative and responsibility of decisions of the
> economic order from the right of ownership over the means
> of production ... In this way the right of economic co-manage-
> ment by wage earners belonging to the enterprise is already
> the beginning of the socialization of the economy. But the
> danger mounts when the exercise of this right devolves in
> fact, through the plant personnel, on organizations subject
> to a central director, exterior to the enterprise and a stranger
> to it [81].

Within a few weeks after the Katholikentag at Bochum
first formulated the right to co-management, the newly
founded Catholic employers' association of Germany, then
only a few months old, formally voiced its opposition. Meeting at Bad Neuenahr, October 30, 1949, the national assembly
of B.K.U. adopted a resolution on the issue. Citing the al-

---

the pontiff are: « Pourquoi ne serait-il pas legitime d'attribuer aux ouvriers une juste part de responsabilité dans la constitution et le développement de l'économie nationale? ... Cette communauté d'intérêt et de
responsabilité dans l'oeuvre de l'économie nationale, Notre inoubliable prédécesseur Pie XI en avait suggéré la formule concrète et opportune lorsque, dans son Encyclique *Quadragesimo Anno*, il recommandait ' l'organisation professionnelle ' dans les diverses branches de la production ».

[80] Brouwers, *op. cit.*, p. 111; emphasis is in original. The reference
is to Pius XII, « Allocution au Congrès international d'Etudes sociales »,
3 juin 1950, A. A. S., XXXXII, 487.

[81] R. Clemens, « Principes de Politiques sociale et droit de co-gestion économique dans l'Allocution Pontificale du 3 juin 1950 », *Bulletin
Social des Industriels*, décembre 1950, pp. 441-442.

locution of Pius XII to UNIAPAC of May 7, 1949, B.K.U. expressed acknowledgement of the right of workers to co-responsibility as set forth therein. They agreed to the advisability of outside-the-plant co-management through an economic council at the federal (Bund) and provincial (Land) levels. They intimated that beyond this co-management was being mis-used as a slogan [82].

Pius XII in his allocution to UCID of Italy, January 31, 1952, returned to this subject of such moment to the employers themselves. He recalled his own discourses of May 1, 1949 to UNIAPAC and of June 3, 1950, and repeated that the incontestable norms of natural law do not apply to juridic modifications of the enterprise structure in virtue of the work-contract. The pontiff explained that he opposed these reform tendencies, not to favor the material interests of one group over another, but rather to assure the sincerity and tranquillity of conscience to all concerned with these problems [83].

In his conclusion Brouwers makes three precisions, in summary as follows:

1) In all questions concerning the social and technical direction of enterprises — e. g., decisions relative to work operations, hygiene and safety — participation of workers is acceptable and praiseworthy.

2) In the field of economic management — e. g., decisions concerning plant construction, choice and purchase of raw materials and machinery, price determination, publicity and marketing, choice of fabrication techniques, financial administration, etc. — integral co-management, authorizing workers to deliberate and decide with the employers, cannot be legally imposed against the owner's will, because this is contrary to the right of private property and the authority of the employer.

3) There do exist mitigated types of participation in economic management, as, for example, the freedom accorded to workers' representatives of assisting at certain dis-

---

[82] B. Kulp, « Der BKU zur Mitbestimmungsfrage », p. 1. This is a commentary prepared by the B. K. U. secretariate at the present writer's request. Kulp is associate secretary of the German association.

[83] Pope Pius XII, « La Impresa cristiana », Nel quinto anniversario della UCID, 31 gennaio 1952, *Avanzate e Lavorate*, pp. 9-16 (*Discorsi* XIII, 463-466).

cussions and of having a consultative voice, and the right
to information. Such types of worker intervention, which
leave intact the right of property and of authority of the
employer so that he remains master in economic decisions,
do not appear contrary to papal teaching [84].

This presents a concise statement of the general UNIA-
PAC position on co-management. In 1953 Bernard Jousset,
while president of the international federation, speaking of
papal teaching on the subject, stated: « This excludes likewise every form of co-management among collaborators interior to the enterprise except the staff (hiérarchie), which
is the prolongation of the dirccting management, itself set
up by the proprietor of the means of production ... » [85]. And
this straight-forward affirmation of employers' rights in economic management is balanced, as has been seen by an anxious effort to have the worker share in the fruits and
ownership of the enterprise, and in the co-management of
non-economic spheres via the enterprise committees and
councils, all of which contribute to fostering the community-
of-work.

UNIAPAC is extremely conscious of the changing nature of the enterprise. While defending the basic rights of
the employer, it wants him to understand realities beyond
the legal and juridical letter, and that he can no longer exercise absolute sovereignty over the enterprise. A final statement from « The Aims of UNIAPAC » conveys some inkling
of this vision:

> He (the employer) establishes relations, elaborates struc-
> tures, gives responsibilities, enlivens a community, lessens
> frictions, and, if he understands his function, contributes to
> the pride of the workman.
> The enterprise is an entity which is above the employer.
> The enterprise has a different rhythm of life and another
> finality.
> The enterprise is not at the service of the employer, no
> more than it is at the service of the shareholders or the
> workmen, though all of them should gain from it, according
> to their responsibilities, risks and work.

---

[84] Brouwers, *op. cit.*, pp. 114-115.
[85] Bernard Jousset, « Cogestion », *Professions*, no. 316, 4 avril 1953,
pag. 3.

The enterprise has its own life. Once created by the employer it escapes his hold because its own responsibilities are rooted in the finality of its own action.[86]

4. The Human Person and the Family

UNIAPAC affiliates have devoted much concern to the place of the human person and the family in the modern enterprise and the overall economy. For several years numerous conferences of world and local scope have addressed themselves to translating Catholic doctrine on these basics into the employers' idiom. The positions and institutions already examined have as goals, additional to those already signalized, the fostering of the human development of the workers and the protection and amelioration of the Christian family. It would be misleading to imply that UNIAPAC exists primarily to minister to the person and family, but very true to assert that it exists for these purposes mediately: through economic institutions. The enterprise, property, syndicates, collective bargaining, just wages, enterprise committees, job security, « intéressement » — UNIAPAC convictions and positions on all of these are determined ultimately by the nature of man and his dignity.

The effect of technics upon man and human society is of particular interest to Catholics as employers because most often technical advance results from, or at least is applied by, entrepreneurial action. UNIAPAC affiliates are habitually preoccupied with the mechanization of working life and the « dishumanisation » usually attributed to the assembly line, automation and factory environment. UCID of Italy devoted its 1957 congress to the theme, « I fattori umani nello sviluppo economico — dalla zappa alla automazione », and FEPAC's 1959 assembly was on, « Dirigeants Chrétiens et Progression humaine »[87]. UNIAPAC had already explored the issue in its 1952 international session at Brussels, where the major discourses all applied Catholic social doctrine on technics, bringing it to bear on the UNIA-

---

[86] « The Aims of UNIAPAC », p. 6.

[87] *I fattori umani nello sviluppo economico — dalla zappa alla automazione*, UCID, VIII Congresso, Roma, 7-10 marzo 1957; *Dirigeants Chrétiens et progression humaine*, Congrès National de la FEPAC, *Bulletin social des Industriels*, n. 256, avril 1959.

PAC concept and mission. Some titles suggest the direction of development: « Technical Progress and Human Progress, Integrating the Worker in the Enterprise, The Christian Spirit and Economic Humanism » [88]. The lengthy conclusions adopted by the assembly can be summarized as follows:

1) While it is in the order proper to man that he should utilize the prodigious resources procured by technical invention, and that he should thus realize progressively that conquest of the universe which conforms to his God-given vocation to subdue and dominate the earth, man must not allow the desire for efficiency to become an absolute.

2) In considering man only under the angle of his technical usefulness, in considering him to be only that which he does, and disregarding him for that which he is, we empty man of his human quality. Furthermore, experience shows that if we submit man to the constraints of passivity, we suppress his need for freedom and we accelerate the collectivist trend of society.

3) For these reasons employers must advert to the possible results coming from an exclusive concern for economic advantages from technical progress. While seeking industrial advance, they must devise methods which adapt the machines to human beings. Production procedures which submit the worker to an obligatory and collective rhythm, dictated by the machine, must keep in mind also the rhythm proper to individual men. These procedures must reduce muscular and nervous fatigue. This « tristesse du travail » must be the more combatted to the extent that it is monotonous and without perceptible proximate purpose.

4) Further, the machine has caused the massive entry of women and youth into industrial plants, because their labor is cheaper and the machine has reduced the need for physical strength. There has resulted a disintegration of the home and intellectual and moral decadence of the working girl. As a matter of principle Christian employers must declare themselves adversaries of wage work by the wife

---

[88] *Progrès économique et progrès social*, 4e Session, UNIAPAC, Bruxelles, février 1952, pp. 57-70, 71-84, 85-108, 121-144 respectively; the authors are Giuseppe Prever, then vice-president of UCID; Joseph Höffner, chaplain of B. K. U.; Georges Henry, FEPAC; and Léon Bekaert, president of FEPAC.

and mother. They must strive for an organization of industry which procures for the heads of families the income necessary to permit the wife and mother to carry out her indispensable role in her home and to her children.

5) Employers must aim not only at assuring security of work, but also at giving human dignity to work. In addition to the means already noted this involves, further, the architecture and layout of plants and research in methods of decentralization. These can suppress that passivity and isolation imposed by technical progress, and help to render the enterprise a center of collaboration and solidarity, rather than a breeder of division and class struggle. All this, in brief, calls for the creation of a psychological climate favorable to a real community-of-work, to be attained in a common effort, where each person finds his own *raison d'être* in the overall picture and experiences a shared pride of achievement [89].

In its 1957 congress UNIAPAC returned to this problem of technics and women workers [90], and FEPAC in its 1959 national session on the theme « Dirigeants Chrétiens et Progression humaine » re-emphasized that « ... concern for human values must persist irregardless of the effect on productivity » [91]. C.F.P.C. brought the issue to the local level by devoting part of their « Programme de Travail » for 1959-60 to humanizing the enterprise with stress on delega-

---

[89] Charles Harmel, « Conclusions de la 4e Session », *ibid.*, pp. 145-151. These are not direct quotes, but a synthesis; the enumeration of points is not in the original; Harmel was then president of UNIAPAC. The allocution of Pius XII to the Associazione Cristiana Lavoratori Italiani (ACLI), June 7, 1957, on automation, is frequently commented on by UNIAPAC writers and speakers. It is reproduced in full in *Bulletin d'Information de l'UNIAPAC*, no. ii, août 1957, pp. 69-74. (A. A. S., XLIX, 621-629). The same issue reports on assemblies treating automation by the International Labor Office and the Confédération Internationale des Syndicats Chrétiens, pp. 18-19, 21-23 respectively.

[90] « Résolutions, le XIVe Congrès Patronal de l'UNIAPAC », Montreal, 15-21 septembre 1957, *Bulletin d'Information de l'UNIAPAC*, no. iii, p. 118.

[91] « Conclusions », *Dirigeants Chrétiens et Progression humaine, op. cit.*, p. 180. Cf. also. « Adapter le Travail a l'Homme », *Promotion*, no. 8, juin 1958, pp. 2-4; this is the monthly publication of the « Ingénieurs et Cadres Supérieurs » of APIC. Cf. further. a symposium, « Les conséquences sociales de l'Automation »; F. Rogiers, « Le Travailleur et l'Automation »; R. DeBie, « Automation et Emploi »; J. C. Pierre, « Automation et Revenu »; W. Matthys, « L'Elargissement des Tâches », *Bulletin Social des Industriels*, no. 255, mars 1959, pp. 98-104, 105-108, 109-117, 118-120 respectively.

tion of authority, recognizing legitimate aspirations of the
workmen and their need for information, and fostering their
spirit of initiative and sense of responsibility [92]. These points
are developed in discussion notes to be used by the local
sections at their monthly meetings. Articles on the « dishumanisation » of work occur frequently in the organs of the
associations. One case history presented by C.F.P.C. reports,
« ... a veritable revolution: (this firm) shows that 3600 persons, staff and workers can find their place and live as persons and individuals in a complex organism. The abdica-
tion of one's own personality at the factory gate is no longer
of obligation ». The key here is to ask, « Why? ... Why do
this work? Why follow this method? Why use this machine? » [93].

Several of the national affiliates have taken strong positions against Sunday work. The motives are the Christian
observance of Sunday and the need for a rest day, giving
leisure to all the family together. Particularly have B.K.U.
and FEPAC devoted attention to this issue. B.K.U. has published a booklet, *Unsere Meinung zur Frage dur Sonntagarbeit*, giving technological, economic and moral considerations [94]. FEPAC, after a survey, states that Christians, both
managers and workers, should reach accords of an inter-in-
dustry and international scope to assure the universal observance of the Sunday, based upon respect for the human
person [95].

It will be recalled that the ancestor of UNIAPAC, Léon
Harmel, held strong convictions on the necessity of a family
wage, positions which were very advanced for their time [96].

---

[92] *Programme de Travail Année 1959-1960, passim,* and especially·
pp. 20-21. The 1954 joint congress of the Spanish and Portuguese associations was on the theme, « Relaciones Humanas en la Empresa », « Cuestionario UNIAPAC », UNIAPAC Archives, p. 5.

[93] « L'Homme et le Robot peuvent s'entendre », *Professions,* no. 392,
9 juin 1956, pp. 7-8.

[94] Wilfrid Schreiber, *Unsere Meinung zur Frage de Sonntagarbeit,*
passim.

[95] C. Steenhoudt-Bosteels, « Les différents problèmes posés par le travail du dimanche », « Le travail du dimanche en Belgique: Premier résultats d'une nquête », R. Spitaels, « Le travail du dimanche en sidérurgie »,
Bulletin social des Industriels, no. 259, juillet-août 1959, pp. 283-284, 285-
286, and 287 respectively. Cf. also, M. Thiefry, S. J., M.M. Dupuis, A. Thomas, « Le repos dominical et la semaine ' mobile ' du travail », *Promotions,*
no. 1, février 1959, pp. 2-6.

[96] Cf. chapter II, section 2, part D, above.

He also worked out one of the very first family subsidy systems (allocations familiales). These concepts are continued today by his successors in the Catholic employers' movement. In his doctrinal exposition Brouwers bases his presentation of « salaire familial » on *Quadragesimo Anno*[97]. He develops in some degree the discussion between the relative and absolute family wage, and states that in most modern nations the just wage is an amalgam of both, based on commutative and social justice. In 1956 FEPAC published a seventy-seven page study, *Politique familiale et responsabilité patronale*, setting forth an overall family policy for the state and industry, the enterprises and employers[98]. After a review of the harm done to the family through the industrial revolution, « dominated by errors of economic liberalism and by the influence of an individualism which, in acknowledging only the rights of individuals, ignored totally the reality of the family », FEPAC states that defense of family values falls heavily upon employers because of the responsibility which is theirs from the authority they exercise in society through their enterprises. These responsibilities of employers toward their personnel cannot be shoved off to the collectivity. The demands of these responsibilities are then analyzed : family wage, keeping mothers at home, housing, family allocations, and others.

After the first Harmel experiments in the 1890's family allocations became generalized in France largely through the initiative of a C.F.P.C. leader, Emile Romanet, immediately after World War I. C.F.P.C. has found it necessary to continue a running battle to support their convictions. As late as 1954 they were moved to issue a « Déclaration sur les allocations familiales et la sécurité social ». Condemning « concepts of short-sighted individualism », the declaration insists upon the necessity of a policy of « family wage and family allocations, making possible the presence of the mother in the home, not only in privileged circles, but in all households »[99].

---

[97] Brouwers, *op. cit.*, pp. 80-87.

[98] *Politique familiale et responsabilité patronale, passim*, and especially pp. 7-11.

[99] « Déclaration sur lse allocations familiales et la sécurité sociale », C.F.P.C., 1 juillet 1954. In the next chapter some details of Romanet's influence in the spread of family subsidies will be given.

In the discussion above some reference has already been made to the movement's position on housing for workers. The emphasis so far was on the effect it would have in mitigating class struggle, defending private property, promoting worker security and the community-of-work. Another great motive for provision of housing, is, of course, UNIAPAC's concern for the family. In this field the convictions of the national organizations are best demonstrated by their espousal of state and private mutual-aid construction schemes. This is widespread; in 1953 A.K.W.V. of Holland published a booklet on cooperative housing, *Samen Bouwen* (Building Together), and Sergio Ossa Pretot, leader of the Chilean USEC and UNIAPAC vice-president, has been for several years president of « Fundación Mi Casa », a cooperative for providing financing and materials for homes for workers [100].

UNIAPAC, in brief, seeks to return the enterprise and the overall economy to a concept of its finality, a finality centered in the human person, living in the family. The address of Paul Cardinal Léger of Montreal to the world congress held in that city in 1957 is much quoted by UNIAPAC leaders as an excellent development of this theme. Cardinal Léger says that the crisis of our times can be defined without hesitation as a « crise de finalité », a complete forgetfulness that things and men have a destination. He attacks the error of « technics for the sake of technics, science for the sake of science, art for the sake of art, leisure for the sake of leisure ». He asserts that the contrary of poverty and unhappiness (misère) is not necessarily abundance, but value: « ... the great necessity is not above all to produce wealth, but to give the proper value to man, to humanity, to the universe » [101].

UNIAPAC and affiliates believe that Catholic employers have the duty of giving the economic world this human person — and family — centered vision, an understanding of its true finality.

---

[100] « Pays-Bas: Comment acquérir la propriété d'une maison pour les ouvriers »? *Bulletin d'Information de l'UNIAPAC*, no. 5, avril 1953, pp. 7-8; UNIAPAC archives, « Version Grabada del Historial del Movimiento Patronal en Chile », p. 2.

[101] S. Em. Cardinal Léger, « La mission sociale d'un patronat chrétien », *Bulletin social des Industriels*, no. 242, décembre 1957, pp. 392-398,

5. Industrial Organization
(Organisation Professionnelle)

Frequent reference has already been made to UNIAPAC's doctrine on industrial organization, known in French as « l'organisation professionnelle », and in papal documents as « ordines ».   In a sense the Catholic employers' movement has espoused and developed this concept as their key platform, especially since Pius XII directly exhorted them on the subject in 1949.   The pontiff, speaking to UNIAPAC during its constitutive assembly in Rome, stated:

> For this community of interest and responsibility (among employers and workers) in the operation of the national economy, our well-remembered predecessor, Pius XI, had suggested the concrete and opportune formula, when in his encyclical *Quadragesimo Anno* he recommended « l'organisation professionnelle » in the diverse branches of industry.   In effect, nothing appears to him so likely to triumph over economic liberalism as the establishment for the social economy of a statute of public law based precisely on the community of responsibility existing among all those who take part in production [102].

UNIAPAC took the papal allocution seriously; the following year, 1950, they devoted their international session to the doctrinal and practical aspects of the subject.   The ten conferences given by members of five national associations are published with commentary in book form, *L'Organisation Professionnelle* [103].   During the ensuing decade

---

quote from p. 393. This address has been frequently cited to the present writer by UNIAPAC leaders, and particularly praised by the secretary general, Rik Vermeire.

[102] Pope Pius XII, « Allocution du 7 mai 1949 aux membres de l'Union Internationale des Associations Patronales Catholiques », Marcel Clément, *Le Chef d'Entreprise*, p. 240 (A. A. S., XXXXI, 284-285). « Cette communauté d'intérêt et de responsabilité dans l'oeuvre de l'économie nationale, Notre inoubliable prédécesseur Pie XI en avait suggéré la formule concrète et opportune lorsque, dans son Encyclique *Quadragesimo Anno*, il recommendait l'organisation professionnelle dans les diverses branches de la production. Rien, en effet, ne lui semblait plus prope à triompher du libéralisme économique que l'établissement, pour l'économie sociale, d'un statut de droit public fondé précisément sur la communauté de responsabilité entre tous ceux qui prennent part à la production ». (Translation into English is by the present writer).

[103] *L'Organisation Professionnelle*, 2e Session UNIAPAC, Paris, avril 1950, *passim*. The lecturers were from France, Belgium, Holland, Great

this volume has been repeatedly cited and has become a
basic source of UNIAPAC thought. Again, this broad, complex subject can only be briefly reviewed.

UNIAPAC rejects the basic theories of economic liberalism. The movement does not espouse the abstract concept of full economic freedom for employers or workers,
singly or in groupings, as leading mechanically to automatic
harmony. Rather these partners in production should associate, not only within the enterprise community, but also
should reach outside the firm to form councils or boards,
in keeping with their respective industries or products.
Each industry board should have power to supervise and
regulate various relations within the industry, and represent
the industry as a whole vis-à-vis other industry boards, the
economy as a whole, the state and society. In this system
the various industry boards are themselves supervised by
an overall national council which moderates the policies of
the industry boards in view of the whole economy and
toward the common good. This top national body is to be
composed by representatives of management, labor and the
public — the last by government appointment, or selection
by designated non-official bodies. The industry boards at
all levels would be composed of management and labor
representatives selected by their own bodies, i. e., employers'
associations and labor unions. The whole system would
have juridic status, being brought into being by public law.
UNIAPAC seeks an economic order which is neither liberal
anarchy, nor socialist statism; for that reason these bodies

Britain and Italy. This present day position of UNIAPAC must be sharp-
ly distinguished from the corporatist concept originally espoused by Léon
Harmel, already discussed above, chapter II, section 2, part D. Likewise,
it is a theory of industrial organization much different from the corporative regime, hotly debated in the 1930's, and discredited by the memory
of authoritarian structuring of the industrial branches into veritable bu-
reaus of totalitarian states. As will be seen in due course, UNIAPAC's
proposals aim at the very opposite: free labor unions and employers'
syndicates forming a self-regulating institution for the purpose, among
others, of avoiding absorption by the state. For a history of the corporatist concept, cf. Georges Jarlot, S. J., *Le Régime corporatif et les
Catholiques sociaux, passim,* and for the debate of the 1930's, see especially chapter XII, « Regime Corporatif 1938 », pp. 221-235. Treatment in the
present study is confined to the current position of UNIAPAC. Cf. also,
Semaine Sociale de France, XXVII Session, Angers, 1935, *L'Organisation
Corporative, passim.*

are often called intermediate institutions, occupying a position between the state and the individual.

Here and now, the writer interjects that this presents his version of his understanding of UNIAPAC's concept of industrial organization. Nowhere is there to be found in their declarations an exact blueprint of the system. This is a summary generalization from conversations and interviews with leaders, from study sessions and congress reports [104]. While pressing for the development of industrial organization, UNIAPAC admits readily the possibility of many variants and even their desirability, in keeping with the diverse historical and social traditions and existing institutions. A gradual evolution of forms is also stressed.

The Catholic employers' associations of France, Belgium and Holland have played important roles in bringing about first experiments with industrial organization in their respective lands. Holland's « Publiekrechtelijke Bedrijfsorganisatie (P.B.O.) » — Public Law Industrial Organization — is by far the most advanced, in effect since 1950. A cursory look at P.B.O. will give a better idea of how the general concept can be concretized in a given nation.

P.B.O. has three types of interrelated bodies [105] : industrial boards (bedrijfschappen), commodity boards (productschappen), and a single national social and economic council (Sociaal-Economische Raad), which supervises the whole system. The industrial boards are horizontal bodies, dealing with issues inherent to enterprises which perform similar or equal economic function; the commodity boards are vertical, organizing enterprises which perform a different function in regard to the same product. To date some thirty horizontal industrial boards have been set up, e. g., for agri-

---

[104] These interviews have already been cited; those with Albreghts, Marijnen, Elsen, Linnebank, Spoorenberg, Lombaers and Vermeire have particular pertinency here. A recent presentation of Catholic doctrine on this subject is found in Calvez and Perrin, *op. cit.*, pp. 499-536.

[105] Interview with E. A. V. Vermaas, secretary of « Sociaal-Economische Raad », September 16, 1959, The Hague, and interviews already cited. Also, *Sociaal-Economische Raad*, Verslag over 1957 en 1958, *passim; De Publiekrechtelijke Bedrijfsorganisatie in Nederland*, B. M. Telders Stichting, pp. 146-153 (original contains an English summary); *The Industrial Organization Act in the Netherlands, Sociaal-Economische Raad, passim;* « The Social and Economic Council in the Netherlands », *passim;* A. H. M. Albreghts, « Le Statut de la Profession », *L'Organisation Professionnelle*, pp. 143-162.

culture, forestry, coal mining, hotel and catering services, various branches of the retail trade, banking and insurance. On the other hand, an exemple of the vertical body is the livestock and meat commodity board, which covers enterprises of livestock production, the packing-house industry, livestock markets, wholesale and retail butchers and retailers of meat products. A second vertical example is the beer commodity board, concerned with the brewing industry, the wholesale and retail trade in beer.

An industrial board cannot be established except with agreement of the employers' economic associations and workers' syndicates in the branch of industry affected. These private law organizations determine the composition of the industrial board of their sector, and in effect transfer to this body of employers' and workers' representatives certain powers for the regulation of their industry. This might include setting of wages, work conditions, worker classification by skill and age, rationalization of production, quality standards, competition practices, and power to regulate sales, delivery and payment conditions. Commodity boards are given regulatory powers regarding economic relations between the various production, processing and distributing phases of a given item. They are not, however, allowed to make price regulations unless that faculty is especially granted by the government. The principal single power so far granted commodity boards is capacity to establish and administer social security funds. This board's members are also selcted by employers' and workers' associations, usually in paritary fashion. The president of each commodity board is appointed by the government, and whereas the industrial boards are voluntarily formed by the employers and workers affected, the commodity board can be created by the government. This, however, has occurred only once, in the forming of a board for agricultural produce, and this was not against the will of a large sector of those affected.

The overall purpose of both horizontal and vertical boards is « promoting such conduct of business by the enterprises for which they have been instituted as shall serve the interest of the Netherlands people, and protecting the common interests of those enterprises and the persons en-

gaged therein » [106]. The board members are not mandatories
of the organizations by whom they were appointed; they
must vote without orders from, or consultation with, third
parties.

Their operation is supervised by the overall national
body, the social and economic council (Sociaal-Economische
Raad). Various decisions of the boards, particularly of a
financial nature, like their budgets, are subject to approval
by this national council. This important body is composed
of forty-five members, fifteen of whom are appointed by
employers' organizations, fifteen by workers' syndicates, and
fifteen by the government as representatives of the public
at large.

Besides this responsibility over the horizontal and vertical boards, the social and economic council has other important duties. It exercises certain administrative power
over the enterprise councils, which must be established in
all firms employing more than twenty-five workers, as already outlined in section 3 of this chapter. And most noteworthy, the « Raad » has an advisory function toward the
government: governmental ministers must ask the council
to advise them on any important measures or legislation
being contemplated in the social and economic fields. Such
consultation in recent years has been relative to cartels and
competition regulation, price control and inflation, export-
import regulation, agricultural policy, old age and survivors'
pensions, family subsidies, work hours' reduction, and international economic policy.

This overall system of industrial and commodity boards,
together with the « Sociaal-Economische Raad », is known
as the « Public Law Industrial Organization — Publiekrechtelijke Bedrijfsorganisatie », or P.B.O. It has been warmly
supported by the Catholic employers' movement in the
Netherlands, which made a distinct contribution to its constitution during the post-World War II years. A.H.M. Albreghts, former secretary general of the Dutch Catholic associations and of UNIAPAC, and still today a dominant UNI-
APAC leader, was one of the important creators of P.B.O.
In a discourse on P.B.O. to the 1950 UNIAPAC session on

---

[106] *The Industrial Organization Act in the Netherlands, op. cit.*, art.
71, p. 25.

industrial organization, already drawn upon heavily in this
exposition, Albreghts asserts the necessity of abandoning the
negative *laissez-faire* of liberalism and the pressing danger
of state collectivization, and that: « Industrial organization
is the alternative to serfdom. We conclude that cooperation
between workers and employers is indispensable... Such
cooperation will find its most perfect realization in an order
like the one we have just described (Holland's P.B.O.). We
see in this socio-economic order the best means to combat
Communism and also the road ... (against) monopolist tendencies » [107].

Albreghts repeats that a healthy economic development
is impossible in a regime of absolute freedom, and that,
further:

> ... a certain rationalization of socio-economic affairs is neces-
> sary to assure to labor a just legal and social position ... to
> favor economic advance without wastage of capital and hu-
> man energy. It is the industrial and commercial groups who
> must, as much as possible, themselves regulate these activities
> in the framework of industrial organization ...
> The road we follow is not without difficulties, but it is
> fitting that we, Catholic employers, must not fear for the
> future. It is up to us to convince our Liberal colleagues of
> the value of our principles and the possibility of their reali-
> zation, to show them that this is the unique way outside the
> totalitarian system of Communism [108].

The Netherlands have gone much further along the road
toward « l'organisation professionnelle » than have other
countries. Brouwers explains the progress attained in Belgium. After exposing Catholic teaching *in re*, the FEPAC
chaplain outlines « the important law passed in 1948 which,
without realizing the *ordines*, or industry councils, spoken
of by Pius XI, does, however, proceed along the line of
' l'organisation professionnelle ' proposed in *Quadrafesimo
Anno* » [109]. Brouwers reviews these public law bodies which
function in Belgium on three planes: enterprise councils at
the local firm level, already treated at length above; industrial councils (conseils professionnels) formed by employers'
and workers' representatives in each branch of industry;

---

[107] Albreghts, « Le Statut de la Profession », *op. cit.*, p. 160.
[108] *Ibid.*, p. 161.
[109] Brouwers, *op. cit.*, p. 130.

and the central economic council, « Conseil central de l'économie », at the national level. The last named is composed of fifty members, twenty-one from workers' syndicates, an equal number from employers' organizations, and the remaining eight members being chosen by these forty-two members themselves. The great mark of difference from the Dutch P.B.O. is that in Belgium these industry and national level bodies have only a consultative role[110].

In its response to the UNIAPAC questionnaire on social peace, FEPAC states flatly that despite these hopeful tendencies and papal teaching, « ... our country has not really entered the path toward a veritable ' organisation professionnelle de droit public ', and Christian employers ... have not formulated concrete propositions for such a system »[111]. Some portion of management, FEPAC continues, pleads for the multiplication of collective contracts between employers and workers at the industry-wide level, either within or at the margin of existing organizations; these collective agreements could establish the guide lines of labor relations in each. « It is to be hoped », FEPAC concludes, « that such a conception, while fostering social peace, would at the same time foster the upbuilding of an industrial order according to the sense of papal teaching »[112].

France's progress toward « l'organisation professionnelle » is at a stage comparable to that of Belgium. Its national council, however, has two hundred and five members, representing nine economic and social categories, e. g., family associations and cooperatives, in addition to labor and management[113]. Like FEPAC, C.F.P.C. also regrets the non-realization of a more all-embracing structure. Shortly after the new French constitution was proclaimed in 1959, André Aumonier, secretary general, made the following observation:

> So far nothing allows us to foresee (the establishing by the new government of) that « organisation professionnelle »

---

[110] Interview with Victor Van Rompay, deputy secretary general of « Conseil central de l'économie », September 7, 1959, Brussels. Another difference is that a separate consultative council has been established in Belgium for worker and social issues.

[111] « La Paix sociale et les responsabilité patronales », *op. cit.*, p. 23.

[112] *Ibid.*

[113] « La mise en place du Conseil économique et social », Conseil national du Commerce, p. 2.

empowered by public law, such as we have promoted so many
long years in accordance with papal teaching, which in the
economic and social field has never been tellingly contradicted
by any other doctrine, not by any other experience [114].

After commenting on the newly set up national economic and social council, Aumonier cites the hope expressed
by some that this body will become the brain and motor
capable of conceiving, bringing to life and animating such
an organization of the industries: « Nothing prevents us
from hoping that, thanks to the government and the influence of its future members, the economic and social council
will become in fact the instrument of economic and social
policies as far removed from absolute Liberalism as from
totalitarian ' dirigismé ', that is to say, ' une organisation
professionnelle ' » [115]. A few weeks later Aumonier, with
representatives of three other management movements, was
received by President Charles De Gaulle. Aumonier reports
that active participation by labor in economic responsibilities at the industry and national levels was discussed, with
a declaration of agreement among the four movements that
parity voice and authority must be given labor at those
levels [116].

The *Programme de Travail* of C.F.P.C. for 1959-60 directed to its local sections, treats of « l'organisation professionnelle ». It states that:

---

[114] André Aumonier, « L'Organisation professionnelle et la 5ᵉ République », *Professions*, no. 429, october 1959, p. 6. Aumonier is a member of
the newly established « Conseil économique et social ».

[115] *Ibid.* In 1956 C. F. P. C. devoted an entire issue of its quarterly
review to « l'organisation professionnelle », *Documents et Commentaires*,
no. 15, septembre 1956. Authors include Roger Reynaud, member of the
« Comité Confédéral » of the Confédération française des travailleurs chrétiens, who writes on « Vues syndicalistes sur l'organisation professionnelle », pp. 23-24, and Philippe Laurent, S.J., on « Les qualités nécessaires
dans l'édification d'une organisation professionnelle », pp. 27-31.

[116] « Les ' Quatre ' chez le Général De Gaulle », *Professions*, no. 430,
novembre 1958, p. 7. The other movements joining C. F. P. C. in the
discussions were Association des Cadres Dirigeants de l'Industrie (ACADI),
Centres des Jeunes Patrons (C.J.P.), Union des Chefs d'entreprise pour
action pour des structures humaines (UCE-ACT). Cf. also, « Penser et
Prévoir pour le Gouvernment », *Professions*, no. 434, mars 1959, p. 16,
which reports an address given to C. F. P. C. by Emile Roche, president
of the national economic council. In thanking the speaker, Emile Decré,
president of C. F. P. C., pointed out that the difficult role of the national
council would be effectively strengthened « to the degree that ' l'organisation professionnelle ' as a solid structure becomes an intermediate body
between the enterprises and the Economic Council ».

The process which will permit the attainment of a veritable organisation of industries goes forward via « mutual
engagements » between employers and wage earners on those
concrete problems which common good demands that they
settle, engagements which must be developed, multiplied and
extended. This organization must not be « planified » *a priori*.
It must not be directly imposed by public authority, but only
encouraged. In relation to it (organisation professionnelle),
industrial employers' bodies and workers' unions in their
present actual state appear as necessary but « provisory »
forms. This (organisation professionnelle) should grow and
develop progressively [117].

By and large UNIAPAC affiliates other than these three
surveyed here appear to put less stress on industrial organization. Occasional reference is found, but no promotion
of like constancy. UNIAPAC itself does not attempt to force
an implementation of this concept. The world federation
merely nourishes and fosters, well aware that the idea must
implant itself in local terrain and come to term only after
variable periods, and then in diverse forms. At the same
time the national affiliates do strive to build up acceptance
of workers' unions, employers' associations, collective contracts, enterprise councils and the like, which to UNIAPAC
are all building blocks and bonds for the future overall
structure of « l'organisation professionnelle » [118].

---

[117] *Programme de Travail, op. cit.*, pp. 36-37.

[118] *La Paix sociale, op. cit., passim*. In the United States the closest
approximation to these concepts is expressed as « the industry council
plan ».

Whereas industry boards as such do not exist in the United States and
are seldom even discussed, very recent reports seem to presage industry-
wide meetings. Bob Senser, « The White House will put Heads Together »,
Work, February 1960; p. 1 ff, reports: « A top-level labor-management conference will be held under White House auspices late in February or
early in March ». The article quotes the American secretary of labor,
James P. Mitchell, as having expressed the hope that this conference will
be followed by « conferences on industry levels, where employer representatives and labor representatives can sit down, outside the bargaining table, and talk about common problems in the industry ».

The concluding part of the article refers to UNIAPAC. After stating
that automatic results must not be immediately expected from these exchanges, the article concludes: « Disillusionment can be forestalled by
learning from the experience cited by a recent visitor to the U. S., Rik
Vermeire of Belgium, secretary-general of the International Association of
Catholic Employer Organizations. Vermeire pointed out that in Belgium
union and management meet continuously, at the plant level and on up
to the national level, to iron out not only existing problems but future
ones (automation falls into both categories). All wasn't lovey-dovey at

The very gradualness of this realization is also **UNIAPAC** doctrine.

6. THE NATIONAL AND INTERNATIONAL COMMUNITIES.

The **UNIAPAC** position concerning the state and public authority has often been adverted to, particularly in treating nationalization of property, social legislation and « l'organisation professionnelle ». While constantly on guard against an encroaching collectivization, the Catholic employers' associations fully admit that the state has an important role to fulfill in economic and social affairs, that as the custodian and promoter of the common good it must be always vigilant and actively contribute to social order. It will be recalled that Léon Harmel, « with his antennas on the future », during his lifetime evolved from a rather intransigent non-interventionist of the old liberal school, to the view that the state must not only protect individual freedom, but should also promote the common good of society [119].

UNIAPAC circles acknowledge readily that the role of the state has greatly expanded, that, as C.F.P.C. puts it in a statement entitled « L'Etat et son rôle », the justice to be realized today is no longer that which preoccupied Saint Louis. Rather: « It is in the formidable dimensions of the modern world, of the dense and complex network of economic relations, and of the distribution of power among men and the social groupings » [120]. The state must combat

---

the start, Vermeire said. 'At first when Belgian labor and management met they quarreled a great deal. They weren't used to working together. Now, after 10 years under this system they agree eventually in about 95 % of the cases'. The U. S. is now starting out where Belgium was 10 years ago ».

[119] Guitton, *op. cit.*, vol. II, pp. 50-51. This is reviewed in chapter II, section 2, part D, above.

[120] « L'Etat et son rôle », *Professions*, no. 427, juillet-août 1958, p. 4. This is one of several doctrinal statements in the same issue, occasioned by French civil crisis of 1958; other statements are entitled: « Autorité, Obéissance et Bien commun; Le citoyen dans la nation; Le Chef d'entreprise au service du pays; Refaire les Tissus ». The last treats of « l'organisation professionnelle ». Cf. also, Jean Marie Louvel, « Les Rapports entre l'Etat et l'Entreprise, *L'Organisation professionnelle, Documents et Commentaires*, no. 15, septembre 1956, pp. 61-69. The « assises », national assembly of C. F. P. C., in 1958 was on the theme: « Le Chef d'entreprise au service du pays »; it is reported in *Documents et Commentaires*, no. 22, juin 1958.

privilege and exploitation, the statement continues, and must supervise justice between sectors of the economy, between the various industries and among those who contribute to the economic life; all because: « Social justice is necessary for the cohesion of a people ... Managerial leaders more and more recognize and affirm these truths ». As has been seen, in UNIAPAC doctrine « l'organisation professionnelle » as a public law organism is the economic power structure best calculated to procure social justice with a minimum of direct state authority.

Their lines of doctrine and of program having been clarified at the national level, a growing concern within the UNIAPAC movement today is with extra-national issues and institutions.

In 1957 C.F.P.C. issued a « Déclaration sur l'Europe à propos du Marché Commun », manifesting its approval of all measures to strengthen solidarity among European nations, provided these conform to Christian concepts and build up a greater justice among all men. « The evolution of the world », C.F.P.C. continues, « shows the peoples of Europe that unity is urgent, if they want to maintain living economies and to conserve those intellectual and moral values which are most precious to them » [121]. The European Common Market is a stage in this unification. C.F.P.C. expresses apprehension over liberal and technocratic influences in this creation of a European economy; C.F.P.C. believes, on the contrary, that the European economy must be founded on « organisations économiques professionnelles et sociales », representative of all groups concerned, not only of employers, but of workers as well.

UCID's national congress in 1959 dealt with « Problemi dello sviluppo economico sociale nella Comunità Europea » [122], and the 1958 UNIAPAC conference at Knokke-Brus-

---

[121] « Déclaration sur l'Europe à propos du Marché Commun », *Documents et Commentaires*, no. 17, mars 1957, pp. 19-20. Cf. also, *Programme de travail Année 1959-60, op. cit.*, p. 38, which projects « l'organisation professionnelle » to the European level.

[122] Some of the addresses were: Giuseppe Cardinal Siri, « Responsabilità morale della collaborazione internazionale », Vittorio Vaccari, « Responsabilità della dirigenza ed integrazione europea », Gino Gastaldi, « La formazione degli operatori all'integrazione europea », 9 UCID Congresso Nazionale, Venezia, 7-10 maggio 1959; Gastaldi is general manager of Necchi. The writer was in attendance at this congress. In 1950 UCID

sels was on « Economic and Human Perspectives of the Common Market ». In the conclusions of this conference UNIAPAC sees in this opening of a new era responsibilities for constructing a « more human Europe ». Social objectives must be re-appraised, e. g., regarding family remuneration, access to property for all categories of people, and means for benefitting employers, workers and consumers through the advantages of a wider marker. « But », UNIAPAC asserts, « the economic advantages resulting from the Common Market will not be destined uniquely to bettering the standard of living of the European people, they will be utilized to an increasing degree in favor of the economic and human development of the underdeveloped regions of the whole world » [123]. These objectives, the conference concludes, imply study and action in common, not only by Catholic employers, but also by employers and workers, by Catholics and Protestants and all men of good will who, while not embracing specifically Christian principles, concur with solutions in keeping with natural law.

UNIAPAC returned to the question of aid to the underdeveloped countries in its 1959 congress at Luzern. Much time was given to discussing the issue. The necessity of assistance was accepted by the assembly without question, and rather concrete plans were advanced for effectuating this conviction. Jacques De Staercke, administrative delegate of FEPAC, proposed the creation of an international fund which would dispose of sufficient capital to push beyond the current experimental stage, and, most importantly, this fund « would be managed by representatives of the underdeveloped countries and by representatives of the industrialized nations. Such a management, strictly paritary, is absolutely necessary if we want to avoid that the programs, decisions and recommendations of the fund be interpreted

---

devoted its congress to: « Problemi della cooperazione economica e sociale europea ».

[123] « Conclusions », *Perspectives humaines et économiques du Marché Commun, Documents et Commentaire*, no. 23, septembre 1958, pp. 84-85. UNIAPAC affiliates of Latin America are promoting consideration of a common market treaty among some of their nations, according to reports made by Rik Vermeire to this writer, January 1960. Cf. also, « Communiqué de Presse », UNIAPAC Comité central des Délégués, Paris, 28 février 1959.

as the mark of an imperialist policy » [124].   The Belgian leader goes on to assert that continuance of fragmentary, unitary aid will only salve the consciences of the « have » nations and fire the hopes of the « have-nots » without meeting the problem and without filling the daily widening chasm between industrialized and underdeveloped nations.   To De Staercke it appears necessary that UNIAPAC make this its « number one problem ».

In the same discussion, Bernard Jousset, UNIAPAC vice-president and former president, emphasized the role to be fulfilled by private capital, he seeing the international fund proposed by De Staercke principally in function of guaranteeing the risk taken by private initiative.   Jousset suggested countering the charge of imperalism by having indigenous citizens on the boards of directors of the developing corporations, these last remaining in foreign hands only as a concession for a set term of years sufficient to justify the investment [125].

UNIAPAC closed this 1959 congress with the following resolution: « Within the international community social peace, the fruit of justice, cannot be attained as long as the greater part of humanity is plunged in misery ... Christian employers consider it their duty to work together with all their influence for the development of the under-equipped nations » [126].   Following this session, a commission on aid to technically underdevelopped countries was appointed, chaired by A. H. M. Albreghts.   It first met in September 1959 and has set out to elaborate UNIAPAC's position with a series of seminars and conferences, and to make that position felt through exterior influence amidst other employer and public groupings [127].   Also, it is seeking to arouse a grass roots understanding and support for aid to the « have-nots ».   Articles and editorials on the matter increasingly appear in their publications [128]; local groups

---

[124] « La Paix sociale sur le plan national et international », *La Paix sociale, op. cit.*, pp. 122-123.

[125] *Ibid.*, p. 124.

[126] « Resolutions », *ibid.*, p. 154.

[127] The writer participated in the commission's first meeting, September 23-24, 1959, Brussels. The writer also attended a session on the issue at Angers, France, conducted by the local section of C.F.P.C., in conjunction with the annual Semaine sociale, July 1959.

[128] Cf. for example, P. Lebret, « L'Intelligence et la Charité des Chré-

grapple with the issue; the study material of Switzerland's
V.C.U. during 1959-60 was on this subject.

And on the occasion of the meeting of its governing
council in Rome, October 1959, UNIAPAC issued a press
communiqué urging the creation of a « Fonds Mondial » to
provide financial resources to the underdeveloped nations.
This fund would be managed within the framework of the
United Nations, on a basis of paritary voice among the
assisting and the assisted countries. Further, « UNIAPAC
is persuaded that the equipping of the new nations constitutes the most immediate and most important problem
of our epoch. It is determined to cooperate with all inter-
governmental organizations which take initiatives in this
matter, and notably with F.A.O. (the Food and Agriculture
Organization), which this year organizes the world year
against hunger » [129].

7. The Role of the Entrepreneur and Enterprise.

The optimistic doctrine of indefinite linear progress of
the human race has been heavily discredited since the two
World Wars. The present generation lives the anomaly
that, in a period of dramatic political, technical and economic change, the former naive acceptance of any change
as automatically good has been moderated by many disillu-
sions, and even skepticism.

Proprietors as a class are generally identified as the
conservatives of society, tending ever toward retaining the
status quo, toward maintaining — their attackers allege —
the authority and security their property gives them.
Whether it be justified or not, employers and managers
often share this label.

UNIAPAC and affiliates strive against this mental construct of conservativism, be it fictional or factual. Particularly since World War II these Catholic employers' as-

tiens contre la faim du monde », *Professions*, no. 433, février 1959, p. 16;
André Piettre, « Suicide ou Survie de l'Occident? » *ibid.*, no. 426, juin
1958, pp. 4-5; Philippe Laurent, S. J., « Comment aider les pays sous-équipés? », *Bulletin social des Industriels*, no. 254, février 1959, pp. 70-79.

[129] « Projet de communiqué de presse », Conseil central des Délégués, Rome 9-10 octobre 1959.

sociations have to a marked degree made progress and dynamic change into a high value and quasi doctrine. This ingredient in the UNIAPAC concept of the role of the entrepreneur and enterprise must be signalized without lengthy analysis.

Problably UCID of Italy is the national association most vocal in this sphere, and their general secretary, Vittorio Vaccari, is its most eloquent spokesman [130]. His many addresses and editorials abound in exhortations for breaking with the past, favoring imaginative re-thinking of the role of the entrepreneur and enterprise in today's context, with anticipation of the future, and taking the risks required for creative renovation. Research, automation and new techniques must be undertaken in a spirit of pioneering. Vaccari pleads for an openness on the part of employers and managers, that they grasp their vocation as overflowing the boundaries of their own enterprise and industry and nation. Vaccari and UCID, together with other affiliates, notably those of France, Belgium and Switzerland, stress the necessity of management development and strongly support the managerial training centers which have arisen in Europe after the Second War. They want an expanding economy, although this might mean state stimulus to investment and capital formation.

In setting forth « The Function of the Employer », UNIAPAC states:

> To answer effectively the basic needs of men who want a higher standard of living, there must be men who concern themselves with these needs, those of today as well as those of the future.
>
> There must be men who take on the worry of a constant progress, by creating new goods, or by maintaining production of improved quality and at lower prices.

---

[130] Among other addresses and articles by Vaccari are: *Una dirigenza cristiana per un progresso sicuro, passim; UCID Dieci anni, passim,* especially pp. 4, 7-8; « La produttività del moderno atto direttivo », *Operare,* xiv, 3, maggio-giugno 1958. pp. 29-34; « Dirigenza economica e responsabilità politiche », *ibid.,* no. 4, luglio-agosto 1958, pp. 29-32; « Una filosofia per la nuova dirigenza », *ibid.,* xiii, 5, settembre-ottobre 1957, pp. 28-32; also by the director of UCID's study center, Anacleto Benedetti, « Autorità e libertà nell'esercizio dell'atto direttico », *ibid.,* xiv, 6, novembre-dicembre, pp. 29-32.

There must be men who abandon routine, who dominate and orient progress, who by their imagination, intelligence and perseverance bring about the upbuilding of the world [131].

The UNIAPAC movement is especially *avant-garde*, as has been seen, in experimenting with new forms of economic and social institutions. Emile Decré, president of C.F.P.C., in the closing report of the 1959 UNIAPAC congress, sums up this overall concept [132]. In his view the employer is invited to surpass himself (à un dépassement), in that his personal vocation constantly draws him into taking on further responsibilities. His performance will improve to the extent that he possesses knowledge and, more simply, the appetite to know. Further yet, an inventive spirit, and above all imagination, head up the qualities which the employer must possess, for imagination nourishes progress. For Decré imagination remains first of all a moral disposition, expressing the demand to improve our activity and our life. The UNIAPAC leader notes that Léon Harmel needed a great imagination to discover that the welfare of the worker must come about through the worker himself, that it was up to the worker, and not the employer, to take on new responsibilities. « Today again », Decré asserts, « we must discover that the atmosphere of the firm reposes upon the knowledge and respect of men and of the institutions they have created for themselves. But we have to advance beyond this ... *Conscious of these new frontiers ... we* (Catholic) *employers must take on collective responsibilities both at the national and international planes* » [133].

Decré goes on to show that the UNIAPAC movement, through the solidarity it begets among employers, sustains the courage needed by individuals to advance the kingdom of God. The movement makes possible the substitution of a defensive mentality by a mentality of conquest: an intellectual conquest over mental routine, a social conquest to overpass class egoism: « It is in this sense that our movement is dynamic, animated by a forward force which pulls along a milieu » [134].

---

[131] « The Aims of UNIAPAC », p. 4.

[132] E. Decré, « UNIAPAC et la Paix sociale », *La Paix sociale*, *op. cit.*, pp. 144-145.

[133] *Ibid.*, p. 145. Emphasis is in original.

[134] *Ibid.*, p. 146.

UNIAPAC develops then an entrepreneur's ethos [135]: the leader who takes on responsibilities and organizes initiatives; who breaks with the past and looks to the future; who, being familiar with the exact and social sciences, creates new technics and institutions; who serves man, society and civilization. The peculiar feature, of course, of the UNIAPAC image of the employer and manager is that his intentions and acts are directed by the finality of the enterprise. The enterprise is an entity which is above the employer; he must engage his person and his goods, and, ultimately of greater gravity, the goods of others, in a risk-filled activity, developing this activity according to the exigencies of the common good [136]. And to UNIAPAC, in keeping with the teaching of Pius XII, the final goal of the enterprise and economy is « to place at the disposal of all humans those material conditions necessary for man's cultural and spiritual life » [137].

It is small wonder that UNIAPAC concludes that, « The profession of an enterprise manager is arduous, even repellent ... To accomplish these tasks and face those employer responsibilities, it is undeniable that the employer must have an adequate formation » [138].

It is this image of himself and this formation that the UNIAPAC member seeks to attain, and that the movement seeks to impart.

---

[135] Cf. Joseph Höffner, *Das Ethos des Unternehmers, passim.*
[136] « The Aims of UNIAPAC », p. 6.
[137] « UNIAPAC, International Union of Catholic Employers' Associations », p. 10. The reference to Pius XII is from radio message of June 1, 1941, A.A.S., XXXIII, 199. Cf. « Résolutions du Congrès-UNIAPAC », (Montréal 1957), *Bulletin social des Industriels*, no. 241, novembre 1957, p. 362: « Les membres de l'UNIAPAC déplorent que trop souvent, l'économie contemporaine et l'entreprise moderne soient detournées de leur fin qui est de mettre à la disposition de tous, les conditions matérielles de la vie culturelle et spirituelle. En consequence, ils considèrent comme un impérieux devoir de prouver, dans la pratique, qu'il existe une conception chrétienne de l'entreprise ».
[138] « The Aims of UNIAPAC », pp. 10-11.

CHAPTER VI

PRESENCE, INFLUENCE AND FORMATION

The last chapter gave a summary of the doctrinal positions of the Catholic employers' movement. It was seen that UNIAPAC and affiliates study and elaborate Catholic social teaching, striving towards its integral interpretation in socio-economic life, applying it to concrete conditions in their respective enterprises and industries, local and national economies, and concerned as well with implications for the international community and overall society. Something must now be said of the means by which UNIAPAC members communicate these ideas, ideals and projects to the entrepreneurial and economic world.

This is accomplished through their contact with and influence upon other employers and social leaders, influence exercised by UNIAPAC adherents singly as individual members or collectively as groups, and directed toward other employers and leaders as individual persons, or as grouped in their economic, political, labor or other social bodies.

It is inevitable that much of this ground has already been covered. At the start the writer chose not to segregate treatment of history, policies and doctrine in an abstract piecemeal manner, devoid of concrete exemplification. Consequently, there has already been considerable demonstration of the manner in which UNIAPAC exercises its influence: the role of an individual like Bakaert in Belgium — and now throughout Europe — as head of top secular organizations, the role of Harmel on enterprise organization and worker participation, and of Steenberge and Albreghts in industrial organization in Holland. Reference has also been made to non-official and personal links with political bodies, and quasi official relations with labor unions. It was seen that associations sometimes promote programs affecting national policy, as UCID's sponsorship of top-level sessions on the European Common Market, which included participants of ministerial rank, and having influence upon social legislation, as B.K.U. relative to pensions and C.F.P.C. on profit-sharing.

It is useless merely to repeat these citations, already seen in the context of the doctrinal and social positions involved, and it is equally vain to catalogue further examples indefinitely[1]. Rather these efforts at presence and influence will be reduced to two classifications: influence exercised by by UNIAPAC members as individual men, and influence exerted by UNIAPAC and its national affiliates as collectivities, as organised bodies. Each of these will be subdivided into two types, and appropriate examples will be given.

First, individual members of UNIAPAC affiliates exercise influence upon individuals who are not adherents. They accomplish this not only by conversation with or persuasion of other employers, but principally by the way they conduct their own enterprises and by the initiatives they undertake. The first example of Léon Harmel, already seen at length, is eminently applicable here, especially before the persons he influenced gathered into associations. His concept of the worker as being more than a production cost, as a person who should be given at least consultative voice, and his experimentation to devise techniques which would assure that voice, leading to the factory council — all these were pioneering initiatives which deeply influenced other entrepreneurs. Pope Leo XIII recognized and encouraged these new orientations; he asserted that Harmels must be multiplied.

Comparable efforts today are in the fields of profit-sharing and property acquisition by workers. Here, as was seen, the example of a given enterprise is not only passed on by haphazard contact among employers, but through detailed citation by the movement itself which explains a

---

[1] Much of the material covered in this chapter has already been treated under some other aspect. Because of this, previous documentation will not be repeated in footnotes. This data is mostly from interviews already cited and from UNIAPAC archives, especially « Fiches et Personnalités », in the dossiers of the respective national associations. New citations will be made in footnotes only when fresh facts are brought into the text.

plan elaborated and proven out by one of its members, and
which draws inspiration from non-members also.

Emile Romanet, a C.F.P.C. leader, had, as an individual,
inestimable influence in developing family allocations. He
recounts this experience in the French association's organ,
Professions[2]. Back in 1916, as a young manager in a metal
fabrication plant of Grenoble, he noted that single workers,
or those having only one child, fared sufficiently well: « But
starting from two children, fathers of families, who had no
farming relatives to help with food, knew real poverty and
need ». Under this aspect Romanet made a study of the
plant's personnel and reported his findings to his superiors.
Moved by this, the firm began on November 1, 1916 to increase the monthly wage of fathers of children at the rate
of twelve hundred francs (about two dollars eighty cents
in American money) for each child under thirteen years of
age. Within a few months several neighboring plants followed suit, and by 1918 the industrial syndicate of metallurgical
firms set up a central fund to make the allocations uniform
to prevent the selective hiring of single workers by a given
enterprise. Romanet travelled widely in other parts of
France, and to Geneva at request of the International Labor
Office, publicizing and explaining family subsidy plans.
They became obligatory in France in 1932, and, as was seen
above, are still staunchly and proudly defended by C.F.P.C.

It is easy to record Romanet's initiative because it gained international reknown. On the other hand, it is impossible to discern the number of occasions that a similar influence has been exerted in some other field on less impressive scale. UNIAPAC affiliates move their members as
as individuals to show similar imagination and courage in
the whole broad effort toward a just social order, embracing collective bargaining, labor unions, enterprise committees, human relations, delegation of authority, « intéressement », industrial organization and the rest.

A second type of influence is that of the individual
UNIAPAC leader upon existing economic, social and polit-

---

[2] Emile Romanet, « 36 Ans après: Emile Romanet, le Père des allocations familiales nous parle », *Professions*, no. 311, 24 janvier 1953,
pp. 1-3. The subsidy in francs in 1916 was of course less; Romanet
calculates its equivalent in 1953 currency value at 1200 francs per child
per month.

ical institutions. It would be more proper to term this « presence », because in this concept the movement does not *send* a member into an organization in order that the movement can itself wield influence. Rather the movement wants its members to be *present* in other organizations so that they — the individual men — can express their own ideas and ideals *as Christian* employers and managers. They are in no way to speak as mandated emissaries of UNIAPAC. The movement gives them no mandate whatsoever. To the extent that members do exercise influence in the day to day and month by month activity of an organization, they do so only as entrepreneurial leaders who possess certain convictions as Christian men.

An impressive number of UNIAPAC members, many of them well formed and dedicated leaders, occupy important positions in economic and political organizations at local, national and international levels. A few examples will suffice.

Léon Bekaert, already cited, is president since 1952 of the Fédération des Industries Belges (FIB), the over-all industrial association of his land, and is president, too, of the Union des Industries de la Communauté Européenne, formed in 1958 by the economic organizations of the six Common Market countries. Other UNIAPAC leaders occupy positions all the way along the ladder of economic institutions. L. F. H. Regout, for instance, a past president of A.K.W.V., served until 1958 as president of the coal mines' council in Holland's P.B.O.[3]. Franz Greiss, B.K.U. president, also heads up the German association for the preservation of a market economy. Willy Büchi, a founder of the Swiss V.C.U., has been secretary general of the national association of textile manufacturers. France's C.F.P.C. counts several of its leaders as officers of national economic associations: its president, Emile Decré, is vice-president of the national federation of department stores; Yves Comar, vice-president of the French pharmaceutical industry; J. Ca-

---

[3] This and other facts on the Dutch movement are mostly from a letter to the writer from H. G. M. Linnebank, A.K.W.V.-K.V.W. secretary, December 8, 1959; and from *De Katholieke Werkgever*, no. 26, 19 septembem 1959, *passim*, which reports on the past year's activities and the coming year's plans; also, from interviews already cited. To these must be added an interview with the national vice-president of the Catholic trade unions of Holland, J. Alders, Utrecht, April 1, 1959.

lan, delegate general of textile industries; and Robert Vas-
seur, vice-president of the printeries' association. Robert
Lemaignen is a minister of the European Economic Community. And at the regional level, a single study group
of a dozen men in Lille's C.F.P.C. count among themselves
the following leaders of employers' associations: president
of the clothing manufacturers of France; regional presidents
of textile manufacturers and of building contractors; regional vice-presidents of the metal fabricators and chemical
industries; and national vice-president of France's building
contractors.

UNIAPAC leaders are also present in political groupings.
Holland's affiliates has supplied several national governmental officers; four A.K.W.V. presidents and secretaries
have occupied ministerial posts. And its first secretary general, L. G. Kortenhorst, who also handled UNIAPAC secretarial needs during its first fifteen years of existence, has
been president of the Dutch parliament (States General)
since 1947. Three Belgium FEPAC leaders have served as
prime minister; one of them, Georges Theunis, was president of UNIAPAC, 1933-36. And while he was ambassador
to the United States in the early 1940's, Theunis' initiative
sparked the Canadian association. Several of B.K.U.'s leaders are members of Germany's Bundestag. One of these,
Friedrich Burgbacher, serves on important governmental
and Christian Democratic commissions, being, for instance,
president of the national energy board, and representing
his land in the parliament of Europe and on North Atlantic
Treaty Organization (NATO) commissions. Active participation by Italian cabinet ministers and heads of « enti statali » in UCID's program has already been noted. Several
UCID leaders have close associations with national political
leaders through friendship and common interests.

This relationship also reaches down the ladder to lower
echelons, to Jacques De Staercke, for instance, FEPAC administrative delegate (head of executive staff), who was until
1958 president of the Christian Social Party's organization
for the Brussels region. It happens, too, that Roger De
Staercke, father of the FEPAC leader, is himself fulltime
administrative delegate of Belgium's FIB, the national industrialist's organization. It was noted earlier that Rik Ver-

meire was national secretary of the Christian Social Party
until his resignation in 1958 to become UNIAPAC's secretary general. Latin American leaders also occupy important
positions in the public life of their nations. It was seen
that Juan Cavo has been very active in the Junior Chamber
of Commence, serving as president of the Buenos Aires chapter in 1957. Another Argentine leader, Francisco Mura de
Nadal, has served as president of his nation's Confedera-
ción de Comercio, and Chile's Sergio Ossa Pretot, UNIAPAC
vice-president, has been president of Fundación Mi Casa and
is a leader of the Christian Democratic Party.

Further examples of these connections, many of them
very close and in high places, could be multiplied. While
it is difficult to appraise their true value, they testify to
the *presence* of UNIAPAC leaders as individuals in economic
and political circles. It must be re-emphasized that in this
type of influence, the individual in no way represents the
UNIAPAC movement. He is an employer-manager carrying
out his personal obligation as a citizen and colleague, and
doing so as a Christian with convictions.

Besides these two types of influence by UNIAPAC members as individuals, the movement makes itself felt by collective action as an organized body. A first way in which
this group influence is exercised is by education and communication directed to the public, aiming at reaching non-
members. This is done through formal courses and study
sessions, and by way of publications, declarations and mass
media.

Many of the affiliates offer annual or seasonal educational programs. That of UCID, directed at managers, has
already been mentioned. In the centers of Milan, Turin and
Genoa, one hundred fifty managers, aged thirty-five to fifty
years, meet twice a week for nine consecutive weeks for
a two hour lecture and discussion given by a well-known
authority. Tuition is usually about thirty thousand lire
(about forty-nine American dollars), and a particular theme
is developed each season, e. g., in 1958, « Problemi della
Comunità Economica Europea ». Some UCID regional
groups offer other night schools for middle and lower staff,
down to the foreman's rank. Milan and Turin draw to these
eight to ten week courses from eighty to a hundred and fifty

participants, who are divided into classes of twenty according to interests.

France's C.F.P.C. has conducted a well-organized night school, « Ecole du Chef d'Entreprise », for fifteen years [4]. The session runs thirty-two class hours, extending over five months; average annual attendance is about two hundred and fifty participants, who are selectively accepted only if they have already exercised some managerial direction over others. Over eighty per cent of these students are not members of C.F.P.C. Besides regular classes the school's directors encourage formation of « équipes » of eight to ten persons who meet weekly in their own homes to discuss the current material of the course. Seventeen such smaller teams were active in 1959. The school also has a correspondence section; these students come to Paris for a week's session toward the end of the school year.

Other UNIAPAC affiliates conduct multifold educational programs. Spain's A.S.P. has created in Valencia a management training center. Here and in other regionals periodic specialized courses lasting a week or so are offered, e. g., for social assistants (on pensions, social security, hospitalization, etc.), for managers on enterprise committees and collective agreements, and, notably, for priests on social doctrine. Many varieties of conferences and study days and seminars have already been referred to above. Periodicals and publications, often cited, also reach non-members to extend this educative actions.

Some educational influences are much more informal and of a private nature, directed to very specialized groups. Thus, the writer found through chance conversation with Giorgio Lausi, vice-director general of IBM ITALIA, that Anacleto Benedetti, director of UCID's study center, had given a series of lectures to fifteen of his company's managers gathered together in a Milan hotel from all parts of Italy for three days [5]. The subject was decision making in management practice. Lausi, who attended the lectures, is not a member of UCID. When met by the writer he was

---

[4] « Ecole du Chef d'Entreprise », 1959-60, 16e Session Annuelle, *passim;* and interview with Micheline Jannor, secretary general of the school, July 2, 1959, Paris.

[5] Interview with Giorgio Lausi, vice-director general of IBM ITALIA, May 8, 1959, Venice. This firm has 1500 factory workers and 500 employees in sales and service.

participating in UCID's national congress. He is the type of executive whom UCID is reaching outside its own membership.

From many citations it was seen that UNIAPAC affiliates now and again employ public declarations to clarify issues, to counter opposition, to set forth their own position, and to influence *ad extra*. Communiqués to the press are also made, and radio and television programs are utilized, although use of these mass media seem remarkably restricted. Very probably this is due to the fact that UNIAPAC and affiliates do not address themselves to the general public. They direct their energies toward economic and social leaders and bodies, particularly those involved in policy formation.

A second type of collective influence is that which results from collaboration by UNIAPAC and affiliates with other organizations. Such collaboration has already been noted, e. g., by C.F.P.C. with other employer groups in making representations to the government and public declarations on profit-sharing and acquisition of property.

UCID sponsors seminars and courses conjointly with other economic organizations. The Milan, Turin and Genoa groups collaborated with the secular Unione Industriale, Camera di Commercio and Unione Agricoltori in 1959 for a series of twelve meetings to work out common approaches toward the Common Market [6]. The Dutch movement maintains permanent relations with other employers' associations through fifteen « contactcommissie », each having two or more Catholic appointees. Each contact commission treats a special subject, e. g., energy, European integration, cartels, long-term wage policy, water utilization, etc. FEPAC in 1958 set up a contact commission with the Jeunesse Ouvrière Chrétienne (JOC) on reception and acclimatization of young workers entering the factory, and joined other groups to form the Fédération Catholique du Logement [7].

Some note has been taken of relations with labor and political movements. Besides influence through individuals, UNIAPAC affiliates cooperate with worker and party leaders

---

[6] « C.E.E. », Secondo Ciclo di Riunioni 1959, UCID Torino, Genova, Milano, *passim*.

[7] « Rapport Annuel, 1958 », FEPAC, mai 1959, pp. 35 and 18 respectively.

by joint study commissions in which they strive to arrive
at common understanding and policy on a particular issue.
Thus, V.C.U. has been sitting with labor leaders in a study
commission of the Swiss Christian Conservative Party to
formulate work contracts which eliminate both *laissez-faire*
liberal and socialist tendencies. Other Swiss commissions
have met on family subsidies and cartels. B.K.U.'s rented
headquarters is located in the building of the German Catholic workers' movement; as a matter of course employer
and labor leaders discuss many issues and participate in
each other's conferences to constitute an almost continous
contact commission. Officials of Belgian and Dutch labor
unions volunteered readily to the writer that these many
interchanges have forged bonds of mutual respect and even
of friendship between themselves and employer leaders.

Sometimes UNIAPAC affiliates are asked by governmental bodies to perform some official role. In September 1959
members of the Uruguayan association, A.P.D.C.E., were requested by the governmental of Uruguay to initiate a study
for the development of a common market among Latin American countries [8]. André Aumonier as secretary general of
C.F.P.C. occupies a post on France's economic and social
council. And again, the Dutch movement names representatives to numerous official bodies, including twelve commissions and five sub-commissions of P.B.O. The general
president of the A.K.W.V.-K.V.W. executive committee, F. J.
F. M. van Thiel, is a member of P.B.O.'s national policy
forming and regulatory body, « Social-Economische Raad »,
and the movement's secretary general is usually a deputy
member, as is Albreghts. Van Thiel is, incidentally, also a
prominent member of the Dutch parliament.

UNIAPAC in the past two or three years has intensified
its participation as an organization in international affairs,
for instance, through consultative status in FAO and through
cooperation with the Council of Europe in the enunciation
of a European Social Charter. A memorandum of March
1959 criticized the preliminary draft of this charter as tending to codify human rights as though these merely arose
from work contracts [9]. Further, the charter goes from in-

---

[8] Letter of Vermeire to the writer, February 16, 1960, p. 1.
[9] « Project for a Preamble to the European Social Charter », UNIAPAC,
March 1959, *passim.*

dividualism on one hand to state intervention on the other,
ignoring personalism and the role of free non-governmental
associations in an organic society. The UNIAPAC criticism
continues:

> The family tends to be considered (by the present draft
> of the charter) as a social risk against which one has to
> be provided for, in the same way as against illness or old
> age ...
> Results from a policy of progress no longer depend today
> solely upon an economic and social state policy, and tomorrow
> upon supra-national power, which will certainly retain all its
> importance, but also and at the same time, upon responsibi-
> lities and duties freely assumed by persons and industrial or-
> ganizations.
> Public authorities should respect and favor society's or-
> ganic structure and encourage all forms of professional or-
> ganization ...
> The *projet* (of the charter), having left aside the rights
> and duties, liberties and responsibilities of man toward the
> enterprise, industry and nation, leads directly to interven-
> tionism. The actual wording appears to suggest that social
> promotion (initiative and progress) should be the work of
> the state [10].

UNIAPAC then offers its own draft of a preamble to the
European Social Charter, incorporating the elements which
it found absent and based on, « The moral and spiritual
values proper to European civilization (which) constitute a
common inheritance of all the nations of Europe » [11].

In summary, then, these are the means through which
the Catholic employers' movement exercises influence: by
individual members acting upon other individuals, by the
presence of single leaders as socially formed Christians in
other organizations, by organizational initiatives addressed
to individuals, and by collective collaboration with other
bodies of economic, social or political character.

The over-all effectiveness of UNIAPAC affiliates is very
difficult to evaluate. Well aware of the possible temerity
of such a judgement, the writer nevertheless classifies the
influence of the national associations as follows: those of
Belgium and Holland exercise a weighty influence in the
socio-economic life of their nations; that exerted by the af-

---

[10] *Ibid.*, pp. 3-4.
[11] *Ibid.*, p. 5.

12

filiates of France, Italy, Canada (Province of Quebec) and
Spain, is less, but is still considerable and widely felt; the
influence of the German, Swiss, Portuguese, Uruguayan,
Chilean and Argentine groups is moderate and growing; in
the other nations influence is as yet small to nearly nil.
UNIAPAC as an international movement is placed in the
third category, moderate but growing, with stress on the
rapidity and solidity of this growth.

Frequently, throughout this study reference has been
made to the importance attached to formation of leaders
by the movement. This formation is educational, apostolic
and spiritual.

The manifold courses and seminars, study days and congresses all contribute to the acquisition by UNIAPAC members of knowledge of the social doctrine of the Church. So
do the publications and study outlines for local meetings.
The imparting of Catholic social teaching is the first purpose of the movement and, without reviewing again all the
means it utilizes, after participation in numerous meetings
and conversations with many members, the writer can pass
judgment that as an educational agency UNIAPAC attains
good results. As a group the men grasp the principles firmly,
apply them capably and are often remarkably conversant
with details and relations, while retaining an integrated, synthetic vision of the whole body of Catholic doctrine.

Apostolic formation is attained to some extent by all
affiliates through their general programs, officers' meetings
and special commissions. But it is best developed in the
small groups of France and Belgium, which meet monthly
or fortnightly in their homes or offices. Training week-ends,
semi-retreat in character, for C.F.P.C.'s « animateurs » have
already been reported. FEPAC began a similar system two
years ago.

The writer attended one such formational week-end conducted by the regional committee of Brussels for its own
members [12]. Thirteen lay leaders, their chaplain, Father Dubois, and Jean Vanderstraeten, national secretary, spent Fri-
day afternoon through Sunday afternoon in a secluded pension near Louvain. Among these were the general managers

---

[12] « Week-end d'études du Comité de la Régionale de Bruxelles de
l'APIC », 4, 5 et 6 septembre 1959, Héverlé-Louvain, *passim*.

of a cement factory employing a thousand men and of a plant which fabricates airplane parts with eight hundred fifty workers; another was the owner-operator of a food processing firm of three hundred employees, a director of a coal mining chain, the head of a technical bureau of a hundred fifty employees of whom some thirty are engineers, and the management counsellor of the Société Générale de Belgique, which controls a hundred fifty enterprises covering twenty per cent of Belgium's industrial production. The development and supervision of managers is the regular responsibility of the last-named, Emmanuel Vaes. He led the first discussion on, « How to work as a team ». Other discussions, all led by the managers themselves, were on the objectives of the movement, obstacles to formation and education and how to overcome them, means of realizing « our objective of exterior influence », the over-all policy of the regional section, and arrival at methods, personnel and contacts to realize that policy. The chaplain led a spiritual discussion; Mass was offered each morning with a homily. The whole was accompanied by many side conversations.

Part of the purpose was to develop a group solidarity among the regional leaders and to come to know one another personally. The vocation of the men as Christian leaders in their economic milieu was, of course, threaded through the whole weekend. Six or more like sessions are in the FEPAC calendar for the current year. So far none of the other associations have begun similar programs of apostolic formation, though some are considering this intensification of activity.

Spiritual formation is directed principally by the chaplains of the movement. Patterns vary greatly. Normally all local and regional sections have chaplains who attend monthly meetings, give doctrinal instruction, offer Mass for the group — sometimes in the evenings as part of the regular sessions —, preach sermons, e. g., six or seven annually in Brussels on particular feasts, conduct or arrange retreats and days of recollection specialized to managers' needs, and give spiritual direction. The Paris section has a full-time chaplain, Father Boyer. The Milan group sponsors a seasonal course in theology for its members. The fifteen regional chaplains of the Belgian Walloon associations, APIC,

are called together for a day long session by the national
chaplain about four times a year to assist one another and
coordinate their initiatives.

The annual public congress of FEPAC in 1959 was on
the manager's spirituality and apostolate in the industrial
world. The public conclusions state in part:

> The multiple problems which Christian managers must
> face in their professional life confront them regularly with
> an apparent antinomy between demands of workaday efficiency
> and demands of an authentic Christian life.
> The basic failure of partial solutions of this antinomy
> force managers to return to the center, to the point from
> which all avenues go forth ... For the Christian this can be
> nothing but Christ: the Son of God ... the Christ Redeemer,
> Head of the Mystical Body, Center of the world and of history,
> in whom alone all things find harmony and equilibrium in the
> fulfillment of their finality ...
> Industrial managers will realize this unity of integrating
> their professional life with their spiritual life ... by a perma-
> nent « prise de conscience » of the Will of God toward their
> professional life.
> While there exists but one sanctity in the Church to which
> all Christians are called, there do exist spiritualities: different
> routes for reaching that holiness. There exists also a spiri-
> tuality of the employer and manager [13].

The conclusions go on to show how this spirituality is
enlightened and nourished by temporal structures and terrestrial realities, how it is related to the primacy of human
and communitarian values, the finality of economic life and
the coming of the Kingdom of God: « An industrial life
oriented toward the coming of God's kingdom requires that
executives and managers bring about such an organization
of the economy that man is given more than a theoretic
freedom to welcome the message (of Christ) ... and that
Christian managers become primarily His witnesses » [14].

---

[13] « Conclusions », *Dirigeants Chrétiens et Progression Humaine, op.
cit.,* p. 178. In the opening address, p. 129, Léon Bekaert says: « For
many years ... Christian managers of our country have willed by their
action and influence to fill a primary role in our social evolution.
However, to the degree that this effort developed there arose in us a
consciousness of a divorce between an authentic Christian life and the
current economic and social life: the immense difficulty of achieving a
Christian committment integrated with daily action burst upon our eves ».
Cf. also, Georges Dubois, S.J., « Dirigeants et Cadres: Leur Mission Chrétienne », *ibid.,* pp. 145-154.

[14] « Conclusions », *ibid.,* p. 180.

CHAPTER VII

EVALUATION AND CONCLUSION

The UNION INTERNATIONAL DES ASSOCIATIONS PATRONALES CATHOLIQUES (UNIAPAC, International Union of Catholic Employers Associations) has been set forth in its history, structure, membership, method of operation, relation to the Church and other bodies, purposes and policies, doctrine and influence. How is this young burgeoning movement to be evaluated? What, in the end, are its notable attributes, its nature, its prospects?

One: UNIAPAC is a form of temporal action by lay leaders in the over-all Catholic social movement. Parallel to, and often in collaboration with, worker, farmer, professional, political, family and other associations of Christian inspiration, UNIAPAC is the entrepreneurial-managerial manifestation of Christian Democracy, understanding this as: that society-wide movement of modern Christianity of, by and through laymen, who are engaged on their own responsibility in the conception, construction and operation of a just and viable political, economic and social order in the light of natural law principles and Christian ideals, and who conclude from these principles and from practical experience that in the modern world democracy is normally best, that government in the firm, social grouping, local community, state and on the international front should be of, for and by the people. In no way then is this broadest concept of Christian Democracy to be identified with particular political parties, which are but one expression of one phase — the political — of the whole social movement. UNIAPAC has no formal or official bonds with these other manifestations; through mutual interests and work on common goals it does collaborate informally with worker, farmer, political and other groups and establishes with them bonds of friendship among members and mutual interdependence.

Two: While based on Catholic social doctrine and initiated by Christian leaders, UNIAPAC is not separatist or ghetto-minded. Quite the opposite, the movement aims at communication and contact with other employer and socio-economic groups. Its leaders seek to know the mind and theories of those outside its own circle, and to transmit as well their own ideas and ideals. They frequent management centers, associations and schools; they study and discuss the ideas of economists and social theorists like Keynes, Galbraith, Drucker, Schumpeter, Briefs, Sauvy, Beveridge and others. Through these interchanges UNIAPAC leaders gladly discover fresh insights, which as true and sound they readily accept into their own synthesis and program.

Three: UNIAPAC is an educative and inspirational movement; it does not exist to defend or promote the economic goals of its members. This necessary role in the ensemble is left to the general secular economic associations, in which the movement encourages its members to participate with devotion and responsibility. UNIAPAC leaders seek by their presence and example to influence the thinking and policy of their colleagues, taken singly or collectively.

Four: Basically UNIAPAC is not defensive in its attitude. Composed of employers and managers it does not see workers and labor unions as antagonists, but as partners and collaborators. The movement does, however, feel it necessary to restrict trends toward increased state action in the economic field, particularly the trend toward collectivization of means of production. It fears state absorption of economic life not only through the swallowing up of property, but also by the state taking over authority and control. UNIAPAC seeks to evolve intermediate institutions in collaboration with workers' syndicates, in order to maximize the freedom of both labor and management vis-à-vis public authority.

This offensive against total assimilation of the economy by an omnicompetent state is not necessarily motivated by self-interest. The effect of totalitarian control on all the institutions of society is a major concern of the movement, because under such a statism the West's free Judaeo-Christian civilization, with its inestimable human, spiritual and cultural values, is imperiled, and its religious sources are undermined.

Five: While composed of men who by profession are in business and industrial affairs, UNIAPAC's goals are not ultimately concerned with economic life. Rather it addresses itself to elaborating a whole society, and particularly to the function of the economy in that society, and the role of the entrepreneur in that economy.

So UNIAPAC is not concerned with profits as profits, or with efficiency, or increase of productivity, or technology, or research and market techniques as such; nor with the macro-economics of national product, monetary and fiscal policy, international terms of trade, inflation and full employment — in themselves. All this to UNIAPAC's universal view is only part of the wole — of the whole of society and of life and of man. UNIAPAC's field might be termed « maximo-economics »; the totality of all micro-economics and macro-economics, their interrelation and interplay and synthesis, as creatures of man and of God, toward attaining their ultimate finality: the service rendered by the economic to man on his way toward God.

Probably besides Marxism, UNIAPAC is the only movement which strives to elaborate and to apply an economic « maximocosm »: an all-embracing, integral view of productive means and work within human life and society.

Six: The society which UNIAPAC envisions has those marks which are usual to the modern Catholic social movement:

a) The integral human person is the basis and norm of society. Man is not to be distorted to fit social, economic and political forms; quite the contrary, these must conform to the spiritual, perfectible, expansive nature of man.

b) Man as a person is social; his solidarity with his fellowmen arises from his spiritual-corporal nature, faculties and common needs, which he seeks to satisfy and fulfill by common action with his fellowmen, giving rise to the social institutions.

c) The family is the first and basic institution of society. Economic organization must not warp or distort it; rather the economy must serve the family.

d) Society is not a necessary evil, but a necessary good. Society should be organic, not amorphous; it ought to be composed of many associations, interrelated according to their function and value to man and his fulfillment.

e) The state is not to be equated with society. The two are not co-terminous. The state is a necessary institution, but it is posterior to man and to the family. While promoting the common good of all persons and groups, the state must not absorb functions which anterior, valid and free associations can and ought to perform. Rather the state ought to protect and, when necessary, coordinate these manifold associations for the common good.

Seven: UNIAPAC's proper concern is not society in itself, but the place of the economy in society and the contribution to be made by economic institutions to society conceived in these personalist, organic, Christian terms.

For the movement: « The ultimate goal of today's economy and modern business is to place at the disposal of all humans those material conditions necessary for man's cultural and sipiritual life »[1]. This repudiates the *laissez-faire* Manchester school of economic liberalism. And while this ideology seldom appears today in pure nineteenth century form, UNIAPAC refutes its disguised remnants and recurring tendencies.

While appreciating its stimulus to initiatives and the need to maximize freedom, UNIAPAC does not believe that individual striving for the self-interest of each will automatically redound to the greatest good of all. Nor does the movement believe in an absolute sovereignty of private property. While asserting private ownership as opposed to state ownership, the movement insists on the social use of property. The goods of this world are created by God for the needs of all human persons. The determination of modalities of ownership and use are adaptable to concrete circumstances of a given people at a given point of history. Goods do not necessarily fulfill their social use through the free market alone, especially if this is a free market of individuals. Monopoly accumulation for the strong and mass misery for the weak are more likely to result, so UNIAPAC

---

[1] « UNIAPAC, International Union of Catholic Employers Associations », p. 10.

defends the right of the individual and the weak to organize,
e. g., workers' unions, cooperatives, credit unions — as well
as the right of employers to organize. In fact, this is a duty
for both. Whether goods attain their end, i. e., filling the
needs of human beings, is subject to constant review, and
to living adjustment, with the articulation of new bodies
to balance changes and to meet new realities. Such a view
of the economy is obviously dynamic.

Eight: In the given historical circumstances of today's
industrial civilization UNIAPAC promotes an economy with
the following structural attributes:

a) Productive property is not government-owned; collective state ownership is to be allowed only in those sectors where basic utilities and energy are more safely ad-
ministered by public authority because of monopoly danger
or common good, or in other exceptional cases.

b) Ownership of property is to be spread to a maximum degree, with management having a special responsibility for enabling workers to acquire property, both personal, as housing, and productive, through share-holding.
UNIAPAC admits that the difficulties of spreading property
ownership are manifold, and that this offers no panacea.

c) Further, the economy is validly based on the wage
system, by which a worker is remunerated in money for
labor or services performed.

d) Workers may and should organize into labor unions
in order to defend their economic interests, to present their
jointly and justly formulated demands, to negotiate collective agreements, to safeguard their fulfillment, and to meet
other worker needs in keeping with the personalist, Christian
view of man and society.

e) Workers and employers are partners in the enterprise. Their joint interests are best served by rendering
the firm productive. It is to their combined advantage to
cooperate, and to this end all remnants of class struggle
and mutual recrimination must be overcome. Labor-management and enterprise committees, delegation of authority,
human relations, profit-sharing and other such means must
be utilized for begetting a community-of-work.

f) Labor unions, furthermore, are necessary prior
bases for the industrial organization (organisation professionnelle) of the economy. Workers and employers are part-

ners in a whole branch of industry. Labor and management should organize themselves into councils or boards on an industry-wide basis, so that they can discuss together — outside negotiation meetings — the problems and plans of their industry, and so that when and where necessary both can have a voice in making certain economic decisions in the conduct of the industry branch. Such industry boards must not be agencies of the government, but freely constituted bodies composed of labor and management representatives, who receive from public authority the juridic right to exist and to self-supervision among themselves. The minimum regulation of the industry boards to coordinate their functions with the common good should be exercised through a national council composed of labor and management delegates, and representatives of the public at large.

h) The principal purpose of such an intermediate industrial organization is the maximum utilization of labor and productive means in a free manner, with a maximum voice assured to both partners, with a view to the common good, and with a minimum of governmental intervention.

i) UNIAPAC does not present a blueprint for such an industrial organization. It merely states principles and points to examples, as to Holland's pioneering P.B.O. And the movement does not advise precipitate action, but rather insists on the need of gradual, free and particularized evolution in this direction by each country, in keeping with its particular history, current institutions and cultural values.

Nine: Besides these structural attributes, the economy envisioned by UNIAPAC has these marks:

a) It is the product of entrepreneurs and managers who are imaginative and forward-looking, who are not bound to the status quo.

b) It maximizes use of research, skills and technology, with due safeguards to dangers of « dishumanisation » and the social effects of the rhythm of automation.

c) The economy itself is dynamic, aiming at increased productivity and the fair distribution of goods to enable all men to acquire the material basis necessary for their cultural and spiritual development.

Ten: Until the last two or three years UNIAPAC affiliates have been preoccupied mostly with striving for social order and peace in their respective nations. While fully aware that social peace has not yet been fully attained — and may indeed never be perfectly reached — in their own countries, UNIAPAC members see the necessity of addressing themselves to evolving a world social order. Toward this end the prime and immediate goal must be the economic advance of technically underdeveloped nations. This, they now assert, is the number one problem in the economic world, and must become the number one concern of entrepreneurs, governments and citizens of the free industrialized world.

UNIAPAC currently seeks to arouse and inform its own adherents on this issue, that they may collaborate with colleagues everywhere in working out creative solutions.

Eleven: Besides cooperating on the world problem of industrializing the emerging nations, UNIAPAC believes that nations should draw together in economic collaboration wherever common goals make this feasible, and that this should lead to economic integration as soon as possible, with removal of trade barriers and lowering of migration restrictions. UNIAPAC believes that enlightened management and labor leaders can through these means make a signal contribution to human welfare by softening inherited national antagonisms and opening the way to political accord and federation. This is especially true of Western Europe, where UNIAPAC is until now best organized.

Twelve: UNIAPAC is still very young as a truly international federation. It has in consequence not yet begun to exert any great portion of its potential influence. It is now growing rapidly and solidly. In its present phase these marks characterize it as an organization:

a) The movement is decentralist, according maximum autonomy to national associations and adequate authority to leaders acting for the world federation in the various continents.

b) The movement is extremely adaptable to national and continental differences. It does not impose structures and programs from above, but strives rather to stimulate and inspire local formulas, both in the organization itself and in positions relative to socio-economic policy.

c) While based on Catholic social teaching, the movement insists that it is not a part of the Church and in no way represents her. While UNIAPAC enjoys the approval of Church authorities, it does so only as a group of laymen, moved by certain convictions, formation and inspiration, who want to upbuild a social order and promote social peace according to the principles of natural law and Christian ideals.

d) Participation in the movement is open in most affiliates to all men of good will who will ascribe to these basic principles. And in recent years the movement tends more and more toward openness.

e) For the past decade UNIAPAC orientation and program have been increasingly directed toward non-owning managers, and present emphasis is toward policy-making executives.

Thirteen: The movement has deep respect for ideas and theories which bring understanding to the entrepreneur, enabling him to give interior order to the multifarious concrete actualities with which he deals, and allowing him to establish integral relations between his enterprise and the economy, and among these and the larger realities of man and society and the meaning of life. Reference to economists has already been made. But besides this expected interest in economic theory, to a degree which the present writer has until now failed to stress sufficiently, UNIAPAC shows concern for the broader ideological views and in the intellectuals who propound them. Particularly does the French association reflect this interest. Thus, it is quite ordinary that André Siegfried and Henri Daniel-Rops should address a regular weekly meeting of C.F.P.C. in Paris, or that Jean Guitton should lecture for two hours at the annual national meeting on « La Pensée, l'Action, et la Prière » [2]. The writer was struck with the familiarity manifested by leaders with the ideas and works of Jacques Maritain, Teilhard de Chardin, Romano Guardini, Henri Bergson, J. Messner, Oswald von Nell-Brunning, and others, to say nothing of those of the recent popes in their most lofty expression.

---

[2] Jean Guitton, « La Pensée, l'Action et la Prière », *Documents et Commentaires*, no. 22, juin 1958, pp. 13-38; Henri Daniel-Rops, « Etre présents au monde », *Professions*, no. 316, 4 avril 1953, pp. 1 ff.; André Siegfried (reported by Paul Bureau), « Libre concurrence et relations humaines », *ibid.*, no. 386, 3 mars 1956, pp. 1 ff.

Fourteen: The movement is educational and inspirational in purpose and method. To a certain degree it might also be termed spiritual, insofar as it seeks to elaborate a deepened spirituality for the Christian employer, a spiritual life which breaks out of departmentalized religion which would isolate the entrepreneur's path toward God from the « downtown » workaday world. UNIAPAC lay leaders feel the need of an integrated spirituality, which pulls together their manifold roles and activities, which is itself nourished by the natural human goods which a businessman creates and experiences through his work. Priests and laity together look for the place of this managerial spirituality in the plan of God for his world, a plan in which the director of industry is, willy-nilly, the instrument of Divine Providence, by which man is fed and clothed, housed and cared for. UNIAPAC leaders see in the complex interdependence of the economy — of managers and workers, industrialists and scientists, professionals and politicians — a natural basis for the supernatural truth of the Mystical Body of Christ. And in the growing economic dependence of nation upon nation they see confirmation of the Christian vision of the one human family. From these elements they seek to evolve a spirituality of the modern manager.

They are well aware that many obstacles hinder such advance, that proximity to the material erodes spiritual sensibility, that, in the words of Thorstein Veblen, « Men trained by the mechanical occupation to materialistic, industrial habits of thought are beset with a growing inability to appreciate, or even to apprehend, the meaning of religious appeals that proceed on the old-fashioned grounds of metaphysical validity »[3]. UNIAPAC leaders, as daily artificers of the physical, believe that the metaphysical is no longer « old-fashioned » to the present psychological temper of the managerial world, a change induced in part by the shock treatment of historical and social currents.

Fifteen: So it could be that UNIAPAC's long-term contribution to the free industrial society of the West will be

---

[3] Thorstein Veblen, *The Theory of Business Enterprise*, p. 259. In a footnote of this page, Veblen says further: « The cultural era of Natural Rights, Natural Liberty, and Natural Religion reduced God to the rank of a 'Great Artificer', and modern technology is, in turn, relegating Him to that fringe of minor employments and those outlying industrial regions to which the handicraftsmen have been retired ».

more profound than the social structure and order which
now justly occupy so much of its attention in manifold
meetings, seminars and publications. It could be that
UNIAPAC's long-term contribution will be in the realm of
the mind and of the spirit, as these relate to the economic
and the social.

In the autumn of 1959 an article in the *Harvard Business Review* asked this opening question: « How can one
explain the almost total lack of enthusiasm on the part of
so many United States intellectuals for an economic and
political system under which they have fared so well? » [4]
To the author, Calvin B. Hoover, this lack of support is
perhaps the greatest weakness of American capitalism, when
viewed in the context of the cold war and a period of com-
petitive coexistence with Soviet Russia; it is a weakness
which « renders us vulnerable to continuous expansion of
state control or ultimately even to loss of our system through
parliamentary or revolutionary means ... »

Hoover shows that the rationale of *laissez-faire* capitalism as set forth by Adam Smith was based on an intellectual model which posited that the pursuit of self-interest
by capitalists maximized the wealth of nations and simultaneously minimized the role of the state and hence the
rule of men over men [5]. But this economic system was
never adopted by majority vote; it protected the vested
rights of property owners and depended on the coercive
power of the state for its continuance; so « How could such
a system be defended as serving the public? ... In fact, rather
than viewing capitalism as an economic system operating
in the public interest, the intellectual has come more and
more to think of the interests of the public and the capitalist as fundamentally in conflict ». Using the greatest good
for the greatest number as his norm, the intellectual « tends
to sympathize with any state action which limits the power
or the income of the capitalist, particularly the capitalist
in corporate form ». So it is that the legislator voting for

---

[4] Calvin B. Hoover, « The Intellectuals and Capitalism », *Harvard
Business Review*, vol. 37, 5, September-October 1959, p. 47. This article
was called to the writer's attention by De Staercke of Belgium; he and
several other top UNIAPAC leaders are alumni of the Harvard Business
School.
[5] *Ibid.*, p. 48.

rent control is thought of as voting for the people. Hoover concedes that the market cannot be relied upon by itself to compel corporate management to act in the public interest, and that an expansion of countervailing power and government regulation has become unavoidable[6]. The author notes that, « Efforts to explain the way in which modern capitalism serves the public interest are being made under the slogan of ' People's Capitalism ' », for instance, in Voice of America broadcasts.

The present writer calls attention to the much-quoted talk of Henry Cabot Lodge, United States ambassador to the United Nations, given in the presence of Nikita Khruschev during his 1959 visit to America. Lodge here offers justification of modern capitalism on the grounds of its service to the people in general and rigid control of monopolistic self-interest. He too suggests a new name : « Economic humanism rather than monopoly capitalism perhaps best describes such a system »[7].

The points which the present writer wishes to draw from the *Harvard Business Review* article are the following : ideals and intellectuals still count in today's industrial world; self-interest as the rationale of modern capitalism

---

[6] *Ibid.*, p. 49. Cf. John Kennedy Galbraith, *American Capitalism, passim,* especially pp. 108-153, for a recent formulation of the concept of countervailing power. If the phrase is new the idea and practice is not; cf. Selig Perlman, *A Theory of the Labor Movement, passim;* pp. 155-156 state: « A labor movement must, from its very nature, be an organized campaign against the rights of private property, even where it stops short of embracing a radical program seeking the elimination, gradual or abrupt, ' constitutional ' or violent, of the private entrepreneur. When this campaign takes the political and legislative route, it leads to the denial of the employer's right to absolute control of his productive property ».

[7] « Economic Humanism », *Time,* Atlantic Edition, September 28, 1959, p. 15. Lodge said further: « American business prospers at the same time that the American government, in ways large and small, pervades our lives — that one adult in five gets regular checks from the Government and that federal warehouses give out food to 5,000,000 persons and that 2,000,000 persons live in Government-subsidized housing. We live in a welfare state which seeks to put a floor below which no one sinks, but builds no ceiling to prevent man from rising ». Commentators have remarked on this use by a spokesman of a Republican « businessman's administration » of the term « welfare state » to describe American society, and on the further statement that « the Federal Government, in ways large and small, pervades our lives ». The talk was given before the Economic Club of New York, a group definitely Adam Smith in its origins. These shadings indicate the changed image today's capitalism projects of itself.

is being abandoned in the abstract as it has to a great extent already been abandoned in the concrete; and, most importantly, modern « People's Capitalism » or « Economic Humanism » will be seeking new intellectual bases for the *de facto* reality and as theoretic guides to future development.

The Church and Christian thought as a whole have never fully come to terms with the capitalistically industrialized society. It might be that in its present doubts and dangers modern capitalism will, for the first time since its appearance on the stage of history, give ear to some promptings of the Christian concept of man and society and life's meaning. UNIAPAC employers and managers could become the most logical bearers to their colleagues of the principles needed for a new interpretation of this modern drama. And UNIAPAC theorists might take up where Max Weber and R. H. Tawney left off in their versions of the interplay of capitalism and Christianity.

Max Weber may have found a certain accord between one type of Protestantism and early capitalism in a few predispositions shared by both, as toward individualism, a break with the traditional, and free association. But Weber stresses that the dominant theme of capitalism is this-world rationalization: « Rational industrial organization, ... rational bookkeeping, ... rational capitalistic organization of labor, ... exact calculation, ... rational and stable structures of law and administration, ... For all the above cases it is a question of the specific and peculiar rationalism of Western culture »[8].

As Tawney has shown, this is a rationalization by which capitalism reasons itself into self-subsistent independence, with-drawing itself from judgment by areas of society beyond itself, and either pretending that family and religion, human and cultural values do not exist, or that these must themselves become servants of the economic « new Leviathan ». Tawney denounces that economic efficiency which converts itself into a primary end instead of an instrument. He calls this a lazy caricature of reason, a caricature « to flatter its followers with the smiling illusion of progress

---

[8] Max Weber, translated by Talcott Parsons, *The Protestant Ethic and the Spirit of Capitalism*, pp. 21 and 26.

won from the mastery of the material environment by a race too selfish and superficial to determine the purpose to which its triumphs shall be applied » [9].

To Tawney such a system and such a society are far from the Christian concept. Rather they are in opposition:

> But the quality in modern societies which is most sharply opposed to the teaching ascribed to the Founder of the Christian Faith lies deeper ... It consists in the assumption ... that the attainment of material riches is the supreme object of human endeavor and the final criterion of human success ..., the negation of any system of thought or morals which can, except by a metaphor, be described as Christian. Compromise is as impossible between the Church of Christ and the idolatry of wealth, which is the practical religion of capitalist societies, as it was between the Church and the State idolatry of the Roman Empire [10].

The present writer believes that UNIAPAC can penetrate into modern capitalism a significant bit of that Christian ferment which transformed the old Roman society.

At times today's capitalism manifests certain symptoms comparable to those shown by the hard-pressed Roman Empire, like parroting dead formulas, maximizing pleasure, fear of structural change and slowness to assimilate new power groups. But the differences are also striking. Side by side with the die-hards, there appear today critics of worn-out ideas, initiators of needed institutions, and acceptance of new partners in the community-of-work. Most of all capitalism in this day of trial may be learning that it must live for something outside itself, that it must find

---

[9] R. H. Tawney, *Religion and the Rise of Capitalism*, pp. 282-283. Cf. also, Amintore Fanfani, *Catholicism, Protestantism and Capitalism*, *passim*, and pp. 93-94: « The first problem for the man who intends to act freely in the capitalistic sense is to detach the means that surround him from the concepts and ideas that make of them obstacles to his free action. In the history of European pre-capitalism these concepts are nearly all created or reinforced by religious ideas ... The capitalist, in his first effort to rid himself of obstacles to his action, works indirectly against religion, attacking the system of precepts that has hitherto governed the tendency of economic action. When he realises that it is vain to look to religion for any sanction of his mode of action, he will abandon religion as far as he himself is concerned, holding, with Turgot, that ' men have no need to be metaphysicians to live honestly ... ' » (Memoire sur les prêts d'argent, *Oeuvres*, vol. I, p. 128). Fanfani, leader of the left wing of Italy's Christian Democrat Party, was prime minister 1958-59 and 1960 to the time of publication.

[10] Tawney, *op. cit.*, p. 286.

13

a *raison d'être* beyond itself, and consciously direct its astounding energies to goals in keeping with truly human needs and aspirations.

UNIAPAC exists to bear such truth and to arouse such inspiration in the very heart of the capitalist body. UNIAPAC might help transmit to this new « People's Capitalism » and « Economic Humanism », now in metamorphosis, a new will to live through a new vision of *the why and the how* it must serve man in a society so constituted that the human person can realize himself and find his way to God.

BIBLIOGRAPHY

Primary Sources

1. PAPAL DOCUMENTS

Acta Sanctae Sedis, Typis Polyglottae Officinae, S. C. De Propaganda Fide, Romae.

Leo XIII, Litterae Encyclicae *Humanum Genus*, XVI (1884), 417-433.

— Litterae Encyclicae *Rerum Novarum*, XXIII (1891), 641-670.

Acta Apostolicae Sedis, Commentarium Officiale, Typis Polyglottis Vaticanis.

Pius XI, Litterae Encyclicae *Quadragesimo Anno*, XXIII, (1931), 177-228.

Pius XII, Nuntius Radiophonicus, Quinto Vertente Anno ab Initio Praesente Bello, Orbi Universo Datus, (September 1, 1944), XXXXVI (1944), 249-258.

— Allocutio, Ad Delegatos Sodalitatis, cui nomen « Union Internationale des Associations Patronales Catholiques », ob nonum Conventum internationalem Romae coadunatos, (May 7, 1949), XLI (1949), 283-286.

— Allocutio, Participantibus Conventui internationali Studiorum rerum socialium et Conventui Sodalitatis internationalis socialis christianae, Romae habitis, (June 3, 1950), XLII (1950), 485-488.

— Nuntius Radiophonicus, Christifidelibus Germaniae, ob « Katholikentag » in Urbe Coloniensi coadunatis, (September 2, 1956), XLVIII, 622-627.

— Allocutio, Iis qui interfuerunt Conventui, a Sodalitate Operariorum Catholicorum Italica (A.C.L.I.) indicto ac Romae habito, de argumento « L'Automazione e il mondo del lavoro », (June 7, 1957), XLIX (1957), 621-629.

— Allocutio, Iis qui interfuerunt Conventui alteri catholicorum ex universo orbe, pro Laicorum Apostolatu, Romae habito, (October 5, 1957). XLIX (1957), 922-939.

Discorsi e Radiomessaggi di Sua Santità Pio XII, Tipografia Poliglotta Vaticana.

« Il Concetto Cristiano dell'Impresa », (UCID, 31 gennaio 1952), XIII. 461-466.

« Al VII Congresso Nazionale della Unione Cristiana Imprenditori e Dirigenti », (5 giugno 1955), XVII, 117-123.

« Norme e Indicazioni alla Unione Cristiana Imprenditori Dirigenti », (7 marzo 1957), XIX, 25-31.

L'Osservatore Romano.

John XXIII, Allocuzione alla UCID, XCIX, 25. 31 gennaio 1959, p. 1.

2. UNPUBLISHED SOURCES

UNIAPAC Archives (all typewritten, Brussels).

  Alvarez, R. P. Felix M., M. sp. S., « Breve Historial del Movimiento de Mexico Representado en la Reunión de Responsables », p. 1.

  « Brief History », (UNIAPAC), pp. 4.

  Cavo, Juan, (confidential report), pp. 12.

  « Cuestionario », (UCIDT of Portugal), pp. 6.

  « Curriculum Vitae ».

  « Fiches et Personnalités ».

  « Informe Historia del Movimiento Patronal Católico, Asociación de Patronos y Dirigentes Católicos de Empresa, Abril de 1959 », (Uruguay).

  Pretot, Serigo Ossa, « Version Grabada del Historial del Movimiento Patronal en Chile », pp. 2.

  « Quelques informations sur l'histoire de l'UNIAPAC », pp. 13.

  Vermeire, Rik, address to B.K.U. Tagung, Bad Neuenahr, October 2, 1959, pp. 27.

C.F.P.C. Archives (typewritten, Paris).

  « Origines lontaines du C.F.P.C. », pp. 4.

Secondary Sources

1. BOOKS

Beltrão, Pedro Calderan, S. J., *Vers une politique de bien-être familial*, Librairie Editrice de l'Université Grégorienne, Rome, 1957, pp. 347.

Brouwers, L., S. J., *Le Problème social*, FEPAC, Bruxelles, 1958, pp. 134.

Calvez, J. V., Jacques Perrin, *Eglise et Société économique*, Aubier, Paris, 1959, pp. 578.

Clément, Marcel, *Le Chef d'Entreprise*, Nouvelles Editions Latines, Paris, 1956, pp. 284.

Dieude, Ch., *Les Allocations familiales*, Editions de la Société d'Etudes morales, sociales et juridiques, Louvain, 1929, pp. 259.

Djilas, Milovan, *The New Class*, Thames and Hudson, London, 1957, pp. 214.

Drucker, Peter F., *The New Society*, Harper & Brothers, New York, 1949, pp. 356.

— *The Practice of Management*, Harper & Brothers, New York, 1954, pp. 404.

Ehrmann, Henry W., *La politique du Patronat français*, Armand Colin, Paris, 1959, pp. 416.

Einaudi, Mario, François Goguel, *Christian Democracy in Italy and France*, University of Notre Dame Press, Notre Dame, Indiana, 1952, pp. 229.

L'Entreprise et son destin, Rapport sur les relations industrielles, APIC, Bruxelles, 1949, pp. 137.

The Executive Life, Editors of Fortune, Doubledeay & Co., Garden City, N. Y., 1956, pp. 223.

Fanfani, Amintore, *Catholicism, Protestantism and Capitalism*, Sheed & Ward, New York, 1955, pp. 217.

Fogarty, Michael, P., *Christian Democracy in Western Europe 1820-1953*, University of Notre Dame Press, Notre Dame, Indiana, 1957, pp. 461.

Galbraith, John Kenneth, *American Capitalism*, Hamish Hamilton, London, 1957, pp. 208.

Guitton Georges, S. J., *Léon Harmel*, Vol. I, *Jusqu'à l'Encyclique Rerum Novarum*, II, *Après l'Encyclique Rerum Novarum*, Editions Spes, Paris, 1927, pp. 344 and 437.

« Léon Harmel », *Anthologie du Catholicisme social en France*, Jean Megret, Pierre Badin, editors, Chronique sociale de France, Lyon, n. d., pp. 131-140.

Léon Harmel et l'Initiative ouvrière, Editions Spes, Paris, 1929, pp. 94.

Hagoort, R., *De Christelijk Sociaal Beweging*, Christelijk Nationale Biblioteek, T. Wever, Franeken, 1955, pp. 229.

Jarlot, Georges, S. J., *Le Régime corporatif et les Catholiques sociaux* Flammarion, Paris, 1938, pp. 260.

Lamoot, J., *Monseigneur Six, premier missionaire du Travail*, Editions Spes, Paris, 1938, pp. 411.

Nell-Breuning, Oswald von, S. J., *Wirtschaft und Gesellschaft Heute*, Herder, Freiburg, 1957, pp. 436.

Newman Jeremiah, *Co-Responsibility in Industry*, Gill and Son, Dublin, 1955, pp. 187.

L'Organisation corporative, Semaines sociales de France, Angers, XXVII Session 1935, Chronique sociale de France, Lyon, 1935, pp. 627.

Perlman, Selig, *A Theory of the Labor Movement*, Augustus M. Kelley, New York, 1949, pp. 321.

De Publiekrechtelijke Bedrijfsorganisatie in Nederland, B. M. Telders Stichting, Martinus Nijhoff's Boekhandel & Uitg., Den Haag, 1958, pp. 153.

Rollet, Henri, *L'Action sociale des Catholiques en France*, Editions Contemporaines, Paris, 1947.

Rubrica Soci UCID, Roma, 1958, pp. 314.

Sociaal-Economische Raad, Verslag over 1957 en 1958, Publikaties van de Sociaal-Economische Raad, n. p., 1959, pp. 176.

Tawney, R. H., *Religion and the Rise of Capitalism*, Harcourt, Brace and Company, New York, 1926, pp. 337.

Vaussard, Maurice, *Histoire de la Démocratie Chrétienne*, Editions Du Seuil, Paris, 1956, pp. 333.

Veblen, Thorstein, *The Theory of Business Enterprise*, Charles Scribner's Sons, New York, 1935, pp. 400.

De Verantwoordelijke Maatschappij, Christelijk Nationale Biblioteek, T. Wewer, Franeken, 1958, pp. 370.

Waar Vor Wij Staan, A. H. M. Albreghts, editor, A.K.W.V., 's-Gravenhage, 1950, pp. 211.

Weber, Max, translated by Talcott Parsons, *The Protestant Ethic and the Spirit of Capitalism*, George Allen & Unwin Ltd., London, 1930, pp. 292.

Zamanski, Joseph, *Nous, Catholiques sociaux*, Etudes, Publications, Editions, Enseignement, Paris, 1947, pp. 188.

— *L'Avenir de l'Entreprise, Un Patronat qui s'engage*, Etudes Publications, Editions, Enseignement, Paris, 1948, pp. 176.

2. ADDRESSES AND REPORTS OF MEETINGS

Albreghts, A. H. M., « Avant-Propos », *Aspects sociaux de la coopération économique*, Conférence Européenne UNIAPAC, Knokke-Bruxelles, 12-14 juin 1958, pp. 5-10.

— « Le Statut de la Profession », *L'Organisation professionnelle*, 2e Session UNIAPAC, Paris, avril 1950, Etudes, Publications, Editions, Enseignement, Paris, pp. 143-162.

Aumonier, André, « L'Influence des Mouvements patronaux catholiques dans le milieu professionnel », Congrès International UNIAPAC, Montreal, 1957, *Documents et Commentaires*, no. 20, décembre 1957, pp. 39-48.

— « Rapport général présenté aux Assises nationales du C.F.P.C. », Paris, 19-21 juin 1953, *ibid.*, no. 4, août-septembre-octobre 1953, pp. 25-37.

Au Service du Pays, Assises nationales C.F.P.C., Pau, mars 1958, *Documents et Commentaires*, no. 22, juin 1958, pp. 96.

Bekaert, Léon A., « Les devoirs du dirigeant chrétien », *Dirigeants Chrétiens et Progression humaine*, Congrès national FEPAC, Bruxelles, avril 1959, *Bulletin social des Industriels*, no. 256, avril 1959, pp. 181-186.

— « Esprit Chrétien et Humanisme économique », *Progrès économique et Progrès social*, 4e Session UNIAPAC, Bruxelles, février 1952, pp. 121-143.

— « La mission du Patronat Chrétien », *Rapport du congrès de Rome*, UNIAPAC, 7-10 mai 1949, Casterman, Tournai 1950, pp. 116-127.

— « La Paix sociale et l'Entreprise », *La Paix sociale*, Congrès Mondial UNIAPAC, Lucerne, 4-7 juin 1949, Bruxelles, pp. 39-55.

Biondioli, Pio, « Dieci anni di Azione sociale UCID », *I fattori umani nello sviluppo economico*, Congresso nazionale Roma, 7-10 marzo 1957, pp. 260-264.

Büchi, Willy, « La Paix sociale et la Profession », *La Paix sociale*, Congrès Mondial UNIAPAC, Lucerne, 4-7 juin 1949, Bruxelles, pp. 59-74.

Burgbacher, Fritz, « La Paix sociale sur le plan national et international », *ibid.*, pp. 77-96.

CADICEC, L'Assemblée générale statuaire du 20 Mars 1958, Liaison, 3ème année, 3, numero spécial, pp. 21.

La Collaborazione nella Impresa, Atti del VI Congresso Nazionale UCID, Rapallo, 29-31 gennaio 1954, pp. 303.

— « Mozione Generale », *ibid.*, pp. 295-303.

Decré, Emile, « L'UNIAPAC et la Paix sociale », *La Paix sociale* Congrès Mondial UNIAPAC, Lucerne, 4-7 juin 1959, pp. 129-150.

De Staercke, Jacques, « Le mouvement patronal catholique, ses tâches et ses moyens d'action », Congrès international UNIAPAC, Montreal, 1957, *Bulletin social des Industriels*, n. 243, janvier 1958, pp. 6-13.

— « Le Rôle de l'UNIAPAC », Journées UNIAPAC, Porto, Portugal, 1956, *Documents et Commentaires*, no. 16, décembre 1956, pp. 21-35.

Dirigeants Chrétiens et Progression humaine, « Conclusions », Congrès national FEPAC, Bruxelles, avril 1959, *Bulletın social des Industriels*, no. 256, avril 1959, pp. 178-180.

Greiss, Franz, « Zehn Jahre B.K.U., Rückblick und Ausblick », Jahrestagung, Bad Neuenahr October 2, 1959.

Guitton, Jean, « La Pensée, l'Action et la Prière », Assises nationales C.F.P.C., Pau, mars, 1958, *Documents et Commentaires*, no. 22, juin 1958, pp. 13-38.

Harmel, Charles, « Conclusions », *Progrès économique et Progrès social*, 4e Session UNIAPAC, Bruxelles, frévrier 1952, pp. 145-151.

— « Introduction », *L'Entreprise privée*, Première Session UNIAPAC, Tilburg, mars 1948, pp. 11-18.

— « Le sens du Mouvement patronal catholique international », *Rapports du congrès de Rome*, UNIAPAC, 7-10 mai 1949, Casterman, Tournai, 1950, pp. 19-21.

Henry, Georges, « L'intégration du Travailleur à l'Entreprise », *Progrès économique et Progrès social*, 4e Session UNIAPAC, Bruxelles, 1952, pp. 85-108.

Jousset, Bernard, « Le discours de clôture du Président : Un inventaire des Moyens d'Action Pratique », *Plein emploi et missions des Chefs d'Entreprise*, XII Congrès de l'UNIAPAC Paris, 18-21 mai 1955, *Documents et Commentaires*, no. 11, octobre 1955, pp. 73-80.

Léger, S. Em. Cardinal, « La mission sociale d'un patronat chrétien », congrès de Montreal (UNIAPAC, septembre 1959), *Bulletin social des Industriels*, no. 242, décembre 1957, pp. 392-398.

Louveaux, Pierre, « L'Entreprise, communauté du Travail », *L'Entreprise et son destin*, Rapport sur les relations industrielles, APIC, Bruxelles, 1949, pp. 49-76.

Manuelli, Ernesto, « Le scelte economico-sociali nell'Industria », IX Congresso Nazionale UCID, Venezia, 8 maggio 1959.

Michiels, Jean, « Le sort du Profit dans les débat ' Salariat et Association ' », *L'Entreprise et son destin*, Rapport sur les relations industrielles, APIC, Bruxelles, 1949, pp. 77-92.

L'Organisation professionnelle, 2e Session UNIAPAC, Paris, avril 1950, Etudes, Publications, Editions Enseignement, Paris, pp. 194.

La Paix sociale, Congrès Mondial UNIAPAC, Lucerne, 4-7 juin 1959, Bruxelles, pp. 169.

Le Patronat devant le Syndicalisme, XIIème Congrès de FEPAC, Liège, 15-16 décembre 1951, *Bulletin social des Industriels*, no. 183, janvier, 1952, pp. 82.

Perspectives humaines et économiques du Marché Commun, « Conclusions », Conférence Européenne de l'UNIAPAC, Knokke-Bruxelles, juin 1958, *Documents et Commentaires*, no. 23, septembre 1958, pp. 84-85.

La politique de l'Emploi et le Chômage, XIVᵉ Congrès de FEPAC, Gand, 21-22 février 1952, *Bulletin social des Industriels*, no. 195, mars 1953, pp. 89-176.

Pretot, Sergio Ossa, « Le rôle des Organisations Patronales Catholiques », (report on discussion groups), *La Paix sociale*, Congrès Mondial UNIAPAC, Lucerne, 4-7 juin 1959, Bruxelles, pp. 107-108.

Productivité et rémuneration de travail, XVᵉ Congrès de FEPAC, Charleroi, 11-12 décembre 1954, *Bulletin social des Industriels*, no. 213, janvier 1955, pp. 72.

Quarantini, Alberto Zanelli, « La Représentation professionnelle », *L'Organisation professionnelle*, 2ᵉ Session UNIAPAC, Paris, avril 1950, pp. 167-185.

Rapport d'Activité année 1954. Assemblée Générale Statutaire, FEPAC Bruxelles, 20 avril 1955, pp. 40; *Rapport annuel 1956*, mai 1957, pp. 59; *1957*, avril 1958, pp. 51; *1958*, mai 1959, pp. 40.

« Resolutions », The XIV World Congress of Employers, UNIAPAC, Montreal, 15-21 septembre 1957, *Bulletin d'informations de l'UNIAPAC*, no. 3, pp. 119-121.

Siri, Giuseppe Cardinale, « Responsabilità morale della collaborazione internazionale », 9 UCID Congresso nazionale, Venezia, 7-10 maggio 1959.

V. C. U. und der Arbeit, Tagungsergebnisse 1949-1956, V. C. U., Zurich, 1956, pp. 93.

Vaccari, Vittorio, « Responsabilità della Dirigenza ed Integrazione Europea », 9 UCID Congresso nazionale, Venezia, 7-10 maggio 1959.

3. PERIODICALS

Albreghts, A. H. M., « Le Père Laureys, aumonier depuis 25 ans », *Bulletin d'information de l'UNIAPAC*, no. 3, mars 1956, p. 28.

— « De la Responsabilité internationale de l'UNIAPAC », *ibid.*, no. 2 février 1956, p. 1.

— « Le Temps et Nous », *ibid.*, no. 1, janvier 1955, p. 1.

— « La Vocation de l'UNIAPAC », *ibid.*, no. 6, mai-juin 1953, p. 1.

Aumonier, André, « Ce qui dépend de nous », *Professions*, no. 431, décembre 1958, p. 7.

— « L'Organisation professionnelle et la 5ᵉ République », *ibid.*, no. 429, octobre 1959, p. 6.

— « Pour un 'Patronat de conquête' », *Documents et Commentaires*, no. 9, avril 1955, pp. 3-6.

Bayart, P., « Analyse du discours de S. S. Pie XII du 3 juin 1950 », *Bulletin social des Industriels*, juillet-août 1950, pp. 290-299; septembre-octobre, pp. 345-352.

Bekaert, Léon A., « Le comportement du Chef d'Entreprise devant l'évolution économique et sociale », *Documents et Commentaires*, n. 21, mars 1958, pp. 23-39.

— « Les perspectives du Patronat Chrétien », *Bulletin social des Industriels*, n; 258, juin 1959, pp. 243-245.

— « Rôle et responsabilités d'un centre du Patronat Chrétien », *Documents et Commentaires*, no. 3, juillet 1953.

Benedetti, Analecto, « Autorità e libertà nell'esercizio dell'atto direttivo », *Operare*, XIV, 6, novembre-décembre 1958, pp. 29-32.

— « Le Classi e la evoluzione sociale », *ibid.*, no. 5; settembre-ottobre 1958, pp. 60-68.

Boyer, B. M., O. P., « Un Chef d'Entreprise chrétien peut-il être contre les Syndicats? » *Professions*, n. 421, janvier 1958, pp. 3-4.

— « Doctrine: Refuser la co-gestion n'est pas bloquer le progrès social », *ibid.*, no. 419, novembre 1957, pp. 3-6.

Brouwers, L., S. J., « La doctrine sociale de l'Eglise et l'Entreprise », *Bulletin social des Industriels*, no. 117, mai 1951, pp. 220-235.

Bruniera, Mgr., « Message de Son Excellence Monseigneur Bruniera, délégué apostolique en Afrique Belge », CADICEC, no. 1, pp. 3-4.

Büchi, Willy, « Die Einstellung des Christlichen Unternehmers zum Gewerkschaftsproblem », *V. C. U. Bulletin*, no. 19, September 1952, pp. 134-135.

Bulletin de Contact, FEPAC, no. 108, 15 mars 1958, pp. 6.

Bulletin d'information de l'UNIAPAC, « Pays-Bas: Comment acquérir la propriété d'une maison pour les ouvriers », no. 5 avril 1953, pp. 7-8.

— « Restauration de la Propriété », no. 2, août 1957, pp. 82-86.

— « Le Révérend Père Arnou, S. J., a quitté le C. F. P. C. », no. 9, novembre 1955, pp. 3-4.

— « Son Eminence le Cardinal Giuseppe Siri et l'UNIAPAC » no. 1, mai 1957, pp. 9-10.

— « Voyage en Amérique du Sud des délégués de l'UNIAPAC », 28 juin-août, no. 7, septembre 1955, pp. 1-6.

Bulletin social des Industriels, « Les Conséquences sociales de l'automation », no. 255, mars 1959, pp. 98-120.

— « M. L. A. Bekaert, Grand-Officier de l'Ordre de la Couronne », no. 258, juin 1959, p. 226.

— « Le travail de dimanche en Belgique: Premiers résultats d'une enquête », no. 259, juillet-août 1959, pp. 285-286.

Clemens, R. « L'Organisation de l'economie et la nature juridique de l'Entreprise dans l'Allocution Pontificale du mai 1949 », *Bulletin social des Industries*, novembre 1949, pp. 383-390.

— « Principes de politique sociale et droit de cogestion économique dans l'Allocution Pontificale du 3 juin 1950 », *ibid.*, décembre 1950, pp. 441-442.

Cliquet, Maurice, « Discussion autour de l'Intéressement », *Professions*, no. 436, juin 1959, pp. 5-6.

— « Trois sujets de réflexions sur les expériences d'intéressement des travailleurs à la vie des entreprises », *ibid.*, no. 436, mai 1959, p. 5.

Daniel, Joseph, René Théry, « Projet d'association du Capital et du Travail », *Revue de l'Action Populaire*, no. 34, novembre 1949, pp. 650-678.

Daniel-Rops, Henri, « Etre présents au monde », Professions, no. 316,
    4 avril 1953, pp. 1 ff.
Deble R., « Automation et Emploi », *Bulletin social des Industriels*,
    n. 255, mars 1959, pp. 105-108.
Documents et Commentaires, « La lutte contre le chômage, vers
    des solutions concrètes », no. 12, décembre 1955, pp. 31-86.
— « Déclaration sur l'Europe à propos du Marché Commun », n. 17,
    mars 1957, pp. 19-20.
Dubois, Georges, S.J., « Dirigeants et Cadres: Leur mission chré-
    tienne », *Bulletin social des Indutsriels*, no. 256, avril 1959, pp.
    145-154.
Feltin, S. Em. Cardinal, « Les responsabilités actuelles des Chré-
    tiens chefs et dirigeants d'entreprise », *Documents et Commen-
    taires*, no. 14, juin 1956, pp. 11-20.
Goris, R., « Het Medeheer », *De Christelijke Werkgever*, July 1951,
    pp. 241-251; August 1951, pp. 275-282.
Harmel, Charles. « Une grande association patronale », *Revue Géné-
    rale Belge*, no. 14, décembre 1946, pp. 207-219.
Hoover, Calvin B., « The Intellectuals and Capitalism », *Harvard
    Business Review*, vol. 37, 5, September-October 1959, pp. 47-54.
Jarlot, Georges, S.J., « Les avant-projets de ' Rerum Novarum ' et
    les ' Anciennes Corporations ' », *Nouvelle Revue Théologique*, t.
    81, 1, janvier 1959, pp. 60-77.
Jousset, Bernard, « Cogestion », Professions, no. 316, 4 avril 1953, p. 3.
— « Qu'est-ce que l'UNIAPAC? » *Documents et Commentaires*, no.
    8, décembre, 1954, pp. 5-11.
De Katholieke Werkgever, Jaarverlag 1958, no. 26, 18 septembre 1959,
    pp. 481-536.
Lamoot, Joseph, « Les Chefs d'Entreprise et la mission apostolique
    de l'Eglise », *Documents et Commentaires*, no. 18. juin, 1957,
    pp. 7-27.
Laurent, Philippe, S.J., « Autorité patronale et syndicalisme ou-
    vrier », Professions, no. 384, 18 février 1956, pp. 9-10.
— « Comment aider les pays sous-équipés » *Bulletin social des
    Industriels*, no. 254, février 1959, pp. 70-79.
— « L'Intégration des travailleurs à l'entreprise », Professions, no.
    430, novembre 1958, p. 16.
— « Les qualités nécessaires dans l'édification d'une organisation
    professionnelle », *Documents et Commentaires*, no. 15, septem-
    bre 1956, pp. 27-31.
Lebret, P., « L'Intelligence et la charité des Chrétiens contre la faim
    du monde », Professions, no. 433, février 1959, p. 16
Levard, Georges, « Perspectives d'avenir du syndicalisme français »,
    Professions, no. 423, mars 1958, pp. 4 ff.
Lienart, S. Em. Cardinal, S. Exc. Mgr. Guerry, « Les licenciements
    ouvriers et le chômage dans le Nord », *Bulletin social des In-
    dustriels*, no. 255, mars 1959, pp. 91-92.
Louvel, Jean Marie, « Les rapports entre l'Etat et l'Entreprise »,
    Documents et Commentaires, no. 15, septembre 1956, pp. 61-69.

Matthys, W., « L'élargissement des tâches », *Bulletin social des Industriels*, no. 255, mars 1959, pp. 118-120.

Nouvelles du Secrétariat Général de l'UNIAPAC, mimeo., « Conventions collectives et Accords C », Régie nationale des Usines Renault, Annexe 1; « Convention: Le C. N. P. F., d'une part, La C. F. T. C., La C. G. T. - F. O., La C. G. C., d'autre part », Annexe 2, no. 10, 15 décembre 1958.

Picard, Gerard, « Le syndicalisme ouvrier », *Les Dossiers de l'A.·P.·I.*, no. 4, pp. 10-16.

Pierre, J. C., « Automation et Revenu », *Bulletin social des Industriels*, no. 255, mars 1959, pp. 109-117.

Piettre, André, « Suicide ou survie de l'Occident », *Professions*, no. 426, juin 1958, pp. 4-5.

Professions, no. 420, décembre 1957, p. 1.

— « Après la déclaration commune, quelques précisions », no. 312, février 1953, pp. 3-4.

— « A propos des Comités d'Entreprise », no. 434, mars 1959, p. 7.

— « A propos de l'intéressement du personnel », no. 433, février 1959, p. 7.

— « A propos de l'intéressement du personnel le cas d'une importante société de la région parisienne », no. 435, avril 1959, p. 7.

— « A propos de l'intéressement du personnel deux entreprises du Bâtiment Nantais font part de leur réalisations », no. 434, mars 1959, p. 7.

— « Au delà des allocations-chômages un effort en faveur du meilleur emploi », no. 434, avril 1959, p. 16.

— « L'Etat et son rôle », no. 427, juillet-août 1958, p. 4.

— « Fiches de travail », nos. 432, 433, 434, 436, 437, janvier à juin 1956, pp. 5, 5, 5, 5, 7, et 6.

— « Le groupe de Patrons Chrétiens du C. F. P. C. de Roubaix-Tourcoing prend position », no. 433, février 1959, p. 12.

— « L'Homme et le robot peuvent s'entendre », no. 392, 9 juin 1956, pp. 7-8.

— « Un moyen inattendu de pénétration communiste », no. 432, janvier 1959, p. 7.

— « Les 'Quatre' chez le Général De Gaulle », no. 430, novembre 1958, p. 7.

— « La vie du C. F. P. C. », no. 436, mai 1959, pp. 13-15.

— « Vingt-cinq ans d'action patronale », no. 262, 27 janvier 1951, pp. 2-3.

Promotion, « Adapter le travail à l'homme », no. 8, juin 1958, pp. 2-4.

Reynaud, Roger, « Vues syndicalistes sur l'organisation professionnelle », *Documents et Commentaires*, no. 15, septembre 1956, pp. 23-24.

Richaud, S. Em. Cardinal, « Comment répondre en chrétiens aux problèmes économiques et sociaux actuels »? *Professions*, no., 433, février 1959, p. 3.

— « Mission actuelle du Patronat Chrétien », *Documents et Commentaires*, no. 4, août-septembre-octobre 1953, pp. 5-24.

Roche, Emile, « Penser et prévoir pour le Gouvernement », *Professions*, no. 434, mars 1959, p. 16.

Rogiers, F., « Le Travailleur et l'Automation », *Bulletin social des Industriels*, no. 255, mars 1959, pp. 98-104.

Romanet, Emile, « 36 ans après: Emile Romanet, le père des allocations familiales nous parle », Professions, no. 311, 24 janvier 1953, pp. 1-3.

Senser, Bob, « The White House Will Put These Heads Together », *Work*, February 1960, pp. 1 ff.

Siegfried, André, « Libre concurrence et relations humaines », *Professions*, no. 386, 3 mars 1956, pp. 1 ff.

Soave, Ettore, « Due idee e molti personaggi nel dibattito per le partecipazioni statali », *Operare*, XIV, 1, gennaio-febbraio 1958, pp. 35-50.

Social Action Notes for Priests, NCWC, « Progress Report on the Activities of the Catholic Employers, Managers and Technologists Study Groups » December 1958, pp. 10-11.

Spitaels, R., « Le travail du dimanche en sidérurgie », *Bulletin social des Industriels*, no. 259, juillet-août 1959.

Spoorenberg, P. J., « Le 25ème anniversaire de *Quadragesimo Anno* et de l'UNIAPAC », *Bulletin d'information de l'UNIAPAC* no. 5, juin, juillet, août 1956, pp. 51-52.

Steenhodt-Bosteels, C., « Les différents problèmes posés par le travail du dimanche », *Bulletin social des Industriels*, no. 259, juillet-août 1959, pp. 283-284.

Thiefry, M. S. J., « L'Apostolat des laïcs dans l'Eglise et le discours de S. S. Pie XII en Octobre 1957 », *Bulletin social des Industriels*, no. 248, juin 1958, pp. 208-214.

Thiefry, M., S. J., M. M. Dupois, A. Thomas, « Les repos dominical et la semaine 'Mobile' du travail », *Promotion*, no. 1, février 1959, pp. 2-6.

Time, Atlantic Edition, « Economic Humanism », September 28, 1959, p. 15.

Vaccari, Vittorio, « Dirigenza economica e responsabilità politiche », *Operare*, XIV, 4, luglio-agosto 1958, pp. 29-32.

— « La Produttività del Moderno Atto Direttivo », *ibid.*, no. 3, maggio-giugno 1958, pp. 29-34.

— « Una filosofia per la nuova dirigenza », *ibid.*, XII, 5, settembre-ottobre 1957, pp. 28-32.

Le Vade-Mecum des Conseils d'Entreprise, Bulletin social des Industriels, no. 250, septembre-octobre 1958, pp. 290-396.

V. C. U. Bulletin, « Zehn Jahre V. C. U. », no. 86, September 1959, pp. 574-577.

Work, « Catholic Employers' Organization Growing », October 1959, pp. 1 ff.

4. BOOKLETS AND PAMPHLETS.

Bund Katholischer Unternehmar Mitgliederverzeichnis, Köln, 1958, pp. 93.

Le Chômage et l'Equilibre production-consommation, Commission des Etudes C. F. P. C., Editions E. P. E. E., Paris, 1952, pp. 55.

Le chômage structurel et la politique régionale, FEPAC, Bruxelles, 1958, pp. 103.

Greiss, Franz, *Das Zeitalter des Menschen, Die Zweite Phase der Industriellen Aera*, B. K. U., Köln, 1955, pp. 106.

Höffner, Joseph, *Das Ethos des Unternehmers*, B. K. U., 1956, pp. 18.

Hommage au R. P. Laureys, S. J., Aumônier de l'APIC, n. p., 1956, pp. 28.

The Industrial Organization Act in the Netherlands, Sociaal-Economische Raad, translation by Public Relations Office of the Ministry of Economic Affairs, The Hague, 1950, pp. 39.

Les Nationalisations, FEPAC, n. p., août 1955, pp. 123.

Perico, Giacomo, S. J., *Il Credente nel mondo economico*, UCID Gruppo Lombardo, Milano, 1957, pp. 38.

Prever, Giuseppe R., *Le relazioni umane nella impresa*, UCID Piemonte, Torino, 1953, pp. 45.

« Programme de Travail », mimeo., C. F. P. C., Paris, 1959-1960, pp. 69.

Schreiber, Wilfrid, *Vermögensbildung in Breiten Schicten*, B. K. U., Köln, 1958, pp. 88.

— *Unsere Meinung zur Frage des Sonntagsarbeit*, B. K. U., Köln. 1958, pp. 44.

Statuten, Vereinigung Christlicher Unternehmer der Schweiz, Einsiedeln, 1950, pp. 6.

Statuto, Unione Cristiana Imprenditori Dirigenti, Roma, n. d., pp. 4.

Statuts, Centre Chrétien des Patrons et Dirigeants d'Entreprise Français, n. p., 1958, pp. 4.

UNIAPAC: International Union of Catholic Employers Associations, Brussels, n. d., pp. 16.

Vaccari, Vittorio, *7 Anni di azione sociale UCID*, Roma, 1954, pp. 39.

— *UCID Dieci anni*, Estratto della Revista *Operare*, no. 1 gennaio-febbraio 1957, pp. 14.

— *Una dirigenza cristiana per un progresso sicuro*, UCID, Roma, 1959, pp. 27.

Van Zeeland, Paul, « Discours de M. Paul van Zeeland, Ancien Premier Ministre, Ministre d'Etat, Membre du Senat », *Hommage au R. P. Laureys, S. J., Aumônier de l'APIC*, n. p., 1956, pp. 28.

Verschuerer, Albert, *Les relations industrielles aux Etats-Unis*, Fondation Maurice van der Rest, Editions de la Fédération des Industries Belges, Bruxelles, n. d., pp. 75.

5. LEAFLETS AND FOLDERS

« The Aims of UNIAPAC », mimeo., International Union of Catholic Employers Associations, n. p., n. d., pp. 12.

« C. E. E. », Secondo ciclo di riunioni 1959, UCID Torino, Genova, Milano, pp. 4.

« C. F. P. C., Son But, Ses Moyens, Ses Réalisations », Paris, n. d., pp. 6.

« Ciclo di riunioni sui problemi della Comunità Economica European », UCID, Milano, 1959, pp. 4.

« Les Conseils d'Entreprise », Bulletin d'information sociales, (FEPAC), juin 1958, pp. 3.

« Déclaration du C. F. P. C. sur l'intéressement des travailleurs à l'entreprise », Communiqué de presse, n. d., pp. 8.

« Déclaration sur les allocations familiales et la sécurité sociale », mimeo., C. F. P. C., Paris 1 juillet 1954, pp. 2.

« Ecole du Chef d'Entreprise », 1959-1960, 16ᵉ Session annuelle, Paris, pp. 8.

« La FEPAC », Bruxelles, n. d., pp. 16.

« General Catholic Employers' Association, Catholic Federation of Employers' Trade Associations », mimeo., Algemene Katholieke Werkgeversverening, 's-Gravenhage, n. d., pp. 7.

« Katholieke Werkgevers in Nederland », (illustrated schema), A. K. W. V. - K. V. W., n. d., p. 1.

Lamontagne, J. B., « Regard sur l'A. P. I., depuis sa fondation en 1943 », Extrait du Bottin de l'A. P. I., juillet 1956, pp. 7.

« La mise en place du Conseil économique et social », mimeo., Conseil National du Commerce, Paris, 1959, pp. 6.

« Le Patron—Cet homme seul ... », Centre Français du Patronat Chrétien, Paris, n. d., pp. 12.

« Positions du Patronat Chrétien », C. F. P. C., Paris n. d., pp. 6.

« Project for a Preamble to the European Social Charter », mimeo, UNIAPAC, Brussels, March 1959, pp. 7.

« Réglement intérieur », mimeo., C. F. P. C., n. d., pp. 16.

« Sessions d'Animateurs des Sections », mimeo., C. F. P. C., 21-24 octobre 1959, pp. 2.

« The Social and Economic Council in the Netherlands », mimeo., pp. 5.

« V. C. U., Vereiningung Christlicher Unternehmer der Schweiz », Zurich, 1955, pp. 6.

« Was Will der Bund Katholischer Unternehmer »?, Köln, n. d., pp. 8.

« What We Believe and What We Do », Verbond van Protestants-Christelijke Werkgevers in Nederland, 's-Gravenhage, n. d., pp. 10.

6. UNIAPAC PAPERS

Questionnaire on Social Peace (mimeographed, unless otherwise noted).

— « Social Peace and Employers' Responsabilities », (List of Questions of UNIAPAC to the national associations), pp. 14.

— Belgium : « La Paix sociale et les responsabilités patronales », FEPAC, juin 1959, pp. 29.

— Canada : « Réponse au Questionnaire de l'UNIAPAC au Sujet de la Paix sociale, (typewritten), pp. 7.

— France : « Réponse du Centre Français du Patronat Chrétien (C.F.P.C.) au Questionnaire de l'UNIAPAC sur la Paix sociale et les responsabilités patronales », pp. 28.

— Germany : « Observations relatives au Questionnaire UNIAPAC, Commentaire Allemand », juin 1959, pp. 15.

— Great Britain : « Reply of the Catholic Industrialists' Conference to the Questionnaire on Social Peace », (typewritten), June 1959, pp. 15.

— Holland: « Réponse A.K.W.V. au Questionnaire », (excerpts typewritten), pp. 5.
— Italy : « Observations relatives au Questionnaire UNIAPAC », pp. 5.
— Switzerland: « Extraits de la Réponse Suisse au Questionnaire UNIAPAC sur la Paix sociale », pp. 37.
— Uruguay: « Commentaire Uruguayan sur le Questionnaire UNIAPAC sur la Paix sociale », pp. 6.

Letters.
— Aumonier, André, to writer, September 30, 1959, pp. 4.
— Kulp, B., to writer with requested commentary: « Der BKU zur Mitbestimmungsfrage », typewritten, December 18, 1959, pp. 24.
— Linnebank, H.G.M., to writer, December 8, 1959, pp. 4.
— Lombaers, Matthew, to writer, March 1, 1959, pp. 2.
— Vermeire, Rik, to writer, January 5, 1960, pp. 7; February 16, 1960, pp. 2; February 19, 1960, pp. 5.

Miscellaneous.
— « Communiqué de Presse », La Haye, 5-6 février, 1960, pp. 2.
— « Note pour le Conseil Central de Délégués », (Paris, February 27-28, 1959), pp. 15; *ibid.* (Lucerne, June 3, 1959), pp. 15.
— « Le Problème de l'accès à la propriété », Rome 9-10 octobre 1959, IV-B, pp. 6.
— « Projet de Communiqué de Presse », *ibid.*, pp. 2.
— Van Heijst, L.A.J.M. « Note concernant la répartition des fonctions entre le Comité de Direction et le Conseil Central des Délégués », *ibid.*, VI/3 pp. 3.
— Vermeire, Rik, « Rapport du Secrétaire Général sur son voyage en Amérique du Nord », La Haye, 5-6 février 1960, II B, pp. 9; « 10ème rapport du voyage de M. Vermeire en Amérique du Nord, Mexique », (December 1959), pp. 10.

INDEX OF PERSONS, ORGANIZATIONS AND SUBJECTS

Imprimatur, e Vicariatu Urbis, die 30 decembris 1960,
† ALOYSIUS Card. TRAGLIA, *Provicarius*.